In *Kant and the demands of self-consciousness*, Pierre Keller examines Kant's theory of self-consciousness and argues that it succeeds in explaining how both subjective and objective experience are possible. Previous interpretations of Kant's theory have held that he treats all self-consciousness as knowledge of objective states of affairs, and also, often, that self-consciousness can be interpreted as knowledge of personal identity. By contrast, Keller argues for a new understanding of Kant's conception of self-consciousness as the capacity to abstract not only from what one happens to be experiencing, but also from one's own personal identity. By developing this new interpretation, Keller is able to argue that transcendental self-consciousness underwrites a general theory of objectivity and subjectivity at the same time.

PIERRE KELLER is Associate Professor of Philosophy at the University of California, Riverside. He has published a number of articles on Leibniz, Kant, Hegel, Heidegger, and Husserl.

KANT AND THE
DEMANDS OF
SELF-CONSCIOUSNESS

PIERRE KELLER

University of California, Riverside

CAMBRIDGE
UNIVERSITY PRESS

PUBLISHED BY THE PRESS SYNDICATE OF THE UNIVERSITY OF CAMBRIDGE
The Pitt Building, Trumpington Street, Cambridge CB2 1RP

CAMBRIDGE UNIVERSITY PRESS
The Edinburgh Building, Cambridge CB2 2RU, UK   http://www.cup.cam.ac.uk
40 West 20th Street, New York, NY 10011–4211, USA   http://www.cup.org
10 Stamford Road, Oakleigh, Melbourne 3166, Australia

First published 1998

Printed in Great Britain at the University Press, Cambridge

Typeset in Baskerville 11/12.5 pt [VN]

A catalogue record for this book is available from the British Library

ISBN 0 521 63077 0 hardback

Contents

Acknowledgments

The contents of this book have germinated in a long process going back to my first Kant seminar with Dieter Henrich in Heidelberg. Although I sometimes criticize his views, his influence is obvious in my work. I am also strongly indebted to discussions with Georg Picht, Enno Rudolph, Harald Pilot, and, especially, Rüdiger Bittner, dating back to my undergraduate days in Heidelberg. As a student at Columbia, I was lucky to be able to take on a new set of intellectual debts. After going to Columbia to work with Charles Parsons, whose influence on my work on Kant is also patent in this book, I was fortunate to find Charles Larmore, Thomas Pogge, Sydney Morgenbesser, and, somewhat later, Raymond Geuss willing and very challenging participants in discussions about Kant's philosophy. I owe a particular debt to Charles Parsons, Charles Larmore, and especially Raymond Geuss for their helpful comments on various drafts of this book. Without Raymond Geuss's constant criticism, encouragement, and prodding, I am certain that this book would never have appeared at all. I owe an almost comparable debt of gratitude to my editor, Hilary Gaskin, who has helped me to see where the book could be improved and kept at me finally to complete it. I also wish to thank Gillian Maude for patient help with the copy editing.

Among my colleagues at the University of California at Riverside, I would be remiss if I did not mention Andrews Reath, David Glidden, Bernd Magnus, and Larry Wright, each of whom was generous in his critical comments on my work, in his support, and in his willingness to engage with Kant's thought. Fred Neuhouser, Steve Yalowitz, and David Weberman have also provided much helpful input, as have the members of the Southern California Kant group, Ed McCann, Patricia Kitcher, Jill Buroker, Martin Schwab, and Michelle Greer. I am especially indebted to many discussions with Henry Allison, who has undoubtedly influenced me more strongly than some of my criticisms of his views might suggest. My new colleague Allen Wood's helpful criticisms have led me to make a number of significant changes. My students have also led me to rethink a number of things. I wish especially to mention John Fischer and Laura Bruce, who also helped me with the proofs and the index.

Finally, I want to thank my parents who instilled an early respect for Kant and love of philosophy in me, and my brother, Gregory, and sisters, Karen and Catherine, for having been so supportive of my projects over the years. My philosophical discussions with Catherine have also undoubtedly had an impact on the present work. My greatest debt is to my wife Edith, who has provided me with invaluable criticism of every draft, and much-needed intellectual and emotional support.

CHAPTER I

Introduction

In the *Critique of Pure Reason* (henceforth *Critique*), Kant draws a famous but elusive distinction between transcendental and empirical apperception. He interprets the distinction between transcendental and empirical apperception as a distinction between transcendental and empirical self-consciousness. He argues that empirical self-consciousness is parasitic on transcendental self-consciousness, and that any empirical consciousness that has any cognitive relevance for us depends for its cognitive content on its potential relation to transcendental self-consciousness. These are strong, but, I want to argue, defensible claims once one understands the nature of transcendental self-consciousness, as it is understood by Kant.

The central aim of this book is to provide a new understanding of the notion of transcendental self-consciousness and show its implications for an understanding of experience. I develop and defend Kant's central thesis that self-consciousness puts demands on experience that make it possible for us to integrate our various experiences into a single comprehensive, objective, spatio-temporal point of view. My interpretation of his conception of self-consciousness as the capacity to abstract not only from what one happens to be experiencing, but also from one's own personal identity, while giving content to whatever one represents, shows how transcendental self-consciousness underwrites a general theory of objectivity and subjectivity at the same time.

The leading interpretations seem to be in broad agreement that Kant's notion of transcendental apperception is largely a disappointing failure. Perhaps the dominant tendency has been to dismiss his notion of transcendental self-consciousness as at best implausible and at worst incoherent. But even those interpreters who have been sympathetic to the notion of transcendental self-consciousness have endeavored to give it an anodyne interpretation that renders it largely irrelevant to a defense of objectivity or even subjectivity. By simply identifying transcendental

self-consciousness with objective experience, those interpreters deprive
transcendental self-consciousness of any substantive role in justifying the
claim that our experience is at least sometimes objective, and make it
difficult to understand how it could sometimes be merely subjective.

It is not surprising that interpreters have had their problems with
transcendental self-consciousness, despite the fact that it is undeniably a
central notion in Kant's philosophy. Part of the problem is that Kant's
notion of transcendental self-consciousness requires a subject of self-
consciousness that is somehow distinct from any subject that we can
experience. The only kind of subject that we seem to be acquainted with
in any sense is a subject that we can experience, an empirical subject,
and so the notion of a non-empirical subject that we could become
conscious of seems to be based on an illegitimate abstraction from actual
experience.[1] And, even if one concedes that it might be possible to be
conscious of a non-empirical subject of experience, it seems that the only
way we have of making sense of such a subject is by thinking of it as a
mere abstraction from actual experience, in which case it is difficult to
see how it could support any substantive claims about what the nature of
experience must be.

Skepticism about whether it is possible to be conscious of a subject of
thought that is somehow distinguishable from the kind of subject that is
knowable through experience leads interpreters to look to consciousness
of personal identity as the only kind of consciousness of self that we
have.[2] Commentators who have resisted the tendency to collapse transcendental self-consciousness into consciousness of personal identity
have often gone to the other extreme of treating all self-consciousness as
a consciousness of judgments that are objectively valid, thus denying
that transcendental self-consciousness is a necessary condition for consciousness of one's subjective point of view.[3] And even those commentators who have tried to conceive of transcendental self-consciousness as a
necessary condition of empirical self-consciousness have not had much
to say about how transcendental self-consciousness could be involved in
empirical self-consciousness.[4]

I claim that Kant's notion of transcendental self-consciousness is
more robust than it has generally been thought to be, but also more
commonsensical than most commentators have allowed it to be. I argue
that the key to a proper understanding of the thesis that our experience
is subject to the demands of self-consciousness is a proper understanding
of the fundamentally impersonal character of our representation of self.
We have an impersonal or transpersonal representation of self which is

expressed in our use of the expression "I" to refer to ourselves. When each of us refers to him- or herself by means of the expression "I," each of us refers to him- or herself in a way that could, in principle, apply to any one of us. This is the basic, minimal, idea that Kant tries to express with his notion of transcendental self-consciousness.

I attribute to Kant and defend several further claims about transcendental self-consciousness that are very controversial. I claim that empirical or personal self-consciousness is parasitic on transcendental or impersonal self-consciousness. I argue that this amounts to the claim that we are only able to grasp our own individual identity by contrast with other possible lives that we might have led. Then I argue that our very ability to form concepts in general is based on our capacity for transcendental self-consciousness. This capacity for concept formation and use is displayed in judgments and inferences that themselves depend on our capacity for representing ourselves impersonally. I then go on to make the even stronger claim that the very notion of a representational content that has any cognitive relevance is parasitic on our ability to form an impersonal consciousness of self. Thus, even representations of the world and the self that are independent of thought, representations that Kant refers to as intuitions, have cognitive relevance for us only insofar as we are able to take them as potential candidates for I thoughts. This claim is the ultimate basis for the Kantian thesis that experience is only intelligible to us to the extent that it is a potential content of impersonal self-consciousness that is systematically linked to other potential contents. It is also the basis for his famous thesis that there are non-empirical conditions on all experience.

For Kant, non-empirical conditions on all experience are conditions under which a self-conscious being is able to represent itself in any arbitrary experience as the numerically identical point of view. This representation of the self-consciousness as a numerically identical point of view through different experiences connects different experiences together in a single possible representation. This representation of the self is the same regardless of the different standpoints within experience that the self-conscious individual might be occupying. In this way, the conditions governing the representation of the numerical identity of the self provide one with constraints on the way that any objective experience must be. And, insofar as these constraints also operate on one's representation of one's personal identity as constituted by a certain sequence of points of view within experience, they also provide the basis for an account of subjectivity.

IMPERSONAL AND PERSONAL SELF-CONSCIOUSNESS

Personal self-consciousness involves an awareness of the distinction between me and my representations and other persons and their representations. In order for me to have some understanding of the distinction between me and my representations, and other persons and their representations, I must have some way of comparing and contrasting my identity as a person with a certain set of representations with that of other possible persons with their own distinctive sets of representations.[5] In order to be able to compare and contrast my representations with those of other persons, I must be able to abstract from the particular identity, the particular set of beliefs and desires, that distinguishes me from other persons. For I must be able to represent what it would be like for me had I had a different set of representations than the ones that I actually ascribe to myself:

It is obvious that: if one wants to represent a thinking being, one must put oneself in its place, and place ones own subject under the object that one wants to consider (which is not the case in any other kind of investigation), and that we can only require an absolute unity of a subject for a thought because one could not otherwise say: I think (the manifold in a representation). (A 354)*

The fact that I am able to represent the point of view of another rational being does not mean that I am no longer the particular individual that I am. But it does mean that I represent myself and other persons in an impersonal manner. For, in representing what it might have been like for things to appear to me in the way that they appear to the other being to which I wish to attribute rationality, I represent myself as an arbitrary self-consciousness, that is, just one person among many possible other persons. But at the same time I am also able to represent myself as the particular individual who I happen to be. For it is only in this way that I can compare the representations that I might have had from the point of view of another rational being with the representations that I have from my own actual point of view.

If I come to have doubts about the states that I am ascribing to myself, or if someone else challenges me concerning my past, I will feel the need to consider the possibility that I might be mistaken in what states I think

---

* References to Kant's *Critique of Pure Reason* (henceforth *Critique*) will be to the pagination of the first and second editions of the *Critique* indicated by the letters A and B respectively. I follow the text edited by Raymund Schmidt (Hamburg: Felix Meiner Verlag, 1930) except where otherwise noted. All other citations of Kant's work are based on the volume and page numbers of the critical edition published by the Prussian Academy of Sciences and later by the German Academy of Sciences (henceforth Ak.) (Berlin: de Gruyter: 1990–). Translations are mine throughout.

belong to my own history and even in who I am. I can only do so to the extent that I am able to abstract from my actual personal identity, and evaluate the reasons for ascribing certain states to myself in a manner that would have weight for other persons as well. Thus, in order for each of us to understand what it is to be a person with beliefs, emotions, and desires, we must have an understanding of what it might have been like to have a different set of beliefs, emotions, and desires. The possibility of the point of view that we must take in order to go through these alternative sets of beliefs, emotions, and desires gives self-consciousness its transcendental dimension, that is, it makes self-consciousness a condition under which we can recognize an object that is distinct from our individual momentary representations of the world.

We can refer to the self that functions as a variable in self-consciousness as the transcendental self:

We presuppose nothing other than the simple and in itself completely empty of content representation: **I**; of which one cannot even say that it is a concept, but rather a mere consciousness, that accompanies all concepts. Through this I, or he, or it (the thing) that thinks nothing other than a transcendental subject = x is represented. This transcendental subject is known only through the thoughts that are its predicates. (A 345–346/B 404)

It might seem that the idea of a transcendental self commits one to a featureless *bearer* of experience. But the dummy sortal x that stands in for different individual constants would be misunderstood if taken to mean that when we represent ourselves by means of I thoughts we are then mere bare particulars, or egos bare of any properties that one could come to know through experience. The notion of a transpersonal and standpoint-neutral bearer of experience would be incoherent. In order to be able to represent something, it would have to have some kind of standpoint from which it represents things or at least some determinate set of capacities with which it represents, but, in order to be a transpersonal and standpoint-neutral subject, it would have to have no properties in particular.

Fortunately, Kant does not think of the subject of transcendental self-consciousness as a particular that has no particular properties, although he thinks that this is a view to which Descartes was attracted in trying to infer substantial properties of thinking beings in general from the conditions under which we ascribe thoughts. For Kant, transcendental self-consciousness is a representation of oneself that abstracts from what distinguishes one from other persons, not a representation of a bare particular:

It means a something in general (transcendental subject) the representation of which must indeed be simple, precisely for this reason, since nothing is determined with respect to it, for certainly nothing simpler can be represented than the concept of a mere something. The simplicity of the representation of a subject is not therefore a cognition of the simplicity of the subject itself, for one has completely abstracted from its properties, when it is merely designated by the completely empty of content expression: I think (which I can apply to any thinking subject). (A 356)

While I represent myself in a simple way when I represent myself by the expression "I" or by means of the expression "I think," and even represent other thinkers simply when I represent them as individuals that can potentially say of themselves "I think," it would be a mistake to infer from this that the ego that is the bearer of such I thoughts must itself be a simple individual or bare particular.

IMPERSONAL SELF-CONSCIOUSNESS AND JUDGMENT

The kind of self-consciousness expressed by the statement "I think p," where p is any proposition, is, for Kant, the basis for all use of concepts, judgments, and inferences. In using concepts, and making judgments and inferences, we commit ourselves to a representation of what we are representing by means of our concepts, judgments, or inferences that is not just true for our own individual point of view, but is also true for any arbitrary point of view. Kant refers to this notion of a representation that is a representation for any arbitrary point of view as a representation that belongs to "a consciousness in general" (*Bewußtsein überhaupt*), as opposed to a representation that belongs to one consciousness alone.

Now Kant does not wish to argue that there are representations that do not belong to the individual consciousness of distinct individuals. His claim is rather that we understand what we are representing when we are able to represent the content of representations that belong to our individual consciousness in a way that, in principle, is also accessible to other representers. The capacity to represent individual representations in this manner that is accessible to other representers is just what Kant regards as the capacity to use concepts. The capacity to use concepts is, in turn, exhibited in the ability to make judgments that have determinable truth value, and to draw inferences on the basis of those judgments that we can determine to be correct or incorrect.

In judgment, we may entertain the possibility that something is the case, but we also commit ourselves to the assumption that what we judge is or is not the case. This commitment expresses itself in a willingness to offer reasons for our belief that something is or is not thus and such. In taking on the obligation to offer reasons for what we judge to be the case, we acknowledge that judgment is governed by normative principles. These normative principles are based on the commitment to truth that one takes on when one makes a judgment. Normative principles provide procedures for distinguishing judgment that succeeds in articulating truth from judgment that is false. These procedures may be articulated in the form of rules governing the behavior of individuals. The norms governing representation express themselves in terms of rules concerning when to token a certain representation if we are to succeed in articulating some truth. Our competence in judgment is then measured against our ability to express truths by means of the judgments that we make.

Judgment actually presupposes both the kind of personal self-consciousness that Kant refers to as empirical apperception and the impersonal self-consciousness that he refers to as transcendental apperception. Judgment presupposes personal self-consciousness insofar as judgment involves an implicit or explicit commitment on the part of the person who forms the judgment that things are thus and such for him, her, or it. At the same time, judgment also presupposes an impersonal self-consciousness, for when one makes a judgment one makes an assertion to the effect that things are thus and such not only for one as the particular individual that one is, but that, in principle, things should be taken as thus and such by anyone.

At least some implicit consciousness of self is built into the normative commitment that a judger takes on for her-, him-, or itself. To judge is to place oneself in the space of reasons and thus to take on a commitment to offer reasons for what one judges to be the case. But this means that, in making a judgment, the judger implicitly takes her-, him-, or itself to be not just conforming to rules but also tacitly or overtly obeying rules. Kant links the capacity for obeying rules that we display in our ability to use concepts to pick out and characterize objects not only with our capacity for judgment, but also with our capacity for self-consciousness. To have an idea that an individual is obeying rather than merely conforming to norms of which s/he has no implicit or explicit understanding, we must regard her or his point of view as one that we might be able to occupy in obeying the rules that we do. This is just to attribute the capacity for self-consciousness to those creatures.

Bona fide norms must be principles that the individual can come to understand as the basis for his or her behavior, and they must be principles that the individual can come to see him- or herself as having chosen to be bound by in his or her behavior. Such capacity for choice is what Kant refers to as "spontaneity." He regards it as a distinctive feature of rational and hence self-conscious beings. Such creatures are rational because they can assume responsibility for their own representations. It is this capacity to take responsibility that is the basis for their possession of full-fledged beliefs. To have full-fledged beliefs, one must be able to take something to be true. And, in order to be able to take something to be true, one must be able to form one's belief in accordance with norms that licence one to take as true what one takes as true.

In forming a judgment, the individual is not merely stating a fact about the way that individual interprets matters, the individual is also making a claim that others ought to interpret things in the same way. The individual is thus committing him-, her-, or itself to the possibility of providing reasons for why he, she, or it has judged in that way rather than in another way. These reasons operate as norms governing the judgments in question. Norms are principles governing the responses of individuals that apply to individuals in different situations.

Now it has often been claimed that normativity could stop at the level of what a certain group or community takes to be true. While a view of normativity that stops at the group allows for a shared communal point of view relative to which individuals could be said to be right or wrong, it fails to address the implicit claim of the group or community to articulate standards that hold for them not because they are the ones that they do use but because those standards are the correct ones to adopt. A conflict of belief or values between different communities is only intelligible if the respective communities take themselves to be committed to something that is not merely true or of value for them. Even if these different communities see no way of establishing the validity of their own point of view to the satisfaction of the other point of view, they still must recognize the possibility of some encompassing perspective from which their own view, in principle, could be justified. Thus, the normative commitment to truth requires the possibility of an impersonal point of view, even if the point of view in question is not one that is ever actually held by any person or group of persons.

Generalizing the point, we may say that, in order for one to be able to recognize norms as norms governing one's behavior, one must be able to recognize principles that transcend a particular point of view. These principles that transcend a particular point of view depend on one's ability to recognize not only one's own point of view, but also the possibility of other points of view to which those norms apply. For this, one must have some understanding of what it would be like to be an individual with such a distinct point of view governed by norms. But, in order for one to be able to represent the possibility of another point of view that is subject to the same principles to which one's own point of view is subject, one must be able to abstract from what is distinctive about one's own point of view. One must be able to place oneself in thought or imagination in the position of another and reflect on what things would be like from that alternative standpoint.

The self-consciousness expressed by the proposition "I think" provides each of us with an impersonal or, rather, transpersonal perspective from which we are able to consider ourselves and others. The transpersonal perspective is just the way that we represent our own activities as particular individuals to the extent that those activities are constrained by norms that apply to absolutely all of us. These norms place us in the space of reasons. This is why Kant insists that our only grip on the notion of a rational being is through our ability to place ourselves in the position of another creature. We are able to do this through the abstract representation of self that we have in the self-consciousness expressed by the proposition "I think."

OUTLINE OF THE ARGUMENT

My task in this book is first to show how Kant understands the notion of transcendental self-consciousness. In the process, I distinguish his understanding of this notion from the understanding of it provided by other commentators. Then I develop the implications for an understanding of the general structure of experience that are inherent in the notion of transcendental self-consciousness. I focus on the role that transcendental self-consciousness has in connecting different spatial and temporal episodes together in a single experience. This experience is distinctive in that it is not the private experience of an individual, but, in principle, is accessible to absolutely all of us. To clarify Kant's conception of transcendental self-consciousness, I begin with a discussion of the texts in the *Critique of Pure Reason* in which Kant first articulates the notion of self-consciousness.

Kant introduces his distinction between empirical and non-empirical self-consciousness in the first edition of the Transcendental Deduction as a way of arguing for the claim that we have non-empirical concepts that may legitimately be applied to experience. In the A-Deduction, Kant tries to establish that all contents of experience depend for their very existence on the possibility of connecting them together in a representation of self that is neutral with respect to the different contents of experience. He argues that this is only possible to the extent to which such contents of experience are subject to rules that connect those representations together independently of experience. He refers to these rules governing the possibility of an impersonal representation of self as the categories of the pure understanding. The Transcendental Deduction is concerned with proving that such rules are bona fide rules in that they must actually apply to all experience. In proving that there are necessary and universally applicable rules governing experience, the Deduction also provides a defense of objectivity. For such rules allow us to form judgments about the objects of experience that must be true not just for me or you, but for anyone.

In the next chapter, I argue that the notion of transcendental apperception that is introduced in the A-Deduction is not to be understood as a representation of personal identity. Instead, it is to be understood as a condition under which it is possible for us to form concepts of objects. As such, it is a representation of self that is the same for all of us. I criticize contemporary interpretations of transcendental self-consciousness as a kind of a priori certainty of personal identity, and argue that Kant was not concerned with providing a direct response to Hume's worries about personal identity. Instead, Kant introduces his impersonal consciousness of self as a condition for the formation of concepts of experience. I argue that the success of this argument depends on conceiving of concept use and representation in general as representing the world in a way that is the same for all individuals and that is also inherently systematic.

We represent items against a background of other representations that give those representations their distinctive content. If representations are to belong together in an impersonal self-consciousness, they must be connectable according to rules that allow us to represent ourselves as having the same point of view irrespective of the differences in representational content that distinguish those representations from each other. These rules have a cognitive content that is the same for all of us under all circumstances because that cognitive content is determined by the inherently systematic and standpoint-neutral notion of functional role in judgment and inference.

A number of contemporary interpreters have understood Kant to be a functionalist about the self and the mind. I argue that Kant can only be regarded as a functionalist in a very circumspect sense; he is concerned with cognitive content as constituted by the functional role of such content in judgment and inference. Thus, unlike most contemporary functionalists, and *contra* most functionalist interpretations of Kant, I argue that Kant only regards the mind as a functional system with respect to the contribution of the active, spontaneous, aspect of the mind, rather than with its passive dependence on causal relations between representational contents.

In chapter three, I argue that Kant's conception of the point of view from which content is to be ascribed is based on his rejection of Hume's fundamental assumption that experience consists only of similarity relations between numerically distinct perceivings. Kant argues that the possibility of being conscious of one's self-identity as a self-conscious being is the basis for any conceptual recognition. He also plausibly argues that conceptual recognition of an object must be possible if any significant similarity relations are to be discerned. Without self-consciousness one would not be able to distinguish a successful from an unsuccessful recognition of an item by means of a concept, for one would have no conception of the possibility that the item might present itself to oneself in a way that is other than it is. And, without the possibility of distinguishing unsuccessful from successful recognition, there would be no basis for claiming that one had picked out relevant similarities in experience either.

The associationist conception of experience developed by British empiricism depends on the idea that we can have a brute recognition of similarities without any underlying capacity for representing our identity as thinkers. I argue that Kant was right that this idea of brute recognition will not work. The postulation of a brute capacity for recognition fails to do justice to the normative character of recognition, that is, that recognition can be successful or unsuccessful. Our associations cannot be completely random if they are to account for our awareness of any regularities in experience.

I note that there are first-order rules that allow us to compare and contrast various perceptual representations and represent them in a standpoint-neutral way. These rules are what Kant calls empirical concepts. There are also, however, second-order non-empirical concepts that make it possible for us to form empirical concepts. These second-order concepts dictate that nature must have the kind of uniformity that allows one to connect distinct representations together in one possible self-conscious experience. They are what Kant refers to as the categories. The categories are sufficient to establish a general uniformity in nature. But they do not tell us what particular form such uniformity must take. They do not tell us which particular laws nature must obey.

This is why our ability to apply second-order concepts or categories to experience is governed by still higher-order concepts, which Kant refers to as ideas of reason. Such ideas of reason project a certain kind of systematic unity onto the whole of nature and thus allow us to identify the particular forms of regularity required for the formation of particular empirical concepts. We apply concepts to experience in ways that always involve some implicit commitments to how other concepts are to be understood. It is only through such systematic representational commitments that we are able to distinguish representations that are true of their objects from those that are not. For our only grip on objects that are independent of us is through our capacity systematically to apply the concepts that we have to experience. We have this capacity systematically to articulate and apply concepts because we are able to connect different concepts together in an impersonal representation of their different contents that expresses what they ought to represent for anyone.

In chapter four, I take up the relation of thought and judgment to the self-consciousness expressed in the proposition "I think." Here, I focus on the revised argument of the B-Deduction. The B-Deduction makes the connection between being a potential candidate for impersonal self-consciousness and being a potential candidate for judgment explicit in a way that is lacking in the A-Deduction. First, I note the importance of the proposition "I think" for cognitively relevant content. I note that contents of representation are cognitively relevant to us inasmuch as they can be thought by us. This means that contents of representation are cognitively significant for us insofar as they are potential candidates for judgment. I then develop Kant's argument that anything that can be thought by us has a relation to a possible self-consciousness "I think" in virtue of the enabling role of such self-consciousness in the formation of concepts and judgments.

Representations have relations to each other that are based on the identity and differences between the objects that they represent. The most crucial of these relations are ones that preserve the truth of a representation. Here, the truth of a representation consists in a representation representing its intended object as that object is independently of that representation. Truth is particularly what is at issue when we make a judgment or claim. And truth is preserved between the contents of representations by means of logical relations. These logical relations constitute the most general conditions under which we can ascribe content to representations. These most general conditions for content ascription are the most abstract conceptual conditions governing the possibility of self-consciousness.

I argue that the key to an understanding of the intellectual preconditions on representation is the constitutive role that both personal (empirical) and impersonal (transcendental) consciousness of self play in our capacity to form concepts and articulate them in judgments. Anything that is to be a concept must be such that it is capable of articulating some content in a way that is in principle accessible to any one of us and, indeed, all of us. This capacity to represent things in a person-neutral way needs to be displayed in judgments that have a truth value that purports to be independent of the way a particular individual happens to respond to a particular situation. In judgments, we are able to use concepts to make objective claims that purport to be true not only for me or you, but for anyone.

Kant maintains that representations must be potential candidates for inclusion in a consciousness of oneself that potentially includes all possible representations; This universal self-consciousness is a possible although never actual co-consciousness of all of one's representations. One never actually surveys all of one's representations, much less all possible representations; instead one is able to represent their distinctive contents by connecting them according to rules that have an implicit reference back to oneself as subject of thought. This implicit self-reference is needed for rules constituting the cognitive significance of various contents, because representations have cognitive significance only to the extent that they are potential candidates for comparison and contrast by some subject. To be compared and contrasted by a subject they must present themselves to that subject, and, as such, they must be something for that subject. The demand that all representations be potential candidates for self-consciousness is the basis for a claim that all represented objects stand under the normative constraint of being potential objects of judgment. As objects of judgment that purport to have objective validity, represented objects may be regarded as objective. Even judgments concerning subjective states must have objective import; this leads to the problem of how to find a place for knowledge of subjective states.

In chapter five, I argue that Kant is forced to introduce a second step in the proof to explain how knowledge of even subjective states is possible. He first argues that our knowledge of objects is restricted to spatio-temporal objects. Then, he argues that even our inner states that are temporal depend on the existence of outer states that are spatial. The dependence of inner experience on outer experience allows him to argue that even our perceptions and other inner episodes are subject to the same necessary conditions to which intersubjectively available objects must be subject. This is because even our perceptions provide us with a way of representing the spatio-temporal world from a certain point of view only because they can be integrated into an impersonal and hence objective way of representing the spatio-temporal world for any arbitrary perceiver. The key here is to understand the manner in which not only empirical self-consciousness, but also representation in general, depend on transcendental self-consciousness and thus allow for judgments concerning even one's subjective states.

The argument that self-consciousness is a source of substantive constraints on experience depends on something more than the very general idea that we are capable of forming concepts and making judgments. Kant's argument for objectivity from the postulation of a non-empirical self-consciousness depends essentially on the assumption that we must represent the world temporally because this is constitutive of our very conception of what is internal to our own point of view. Non-empirical consciousness of self is introduced as an enabling condition of our necessary temporal representation of our experiences.

The idea that all experiences have a temporal structure must be linked to more general conceptual constraints on experience. First it must be seen that we are able to think of representations as being in time because we can order those representations in such a way that we can ascribe them to different individuals who have sets of experiences that constitute different temporal series. These different temporal series can only be compared and contrasted with each other to the extent that they may be regarded as belonging to a single shared time. This single shared time is the temporal form that different experiences have in virtue of belonging to one possible impersonal self-consciousness.

The only way we can account for the regularities in what we perceive is in terms of the assumption that what we are perceiving is connected to what we would perceive from a different spatio-temporal point of view according to laws. It is difficult, if not impossible, to identify any laws connecting sense perception to various kinds of objects. The laws in question must therefore be laws governing the objects that we perceive independently of their being perceived. The problem here is that we have knowledge of the objects perceived only through our perceptions. Kant argues that this problem can be resolved once we realize that the laws governing the objects perceived and indeed governing our associations of different perceptions are nothing but the unifiability of different perceptions in an impersonal self-consciousness. This unifiability of perceptions in an impersonal self-consciousness is just the idea that different perceptions are connected in an individual consciousness in the same way that they ought to be connected in any consciousness that perceives or represents things as they are independently of that consciousness. The regularities in experience that present themselves to all of us as self-conscious beings reflect our ability to combine representations together in consciousness in a manner that is not unique to each individual. It is in virtue of such impersonal consciousness of self that we are able to form empirical concepts of the objects that we perceive and are then able to apply those concepts to what we perceive.

In chapter six, I discuss the theory of time-determination developed in the Analogies of Experience. It works out the implications of the idea adumbrated in the Deduction that the unity of space and time (as forms according to which we distinguish the outer from the inner) is a function of the systematic relations that the different spaces and times represented by different possible individuals have to a possible self-consciousness. Kant's general idea that spatio-temporal representations must make a differential contribution to consciousness if they are to belong to the experiences of a self-conscious being is the basis for the general assumption of the Analogies that times and spaces must be empirically distinguishable. In the First Analogy, Kant defends the need to postulate sempiternal substances as the basis for recognizing changes in objects of experience. These substances underwrite our ability to ascribe a determinate position in time and space to representations and objects represented by us. For we have knowledge of positions in time and space only through differences that can be made out in what we experience. These differences manifest themselves temporally in the differences between events. Kant argues that these differences between events are to be interpreted as changes in the states of things. He can claim that all changes must be recognizable in experience on the basis of his robust theory of transcendental idealism. For this robust theory of transcendental idealism does not allow for radically mind-independent and hence recognition-independent events. Even without this strong version of transcendental idealism, a case can be made for the need to presuppose persistent substances if changes are to be recognizable. However, it cannot be demonstrated that events must be recognizable except insofar as they are to be objects of our experience.

Kant's defense of the general causal principle is based on the idea that the temporal order of episodes in any change must be empirically determinable. It thus builds on the necessity of the recognizability of change argued for in the First Analogy on the basis of the principle that empirical representations must make a determinable difference to experience if they are to be potential candidates for self-consciousness. While Kant rejects the causal theory of time when it is understood to reduce the meaning of temporal terms to causal relations, he argues that causation allows one to determine which of two events occurred earlier and which occurred later.

In chapter seven, I discuss the relation of the general causal principle and the general principle that there must be substances and interactions in experience, to our capacity to formulate specific laws governing causation, interaction, and individual things. The only way we can know that a specific change from event-type A to event-type B has occurred and thus that A must precede B is if this change follows in a lawlike fashion upon some other event type of which we have knowledge. Such lawlike succession is just what we mean by causal connection. Interactions between substances are the basis for our knowledge of simultaneity relations between those substances. By being able to determine the temporal order of what is represented by us, we are able to give empirical content to distinctions between different spatial and temporal points of view. At the same time, we are able to connect anything that is represented by us together with anything else that is represented by us in a single consciousness of the temporal unity and the differences of empirical points of view. Kant seems to think that causation and interaction can only assign determinate temporal positions to objects and events if they are capable of providing sufficient conditions for change. However, he allows for indeterministic causal laws at the level of human action, and, in the light of current fundamental physical theory, it seems more plausible to weaken this assumption so that probabilistic laws governing causal connections and interactions become possible at the level of fundamental natural processes. In the concluding sections of the chapter, I argue that Kant's account of causal laws is compatible with free action. The application of causal laws is governed by causal conditions that we assume to comprise a complete set for the regulative purposes of inquiry. However, the important point to see is that we never are in fact capable, even in principle, of identifying a complete set of such causal conditions. This always leaves space for an alternative account of human action under action descriptions that are independent of actual causal conditions.

After discussing the general relation of substance, cause, and interaction to particular kinds of substances, causes, and interactions in chapter seven, I turn in chapter eight to the temptation to think of the self as a thinking thing that is a substance endowed with personal identity over all time. This temptation or "transcendental illusion," as Kant calls it, is rooted in the nature of our access to the self from the first-person point of view. Because I thoughts are self-verifying thoughts, and because we have access to other rational beings by thinking of them as if we were in their place as I thinkers, we become tempted to think that the first-person point of view of self-consciousness is capable of communicating substantive truths about the nature of thinking beings in general. In chapter nine, I look at how this essentially first-person access to rational beings encourages us to think of ourselves as substances that are independent of material objects and knowable in a more certain way than things that exist outside of us.

In chapter ten, I discuss Kant's refutation of idealism which is a revised version of his critique of the kind of epistemic dualism that takes our knowledge of our inner states to be more certain than our knowledge of outer states. Kant maintains that at least some of the objects that we directly experience must be outside of us in space. He attempts to establish this claim by means of an argument showing that determinate consciousness of one's own inner experience is only possible if there are actual outer objects. The argument thus establishes a necessary link between what can be regarded as internal to the point of view of a particular self-conscious being and what can be regarded as external to the point of view of a particular self-conscious being.

The argument against the kind of skepticism about the existence of the external world that Descartes articulates in his First Meditation is based on the general thesis that one cannot ascribe determinate beliefs to oneself without being able to order those beliefs in a determinate temporal order. It is then argued that one cannot ascribe a determinate temporal order to one's beliefs without some direct consciousness of something that is not inherently successive. One's occurrent beliefs and desires are inherently successive. They pick out different nows of awareness due to their character as different occurrent states of awareness. I maintain that Kant needs to be taken at his word that any determinate consciousness of oneself requires an immediate relation to something outside of that self-consciousness. I contend that the argument against "psychological" idealism has force against the Cartesian skeptic who already accepts the possibility of self-knowledge.

The refutation is not complete until it addresses the manner in which our beliefs depend on not only objects that are outside of us in the empirical, but also things in themselves that are outside of us in the sense of being completely independent of our minds. This ultimately leads Kant to raise the issue of transcendental idealism in coming to terms with the problem of how to refute idealism.

I take up transcendental idealism in chapter eleven. Transcendental idealism is the thesis that the only objects of which we can have substantive representations are objects as they must appear to us according to our a priori forms of sensibility. Sensible pre-conditions on experience restrict our experience to objects as they must appear to us, rather than allowing us access to things as they are independently of the way we must represent them as internal to, or external to, our point of view. I argue that Kant vacillates between a modest version of transcendental idealism according to which we cannot resolve the question of what the ultimate nature is of objects that are independent of the pre-conditions that we bring to experience, and a more ambitious claim that objects as they are independently of our experience cannot be spatial or temporal at all. Only the former idealism seems to me to be defensible. In relating Kant's argument for transcendental idealism to his argument against empirical or psychological idealism, I discuss some of Kant's personal notes (his so-called "reflections") which I try to handle with care, since they cannot claim the same authority as the material that he chose to publish. I conclude with a discussion of the general account of experience implied by my reconstruction.

CHAPTER 2

Introducing apperception

Kant introduces the notion of apperception as well as the notion of self-consciousness in the Transcendental Deduction of the Categories. This is the text of the *Critique of Pure Reason* that is widely regarded as the most central one of the whole *Critique*. It is the section of the *Critique* that Kant said had cost him "the most trouble," presumably because it is "laid out at a rather deep level" (A XVI).

In this chapter, I propose to develop Kant's account of apperception and the general way in which Kant connects apperception to representational content in the first (A) edition of the Deduction. First, I argue that the A-Deduction interprets the notion of apperception as self-consciousness. I then argue that the numerical identity that Kant ascribes to transcendental self-consciousness in the A-Deduction is not to be understood as committing him to any specific claims about my individual personal identity. It is rather to be understood as an enabling condition of conceptual recognition of objects. I discuss Kant's argument that all representational content must have at least an indirect relation to a possible self-consciousness in order to be a determinate representation at all. I argue that this is best understood as the idea that each representation has a distinctive functional role in judgment and inference that is based on its relation to a possible self-consciousness.

APPERCEPTION IN THE A-DEDUCTION

Kant introduces empirical apperception in the following way:

The consciousness of oneself according to the determination of our state in inner perception is merely empirical, always mutable, there can be no standing or persistent self in the flux of these inner appearances, and it is customarily called *inner sense*, or *empirical apperception*. (A 107)

Here, Kant identifies empirical self-consciousness with inner sense and empirical apperception. In interpreting empirical self-consciousness in

terms of the notions of inner sense and apperception, he appeals to
accepted terminology in the Leibnizian tradition. Philosophers in that
tradition identified inner sense with empirical apperception.[1] They took
inner sense to be an experience of inner states, while they took empirical
apperception to be a consciousness of inner states. Since they took inner
states to be states of consciousness, they regarded empirical apperception as a form of self-consciousness, that is, they took empirical apperception to be a consciousness of perceptual consciousness. For Kant
"inner sense [is that] by means of which the mind intuits itself and its
state"(A 22/B 37), where "time is nothing but the form of inner sense,
that is, of the intuiting of ourselves and our inner state" (A 33/B 49).

The implication of these passages is that empirical self-consciousness
involves some kind of intuition. Since Kant defines an intuition as a
representation "that relates immediately to an object and is singular" (A
320/B 377), the implication is that empirical self-consciousness is an
immediate consciousness of oneself as an individual. This immediate
representation is a representation of oneself at a certain time, but it is not
a representation of oneself over time.

Empirical apperception represents the self in terms of the individual
states that replace themselves in the succession of different states of
consciousness in time. When we are conscious of our inner empirical
states, we are not conscious of anything that is identical over time. But it
is important to note that Kant does not deny that we have an intuition of
self through inner sense and that we therefore have some consciousness
of self even in empirical self-consciousness. The important point is that
we do not directly experience anything as something connecting our
various experiences together in time.

The ephemerity of mental episodes encourages Kant to argue that in
order to have a representation of self as the identical subject of different
experiences we must be able to represent something that is not given in
any experience. Thus, it might seem that we could avoid the conclusion
that we need something non-empirical to serve as an identical self by
appealing to an object of outer experience as the experientially accessible bearer of experiences. One might argue that in proprioception of
our bodies, that is, in our immediate experience of our bodies, we have a
direct representation of an embodied self. But even proprioception
provides at best synchronous consciousness of self; it fails to provide us
with a representation of our own identity over different times and
spaces. And most significantly, proprioception does not provide us with
the kind of necessary representation of numerical identity in which Kant

is interested. For his real concern is not with how an identical self can be represented, but rather with how something could be represented as *necessarily* identical in different experiences:

That which should *necessarily* be represented as numerically identical cannot be thought as such through empirical data. It must be a condition that precedes all experience and even makes it possible that validates such a transcendental condition. (A 107)

Several questions arise at this point: (1) What is a transcendental condition? (2) What is the transcendental condition in question? And (3) for what is the transcendental condition a condition? Perhaps Kant's best answer to the question of what a transcendental condition is, comes in a discussion of apperception in the section criticizing the false inferences or paralogisms of rational psychology:

For this inner perception is nothing more than the mere apperception: *I think*; which even makes all transcendental concepts possible, in which it is said: I think substance, cause, etc. For inner perception in general and its possibility, or perception in general, and its relationship to other perception without a particular difference between perceptions and determination being given empirically, cannot be regarded as empirical, but must be regarded as cognition of the empirical, and belongs to the investigation of the possibility of any cognition, which is indeed transcendental. (A 343/B 401)

In other words, a transcendental condition is a condition under which cognition in general, and empirical cognition in particular, is possible. Kant regards transcendental apperception as such a non-empirical condition on what can be known empirically. Indeed, Kant identifies the transcendental condition in which he is interested in the A-Deduction as transcendental apperception. In the A-Deduction, he maintains that transcendental apperception makes it possible to explain the existence of a necessary connection between representations which he argues is involved in any empirical cognition. For this necessary connection is supposed to be nothing but the concept of an object that corresponds to our representations. This provides a general answer to the third question: of what is transcendental apperception a transcendental condition? Transcendental apperception is a condition under which it is possible to have a concept or cognition of an object. What the relationship between concepts and cognitions is supposed to be, and why we should understand the concept of an object in the way that Kant proposes, will have to be determined later. For now it is sufficient to note that transcendental apperception is supposed to account for our capacity to form concepts of objects:

This necessity has a transcendental condition as its ground. Therefore a transcendental ground must be found for the unity of consciousness in the synthesis of the manifold of all our intuitions, hence also of all concepts of objects in general, consequently of all objects of experience, without which it would be impossible to think any object; for this [object] is nothing more than the something the concept of which expresses such a necessity of synthesis. This original and transcendental condition is no other than *transcendental apperception.* (A 107)

When Kant introduces transcendental apperception as a necessary representation of numerical identity, he does not explicitly say that the numerical identity that he is concerned with is that of the self. This has led Andrew Brook to argue that the empirical and transcendental apperception to which Kant refers at A 107 is not a consciousness of self at all, but merely awareness of something.[2] Now Kant explicitly claims that empirical apperception is a kind of self-consciousness. The context also suggests that Kant thinks that the standing self that he misses in empirical apperception must be supplied by a transcendental representation. And he later clearly states that numerical identity is certain a priori with respect to all possible self-consciousness, since nothing can enter cognition except via this original apperception (A 113). Moreover, Kant also talks of an "original and necessary consciousness of the identity of oneself" (A 108), as what makes it possible for us to determine an object for our experiences. If this is not enough evidence, Kant also speaks of "the proposition that expresses self-consciousness: I think" (A 398–399), after already talking of "the mere apperception: I think" (A 343/B 402). So it is quite implausible to argue, as Brook does, that apperception is not self-consciousness and that, therefore, self-consciousness is not crucial to Kant's argument.

Kant's talk of a representation of numerical identity with respect to transcendental apperception encourages one to think of transcendental self-consciousness as consciousness of personal identity in contrast with consciousness of individual states involved in empirical apperception. But, in fact, the notion of transcendental self-consciousness is impersonal in a way that, in principle, is in transpersonal. The necessity of representing oneself as numerically identical does not commit Kant to the existence of a persistent bearer of my states of consciousness, but rather to a way of representing ourselves, a point of view from which what is represented by me and you at different times and places can be unified. Kant maintains that the self is necessarily *represented as* numerically identical; he does not argue that it is necessarily numerically identical over different states.

But how are we to understand the necessity of representing ourselves as numerically identical? And in what sense can we talk of a certainty that our self-consciousness is numerically identical? All of us use the expression "I" to refer to ourselves. The role of the demonstrative expression "I" in connecting together representations that individuals have of themselves at different times and spaces in one unitary experience is what makes for the *numerical* identity of our representation of I. The expression "I" articulates a self-consciousness that remains the numerically same point of view regardless of one's spatio-temporal situation. Now I might be mistaken about who I am, and thus about my personal identity, but not about the fact that I am now self-conscious and that I can represent myself as the same subject in alternative situations. Thus, even though Kant thinks of transcendental self-consciousness as necessary to any consciousness of an object, he does not regard transcendental self-consciousness itself as a personal self-consciousness at all. The necessary representation of numerical identity in transcendental self-consciousness is, rather, the necessary representation of a shared point of view from which we can make sense of an objective space and time and, indeed, of the communicability of the contents of concepts to different spatio-temporal points of view:

This pure, original, unchanging consciousness I will now call *transcendental apperception*. That it deserves this name is already clear from the following: that even the purest objective unity, namely of concepts a priori (space and time) is only possible through the relation of intuitions to it. The numerical unity of this apperception lies a priori as much at the basis a priori of all concepts as the manifold of space and time does of all intuitions of sensibility. (A 107)

The purity of self-consciousness refers to its independence from the content of any particular experience. The original character of self-consciousness is based on the idea that any personal or empirical self-consciousness will depend for its existence on the possibility of that impersonal consciousness of self. The unchanging character of such consciousness is based on the fact that it represents a point of view that must be regarded as identical in any experience. This point of view is the basis for our ability to interpret experience in terms of concepts of objects.

Kant insists that the "numerical unity of this apperception is the ground a priori of all concepts" (A 107). The capacity for consciousness of self-identity makes concepts possible by providing the idea of a representer and hence a representation of that representer that is distinguishable from what is represented and yet represents the representer as an I that, in principle, can be regarded as the possessor of an arbitrary spatio-temporal point of view. Our concepts of space and time have "objective unity" insofar as they capture the way a self-conscious being would represent the world in the same way from any arbitrary standpoint in space and time and in any arbitrary psychological state that the representer might happen to be in.

Concepts are just the way in which things are represented in universal terms, that is, represented in a way that connects different experiences together in the same way for different persons in different psychological states and situations: "All cognition demands a concept but this [concept] is always something universal according to its form, and something that serves as a rule" (A 106). Now "concepts are based on functions" (A 68/B 93), where the functions in question are the functional relations involved in judgments that subsume one representation under another representation: "But I understand under function the unity of the act of subsuming different representations under a common one" (A 68/B 93). The representation under which another representation is to be subsumed is one that represents a feature that the first representation has in common with other representations.

The representation of the common or shared feature is what Kant calls a concept. Concepts, then, have their distinctive cognitive content in virtue of the distinctive functional role that they play in the forming of judgments and the drawing of inferences from those judgments. But what all concepts have in common is that they are representations that play identical functional roles despite differences in the inner states of the different individuals who use those concepts in different situations.

Kant notes that the kind of unity of consciousness that is displayed by our capacity for conceptual recognition would be impossible "if the mind in cognition of the manifold could not become conscious of the identity of function through which it synthetically connects that [manifold] together" (A 108). From the need to be able to represent an identity of functional role in different contents of experiences in order to be able to recognize items in experience, Kant significantly concludes that the "original and necessary consciousness of the identity of oneself is at the same time a consciousness of the necessary unity of synthesis of all appearances according to concepts" (A 108). In other words, for Kant, the necessary representation of the numerical identity of the self is built into our ability to represent things in different situations in ways that have the same cognitive role in judgment and inference for all of us.

Necessary consciousness of our self-identity is something more than the ability to represent ourselves as having a point of view from which things appear in the same way to each and all of us. It is the capacity at the same time to represent our point of view as the same point of view as we compare different items of experience with respect to their identity and differences. It is only in this way that we are able to form concepts with different cognitive roles because they have different functional roles in judgment and inference. In sum, Kant links the necessity that we represent ourselves as numerically identical in different experiences to the possibility of forming an impersonal point of view. By taking this impersonal point of view on our experiences, we are then able to form concepts that have the same distinctive functional role in different experiences. The distinctive functional roles that different concepts have, in turn reflect the different systematic contributions that different concepts make to the understanding of what we experience.

INTERPRETING THE NUMERICAL IDENTITY OF THE SELF

The "impersonal" character of our representation of self as numerically identical has been generally obscured by contemporary obsession with viewing Kant's conception of the identity of apperception as a direct response to Hume's critique of personal identity.[3] Hume's reservations about our knowledge of personal identity are summed up in the following passage:

It must be some one impression, that gives rise to every real idea. But self or person is not any one impression, but that to which our several impressions and ideas are suppos'd to have a reference. If any impression gives rise to the idea of self, that impression must continue invariable the same, thro' the whole course of our lives; since self is suppos'd to exist after that matter. But there is no impression constant and invariable. Pain and pleasure, grief and joy, passions and sensations succeed each other, and never all exist at the same time. It cannot, therefore, be from any of these impressions, or from any other, that the idea of self is deriv'd; and consequently there is no such idea.[4]

Hume's worry is that the representations (impressions) that make up our mental life are continually replacing each other, so that there does not seem to be any representation to which we could appeal in order to provide a conception of our personal identity. Kant never attempts to show that there is a "real idea" of the self, nor does he attempt to find an impression from which such a representation could be derived. He thus does not attempt to meet Hume's demands with respect to personal identity. Kant takes it as a given that we have consciousness of ourselves with respect to our inner states even though the self of this inner experience is in a perpetual state of flux. But he also agrees with Hume's worries about the introspective basis for consciousness of one's identity over time. Given Kant's view that we have an intuition of self in inner sense, I see no reason to saddle him with Hume's view that the self is never itself an object of perception or introspection. However, such a claim would only provide further support for Kant's assumption that the self is accessible only through the formal structure that is inherent in the activity of self-consciousness.

Interpreting Kant's notion that we necessarily represent ourselves as self-identical a priori as a direct response to Hume's worries about self-identity forces one to identify a priori consciousness of self-identity with a priori knowledge of one's identity as a discrete individual. This is very difficult to reconcile with Kant's claim that self-consciousness "according to the determinations of our state" is empirical and does not have a persistent subject (A 107). It also ignores the fact that Kant commits himself only to an a priori representation of numerical identity, not a priori knowledge that we are numerically identical.

Not all of the difficulties with Kant's notion of a necessary representation of self as numerically identical can be traced back to regarding Kant as a direct respondent to Hume's worries about our knowledge of personal identity. Much of this controversy has however been generated by the more general conviction that Kant's talk of the numerical identity of the self must commit him to the claim that I can know that I am the numerically same person through different experiences. It should not be denied that Kant's talk of numerical identity of the self encourages an interpretation that identifies consciousness of numerical identity with knowledge of personal identity. This is part of the reason that it has seemed unclear to commentators whether Kant is concerned in his talk of numerical identity of the self with the identity of a person or with a person's being conscious of identical thoughts.[5]

Elsewhere in the A-Deduction, Kant interprets the numerical identity that we necessarily represent, as a numerical identity of possible self-consciousness. This numerical identity is characterized as a priori certain. Kant makes remarks that have seemed to interpreters to suggest that we might be certain a priori of our numerical identity as persons as a pre-condition for having representations at all:

All possible appearances belong as representations to the whole of possible self-consciousness. But numerical identity is indivisible from it and a priori certain because nothing can come into cognition except by means of this original apperception. (A 113)

In response to passages such as these in the A-Deduction in which Kant ascribes a priori certainty to the numerical identity of self-consciousness, Dieter Henrich has emphasized the fact that we have criterialess consciousness of self-identity. This consciousness of self-identity is supposed to be characterized by a certainty of the kind Descartes discovered in I thoughts. Descartes argues famously that I thoughts are self-verifying, to have those thoughts is already to have sufficient warrant for regarding them as true. But he never argues that this self-verifying character of I thoughts extends to claims that the self is identical over time. However, Henrich's idea that we have a Cartesian certainty of the identity of the self over a sequence of states has an antecedent in Strawson's view that at the heart of the Cartesian illusion that we can infer substantial facts about the self from I thoughts is the fact that we have a criterialess consciousness of self in immediate or recalled experience.[6] There is just no question for me that the states that I ascribe to my present and past consciousness actually belong to my consciousness of self.

However, unlike Strawson, Henrich seems to take Cartesian certainty in the direction of making a self-justifying claim about personal identity. In this way, Henrich's notion that we have Cartesian certainty of our numerical identity through the transitions involved in understanding the different aspects of objects seems to commit him to a priori knowledge of the real persistence of a self.[7] For Henrich insists that we are certain of our numerical identity through changes in states. And only with respect to the real persistence of a self does it make sense to make claims about changes in state.

Henrich argues that the self as subject of self-consciousness can only be weakly or moderately, rather than strictly, identical with itself. For self-consciousness involves acts of consciousness that are changes in state and only the notion of a weak numerical identity of the self is supposed to be consistent with changes in state. On the other hand, Henrich thinks of such identity as identity through atemporal change. But neither the idea that strict identity precludes change nor the idea that atemporal changes are possible has any obvious support in the Kantian text. And both ideas seem to be intrinsically quite implausible.

In response to criticism, in particular from Paul Guyer, that Henrich simply assumes one's self-identity over representational states as a synthetic a priori premise governing the self-ascription of representation, Henrich has distinguished his conception that one is certain of the identity of one's self through different states of self-consciousness from empirical knowledge of personal identity as well as from the notion of identity familiar from logic.[8] Unfortunately, Henrich fails to give a positive characterization of his conception of the identity implied in self-consciousness. This would be less problematic if one could see what alternative to the logical notion of identity there could be. Henrich is probably tempted to argue that there is a non-logical notion of identity by talk of a "loose" as opposed to a "strict" meaning of personal identity. But, properly understood, the "loose" notion of identity involved in such contexts is not really a distinctive notion of identity at all. Philosophers who take the identity of a person to be "loose" regard persons as constituted by a series of individual person-stages rather than being the numerically same individual through the time of their lives. But even if persons were mere series of person-stages, persons would nevertheless be "strictly" identical through time, for they would be the same series throughout their existence.

While Guyer criticizes Henrich for endorsing a kind of a priori certainty of personal identity, he thinks that Henrich is right to attribute to Kant the view that we have a kind of a priori knowledge of our personal identity through different states. Indeed, Guyer thinks that Kant assumes that we can be certain that all of our empirical states are ones of which we can become conscious. This is because Guyer interprets Kant's principle that one can be conscious of one's numerical identity as subject of self-consciousness in respect to all possible representations as a claim that one can have a priori certainty of all of one's representational states and hence of one's personal identity as an empirically knowable individual:

Kant has failed to establish that I must in fact *know*–a fortiori be certain–that I have really had all of a putative series of representations through some period of my continued existence in order to investigate their possible empirical significance. But unless Kant can exclude *a priori* the possibility that one of the results of my investigation could be the very *rejection* of the supposition that I actually had one or more of the representations the possible empirical connections of which I am investigating, he cannot prove that certainty of my possession of any particular representations really is presupposed by any empirical investigation of them.[9]

Guyer rightly disparages the idea that we could be certain that each of the representations that we think we have had are in fact our own. This would entail a priori certainty that all of the beliefs that we ascribe to ourselves really are the beliefs that have belonged to our lives, and this would entail a priori certainty of personal identity. But this interpretation of a priori certainty, as a priori certainty of one's personal identity, is based on his assimilation of Kant's notion of transcendental self-consciousness to consciousness of one's self-identity as empirically knowable, that is, to consciousness of one's individual personal identity. We can hardly rule out a priori that some of the claims to empirical knowledge of our personal identity that we make might be false.

One striking feature of Guyer's interpretation is that it is based on a notion of a priori certainty of self-identity that Kant introduces to account for our capacity to recognize objects that are distinct from our momentary present states of consciousness. While Guyer rejects such a priori certainty, he has made the synthesis of apprehension construed as the interpretation of momentary intuitions of multiplicities the key to his interpretation of the Transcendental Analytic as an analysis of the a priori conditions for empirical self-knowledge. According to Guyer, what Kant calls the fundamental premise of the whole Deduction is the assumption that I am *not* immediately acquainted with any *manifold* of representations insofar as I think of a representation as contained in a single moment. Now Kant does say that one must assume in the rest of his argument that all representations must be in time, since they belong to inner sense, and are hence subject to synthesis: "all representations belong as modifications of the mind to inner sense, and as such all our cognitions are also subject in the end to the formal condition of inner sense, namely time, in which they must be ordered, connected, and put in relations. This is a general remark that one must take as a basis for what follows"(A 99). This is not quite the same thing as taking all representations to be something that I think at a moment. To be sure, Kant maintains at A 99 that to think of a manifold *as a manifold* I must first represent a sequence of one impression upon another, and he also says that every representation "*as contained in a single moment*" can only be an absolute unity.[10] Thus, Guyer is right that Kant thinks that a momentary representation is not a representation of a manifold. But

Guyer draws an implication from this assumption of Kant's that comes from failure to see that the only kind of representations that Kant regards as momentary are sensations. Guyer interprets Kant's statement that intuition offers a manifold, that can never be represented as a manifold, *and as contained in a single representation*, without synthesis to mean that we take a present state and judge it to be a representation of different times.

On the other hand, Guyer rightly insists that the temporal order of what is represented is not *created* out of some kind of diversity that is before the mind in some non-temporal manner. This would confuse the synthesis of recognition by means of which the multiplicity of intuition is determined to be what it is with the synthesis of apprehension by which a multiplicity of data is first given in temporal succession.[11] But this caveat leaves it quite unclear as to what sense we are to give to the idea of judging or interpreting a present state to be a representation of different times. Guyer's use of judgment and interpretation to explicate Kant's account of the role that the synthesis of apprehension plays in our experience of different representations, as such, seems to introduce precisely the synthesis of recognition into his analysis of Kant's conception of the synthesis of apprehension that he instructs us to avoid.[12]

Regardless of the merits of his interpretation of the threefold synthesis of apprehension, reproduction, and recognition, Guyer notes that recognition involves the possibility of interpretative error and thus the possibility that one did not actually recognize something that one thought one had recognized. Guyer is clearly correct to insist that interpretative errors are possible.[13] But, surprisingly, Guyer regards a priori certainty of self-identity as something that rules out the possibility of interpretative error even though it is introduced by Kant as a transcendental condition for recognition. But, when Kant maintains that in self-consciousness we are a priori certain of the self's numerical identity, there is no evidence that he wishes to deny the possibility of error in self-ascriptions, as Guyer alleges. Thus, there is no inconsistency in Kant's position here. If one identifies consciousness of self-identity a priori with a priori consciousness of one's empirical identity, then one cannot indeed allow for the possibility that any of the representations which one takes oneself to have had could turn out to be representations which one did not, in fact, have. But there is no reason to think that a priori consciousness of self-identity is a priori knowledge of my particular identity as an empirically knowable individual. While Kant is interested in a priori knowledge of what makes experience possible, he is loath to argue that we can have a priori knowledge of empirical facts.

Far from thinking that we cannot be wrong in thinking that a particular set of states belongs to our personal identity, Kant insists in the Third Paralogism of Pure Reason that "the identity of the consciousness of my self in different times is only a formal condition of my thoughts and their connection, but does not prove the numerical identity of my subject, in which despite the logical identity of the I, nevertheless a change can have occurred that does not allow its identity to be sustained" (A 363). The point that Kant wishes to make is that consciousness of my self-identity does not guarantee that I am an individual who is actually numerically identical over the time of which I am conscious of myself as being the same person. To make this point in a plastic way, Kant suggests the theoretical possibility that an awareness of the past might be passed from individual to individual in a manner that is analogous to a series of elastic balls that pass on their motion from one to another. The final individual in the series could well have a consciousness of the past histories of all the other individuals in the series, and believe itself to be a single individual that persisted through the series even though this would be an illusion.

Guyer realizes that the identity of self-consciousness, as he interprets it, conflicts with the argument of the Third Paralogism in which Kant rejects the idea that we somehow have a priori knowledge of our personal identity. But he regards the tension between his reading of the Deduction and the text of the Paralogisms as a contradiction in Kant's own views.[14] Indeed, on his reading, Kant is inconsistent even in the Deduction itself, since the central argument for synthesis from recognition that Guyer defends is said by Kant to depend on the necessity of representing one's numerical identity. The inconsistencies disappear once one realizes that Kant is concerned with a necessity concerning the way in which we represent ourselves as experiencers and not with a claim that we have a priori knowledge of our individual identity over time.

Guyer's interpretation of Kant's idea that we are a priori certain that we can represent ourselves as self-identical is linked to his reading of the central task of the Deduction. The Deduction must show that there must be certain kinds of syntheses that we must perform on experience a priori in order to show that a priori concepts of the understanding, the so-called categories, have a legitimate use and one that is restricted to objects of experience. Guyer argues that it is only if we can impose a certain connectedness on any possible representation a priori in virtue of a putative a priori certainty of self-identity that Kant will have provided a successful defense of the existence of a priori synthesis from our consciousness of self-identity. For Kant is supposed to need more than an analytic claim to the effect that I regard all the representations that I take to be mine as belonging to my single self, he is supposed to need a *de re* necessity that whatever my representations may be they can be called mine by me. A *de re* necessity concerning representations would apply to representations independently of how we happen to pick out or characterize those representations. Thus, I would know independently of any conditions governing my recognition of representations that all my representations are mine. For only this kind of a priori certainty of self-identity is supposed to require the kind of synthetic principles a priori governing the connections between representations that Kant is trying to establish.[15] Since Guyer regards the notion of a priori certainty of self-identity as "profoundly questionable," he takes the appeal to a priori certainty of self-identity to call into question Kant's general argument in the Deduction for a priori synthesis from transcendental self-consciousness.[16]

But why does Guyer think that a priori synthesis would have to involve a metaphysical or *de re* necessity, rather than a purely conceptual or *de dicto* necessity? Guyer concedes that Kant sometimes avails himself of a notion of transcendental synthesis as non-empirical conditions on experience rather than as acts of transcendental synthesis that are independent of empirical acts of synthesis: "There is indeed a transcendental synthesis which however concerns nothing more than the conditions under which the perception of a thing in general can belong to possible experience" (A 714/B 747).[17] Guyer rightly argues that in the Deduction Kant is committed to the existence of a guarantee that all representations can be combined in a single self regardless of the content, and this forces him to appeal to a more robust notion of a priori synthesis. It is unclear to me why such a guarantee is not consistent with thinking of a priori synthesis in terms of a priori constraints on empirical synthesis. But it is undeniable that Kant does think that there is a guarantee to the effect that any possible object of experience must be a potential object that can be represented as a representation that can belong to a possible self-consciousness. And that representation is also supposed to be represented as a representation that can be compared and contrasted with other representations of that numerically identical self-consciousness:

But the possibility, yes, the necessity of the categories depends on the relation that the whole of sensibility, and with it all appearances, have to original apperception, in which everything necessarily accords with the conditions of pervasive unity of self-consciousness, that is, must stand under universal functions of synthesis, namely of synthesis according to concepts, in which apperception can alone prove its pervasive and necessary identity a priori. (A 111–112)

It is to Kant's argument linking determinate representations to self-consciousness that I now turn.

REPRESENTATIONAL CONTENT AND THE POSSIBILITY OF SELF-CONSCIOUSNESS

Kant draws far-reaching conclusions from his general claim that we can only make sense of the conceptual component of representations by reference to a numerically identical point of view that is available in all experience. He argues that all representations are not only potential candidates for self-consciousness, but have content and indeed exist only in relation to a possible self-consciousness:

All representations have a necessary relation to a possible empirical consciousness: for if they did not have this [possible empirical consciousness], and if it were completely impossible to be conscious of them; then this would say as much as they would not exist at all. But all empirical consciousness has a necessary relation to a transcendental consciousness (preceding all particular experience), namely the consciousness of myself as original apperception. (A 117n)

Kant attempts to ascribe a differential representational content to different representations in virtue of the distinctive representational role that those representations can play for a possible self-consciousness. But one obvious problem for his conception is that many representations seem to have a content that is independent of the cognitive role that they might play in a possible self-consciousness. It is not even clear that all representations can become conscious to someone. The possibility of attributing representations to beings that cannot become conscious of those representations themselves would seem to be enough to undermine Kant's claim that all representations must be potential candidates for self-consciousness. If animals have representations, but do not have self-consciousness, then it would seem prima facie that there are representations of which self-consciousness is not possible. There is no evidence that Kant thought that non-human animals have self-consciousness. As

Jonathan Bennett has noted, it would be self-contradictory to demand of a being defined as non-self-conscious that it be able to be self-conscious of its own states.[18] Kant concedes that there can be representations of which the creature who has them can have no cognition:

> I would not even be able to know that I have them [sense data], and they would therefore be nothing for me, as a knowing being, at all. They might still exist in me (if I imagine myself to be an animal) a being unconscious of my own existence carrying on their play in an orderly fashion as representations connected according to an empirical law of association, exercising influence upon feeling and desire, and so always displaying regularity without my thereby acquiring the least knowledge of anything, not even of these my own states. (May 26, 1789, Ak. XI, p. 52)

Kant's willingness to allow for association even if a creature has no concepts of objects seems at first to conflict with his account of the threefold synthesis.[19] For it seems to provide a counterexample to the twin theses (1) that one needs the capacity for conceptual recognition in order to be able to distinguish an object from the way it appears to one and (2) that one then also needs the ability to distinguish an object from the way it appears to one in order to have some determinate basis for associations. But, in fact, the existence of associative capacities in animals that do not have concepts is not obviously inconsistent with the account of association in the A-Deduction. One can consistently argue that association requires the kinds of regularities that one can only make sense of by using concepts of objects, while also arguing that association is possible even for creatures that cannot themselves use concepts. This is also the key to understanding how it is possible to accommodate the representations of animals in the possibility of self-consciousness.

An animal representation is a representation of an object from a certain spatio-temporal standpoint. The recurrence of certain perspectival presentations of a spatio-temporal object for that animal is the basis for the associations that Kant regards as key to animal consciousness. Now the animal cannot itself become conscious of the various perspectival presentations of the object with which it is presented. At least it cannot regard those presentations as its own distinctive take on the object. For the animal has neither self-consciousness, nor a bona fide concept of an object that can be identified and re-identified in different circumstances. But the very possibility of thinking of an animal as associating different spatio-temporal perspectives on an object is something that must be intelligible. Animals do not themselves distinguish objects from the way those objects immediately present themselves to those animals. We can make sense of the distinction between the object and the way it appears to an observer only by thinking of the observer as if it were the kind of creature for whom the object could be something. This means we must think of the creature as if the creature were conscious of its own distinctive point of view, and this means that we must think of the creature as if it were self-conscious. To do this, we must, as selfconscious beings, put ourselves in the vantage point of the non-selfconscious being in question. In this way, we are able to treat its non-selfconscious representations as if they were self-conscious representations and thus regard them as potential candidates for selfconsciousness.

Animals have no self-knowledge. In this sense, their representations are nothing for them. While representations in such non-selfconscious animals cannot become self-conscious to the animals that have them, we can only attribute representations to animals based on our ability to imagine what it would be like for us to represent the world in the way animals do. This is why, in discussing unconscious representations, Kant demands that I, who am a self-conscious being, imagine myself to be a being unconscious of its existence. Thus, even though representations may not be candidates for self-consciousness by the animal that has them, they are intelligible to us only in virtue of the fact that we think of them as representations that we might have ascribed to ourselves had our circumstances been quite different. For we only think of a representation as representation to the extent that we think of it as an expression of a sentient point of view. And to think of the representation as an expression of a sentient point of view is already to think of the representation as something that a being could, in principle, think of as its own were its cognitive capacities like our own.[20]

In arguing that all representations are potential candidates for self-consciousness at A 117n, Kant moves from the assumption that a representation is unknowable to the conclusion that it does not exist at all. At A 120 the point is put in terms of objects of representation, that is, that which appears to us: "without the relation to at least a possible consciousness, appearance would never be an object of cognition for us and therefore nothing for us, and since it has no objective reality in itself, and only in cognition, it would be everywhere nothing." Prima facie, there is an important distinction to be drawn between the conditions governing our ability to ascribe content to representations and the conditions governing the very existence of representational content. Kant argues here that representations have no existence that is independent of the capacity of creatures like us to recognize them. Representation is constituted by its function in understanding how sentient creatures react to their environment. As such, it is exhausted by the role it plays in understanding persons, animals, and certain sophisticated automata (*automata spiritualia*). We can regard the premise that representation is exhausted by its cognitive role as analytic to the notion of representation. However, the premise is not simply a verbal stipulation, but a substantive claim about the nature of representations. It can thus equally be regarded as synthetic and even synthetic a priori.

REPRESENTATIONAL CONTENT AND FUNCTIONAL ROLE

Kant insists that representations must make a discernible difference if they are to count as distinctive representations. In fact, he argues that representations "can represent something only in so far as they belong with all others [actually, all other consciousness] to one consciousness, and therefore must at least be capable of being so connected" (A 116). Representations represent in virtue of the different contents that they have. They can therefore only be regarded as representational contents to the extent that they can be distinguished from one another. But, in order to count as *representational* contents, they must also be logically distinguishable from their bearer even if they are not, as in the case of a pain sensation, logically distinguishable from their object. To be logically distinguishable from their bearer, representations must be thinkable as having a subject. As representational contents, they are thus distinguishable from one another only insofar as they can be represented as different possible representations of a subject. They must, however, also be represented as such by a subject because it is only through the possibility of first-person access that we understand what makes a representation the qualitative experience that it is. This leads Kant to conclude: "The abiding and unchanging 'I' (pure apperception) forms the correlate of all our representations in so far as it is to be at all possible that we should become conscious of them" (A 123).

In order to be able to consider any content experienced by us as a representational content, we must be able to recognize that content as a representational content. But we can only recognize anything as a representational content if we can compare and contrast it with other representational contents in one consciousness. Contrastive consciousness involves a representation of many at least numerically different representations. If those representations are to be represented in relation to each other, one must be able to represent oneself as the numerically same subject which is representing them in relation to each other. From this line of thought, Kant infers that the possibility of representing the self as numerically identical through its different possible representations is necessary to the very possibility of representations:

We are conscious a priori of the pervasive identity of our self in respect to all representations which can ever belong to our knowledge as a necessary condition of the possibility of all representations (because these only represent something in me through belonging with all other (*mit allem anderen*) [consciousness] to one consciousness, therefore they must at least be connectable therein). (A 116)

The content of a representation must be a content which can belong to the interconnected representations of some self-conscious thinker. The content must be a candidate for self-consciousness by some possible self-conscious being in order for there to be grounds for the attribution of that representation to a representer. We cannot however represent the identity and differences of these different representations in relation to each other without applying concepts to those representations. A concept just is a representation of an object by means of a feature which may be shared by different objects (including representations themselves). These concepts must themselves have contents which are determined by their relations of identity and difference to each other. Thus, we can only make sense of the notion of a representation insofar as we hold that representation to be conceptualizable within the conceptual framework of a being capable of articulating a set of concepts which it is capable of self-ascribing. The further point to note is that the systematic differences between representational contents can be understood as differences in the functional roles that representations play in judgment and inference. It is here that the categories enter the picture.

LOGICAL FUNCTIONS OF THOUGHT AND CATEGORIES

The categories or pure concepts of the understanding whose legitimacy Kant wishes to defend are supposed to have their ultimate source in the basic logical constants or logical functions of thought. The Metaphysical Deduction claims to be able to derive the categories from the most basic logical functions involved in judgment. This list of categories and basic logical functions is supposed to be complete:

This division is systematically generated from a common principle, namely from the faculty of judgment (which is as much as the faculty of thinking) and has not come to be rhapsodically from a search for pure concepts relying on good luck, of whose completeness one could never be certain, since it is only inferred by induction without considering that in that case one could never realize why these concepts and not others belong to pure understanding. (A 80–81/B 106–107)

Although Kant chastises Aristotle for his rhapsodic approach to a doctrine of categories, it is difficult to identify an argument in the Metaphysical Deduction or elsewhere that the table of logical functions or of categories is complete. Kant seems, however, to have thought that an analysis of the nature of judgment would force one to assume a certain set of most basic syntactical forms of judgment. To such syntactical forms of judgment there would in turn be a corresponding set of most basic extra syntactic constraints on the way judgments can be made concerning objects.[21]

Kant lists twelve categories in four groups, (1) categories of quantity: unity, plurality, totality, (2) categories of quality: reality, negation, limitation, (3) categories of relation: inherence and subsistence, causality and dependence, interaction, (4) categories of modality: possibility, actuality, and necessity (A 80/B 106). These categories are supposed to arise from the different ways in which intuition can be connected together in a unity, just as the twelve basic forms of judgment that Kant attempts to abstract from term logic are supposed to arise from the different fundamental ways in which concepts can be connected together in the unity of a judgment (A 79/B 105). The general idea is that categories constitute the different fundamental kinds of objects that can be thought by the different fundamental functions involved in different kinds of judging. These forms of judgment are (1) quantity of judgment: universal, particular, individual, (2) quality: assertive, negative, infinite, (3) relation: categorical, hypothetical, disjunctive, (4) modality: problematic, assertoric, apodictic. Even if Kant had a completeness proof for the logical constants in his term logic, the connection between the categories and these logical functions is quite loose. Questions would thus remain about the completeness of his list of categories.[22]

While categories have a logical meaning that consists in the unification of representations in judgment even without sensible conditions, these logical forms are not yet concepts of objects (A 147/B 186). They only become full-fledged concepts of objects when they are given an extra syntactical content from our experience. For until then the objects that these forms represent are indistinguishable from those forms of thought themselves. Once logical forms have an object that is distinguishable from the forms of thought, they become categories (A 79/B 105). A concept a priori that did not have a content somehow dependent on experience and that did not relate to experience at all would be "only the logical form for a concept, but not the concept itself through which something would be thought" (A 95). While we can have concepts of objects that do not or could not exist in our experience, even such concepts are formed from concepts that do have a content that is somehow linked to experience. This content must be at least a condition for the possibility of experience (A 95–96). Such concepts need not be acquired from experience, but, in the helpful jargon of Kant's reply to Eberhard, they must at least be originally acquired in response to experience and the spatial and temporal structure which makes our experience what it is. This is what gives such concepts their "objective reality" and such objective reality is required if our use of such concepts is to be legitimate.

Now Kant does not seem initially to be willing to extend functional role to all mental states, but maintains instead that functions consist in ways of subsuming representations under a concept. He notes that "concepts are based on the spontaneity of thought, just as sensible intuitions depend on the receptivity of impressions" (A 68/B 93). In the same context, Kant explicitly contrasts the dependence of concepts on functions with the way in which "all intuitions as sensible, depend on affections." The functions involved in our ability to use concepts are limited to the active taking of things as thus and such to be found paradigmatically in judgment and inference.

But the initial picture of a sharp distinction between spontaneity and receptivity, and function and affection soon breaks down. For it turns out that our experience is inherently concept-laden, so that even when we are not making judgments, what we sensibly experience is already conceptualized. While the Deduction begins with the claim that "intuition does not require the functions of thought in any way" and poses the problem of how categories can apply to objects of intuition given this independence of intuition from the functions of thought (A 91/B 123), the argument of the Deduction in favor of the legitimacy of our possession of categories, that is, what Kant calls pure concepts of the understanding, actually goes through only if Kant can establish the quite different claim that intuition depends for its unity, that is, for its ability to represent determinate objects, on the functions of the understanding:

"The same function that gives unity to the representations *in a judgment*, gives also the mere synthesis of different representations *in one intuition* unity, which expressed generally, is called the pure concept of the understanding" (A 79/B 105).

What we directly experience or intuit has a determinate object, only insofar as it is already conceptualized by us and thus subject to the same functions of unity that underlie different conceptual roles. Indeed, Kant maintains that the relation of different contents of cognition to an object "is nothing but the necessary unity of consciousness, hence also of the synthesis of the manifold, to connect it in one representation through a common function <*gemeinschaftliche Funktion*> of the mind" (A 109). Cognition relates to an object insofar as it involves a necessary unity of consciousness. The necessary unity of consciousness involved in cognition of an object is a way of representing things that is independent of the psychological state one happens to be in, because it must be the same for all of us at all times and places. This way of representing things is provided by a function of the mind that is the same for all of us at all times.

Kant must insist that inner perception (introspection) involves sensibility, indeed, inner affection, but also that it has an active and spontaneous dimension to it that reflects its dependence on the functions of thought that underlie the identity of self-consciousness. And, if Kant is to successfully argue that the content even of intuitions is dependent on the kind of identity of function to be found in concepts, but which ultimately depends on our capacity for representing our numerical identity in different experiences, he must argue that even the representational content involved in intuition is a function of the judgmental and inferential role which that content plays in judgments and inferences using concepts. Thus, even though the Deduction starts out by indicating that objects of intuition might be completely independent of the functions of the understanding, the conclusion of the Deduction must be that we have no way of understanding what it would be for an object of intuition to be an object and yet not subject to concepts.

REPRESENTATIONAL CONTENT AND FUNCTIONAL ROLE

So far I have treated Kant's account of representational content as an expression of its dependence on the functional role that such content plays in inference and judgment. In this respect, my interpretation has obvious similarities to Wilfried Sellars's functional interpretation of thought, apperception, and the subject of apperception. Appealing apparently to the Kantian idea that "concepts are based on functions" (A 68/B 93), and that thoughts are constituted by relations between concepts, Sellars argues that Kant allows for no other characterization of thought *processes* than in purely functional terms.[23] He also insists that Kant's transcendental self is constituted by functional relations. For Sellars, the transcendental self is an epistemic principle to which any true thought must conform. The principle in question is that an I thinks the thought of a temporal system of states of affairs and any actual state of affairs belongs to this temporal system of states of affairs.[24] Sellars notes that the thought of this temporal system involves the thought of a complex; as such it is synthetic, indeed it is the synthetic unity of apperception. But it entails an identity of the I that thinks one content with the I that thinks another content in the system, and thus it entails what Kant in the B-Deduction calls the analytic unity of apperception. Now this identity of the I is something that is characterized purely in terms of its functional role; as such, in principle, it could be embodied in different kinds of real bearers. Since we can characterize the transcendental self only functionally, we cannot infer anything about the specific nature of the transcendent self or ultimate bearer of thought, and thus we cannot claim that it is a material entity.[25]

Because the transcendental self is understood in purely functional terms, knowledge of that self does not presuppose matter of factual knowledge of the self as does our access to the transcendent or noumenal self, that is, the self as an object of understanding alone. Somewhat surprisingly, Sellars maintains that the states of the empirical self, that is, the states of self as it is knowable from experience, are also characterized in purely functional terms.[26] The claim that what we know of our selves empirically is known in purely functional terms has a more tenuous connection to the Kantian text.

Sellars acknowledges that Kant takes the states of the empirical self to be ones which are passive, states that the self is in some sense caused to have. He even thinks that Kant is legitimate in thinking of some states, such as perceptions, as passive in that they can be taken to be caused by the states of material substance.[27] Although Sellars does not do so, he might take such states as functional in the sense that they causally depend on certain inputs. But this would be to use the term "functional" in a new and different sense than the one that has a basis in the Kantian text. Patricia Kitcher thinks of Kant as a functionalist in this causal sense, which she links with the Kantian idea of synthesis. This has two rather paradoxical consequences. Kitcher maintains that judgments have representational character only on the basis of their dependence on intuitions. In other words, as Kitcher interprets Kant, judgments have a functional role in representation only in virtue of their dependence on intuition. And synthesis, which Kant insists is a spontaneous activity of the self, becomes a function of the causal dependence of the self on stimuli.[28]

Kitcher reconstructs Kant's position along the lines of a functionalist cognitive psychology in which personal self-consciousness is a construct out of impersonal activities of information processing. She insists that an understanding of the self as an agency for connecting representations can only be made intelligible by collapsing the transcendental and the transcendent self into the empirical self, where the transcendental self is the self as an enabling condition of experience, the transcendent self is the self as it exists independently of any experience, and the empirical self is the self that we experience through the changes in our representations.[29] Kitcher denies the existence of any subject underlying mental states and giving them unity, but she insists on the reality of mental states and their unity, and tries to give Kant's epistemological doctrines an explicitly psychological interpretation wherever possible.[30] Although Kitcher does not emphasize a priori constraints on representation, she tends to regard such constraints as expressions of innate dispositions of the mind.

For Kitcher, the self does not determine the content of representations. Instead the self arises out of that content. The self is nothing but a system of representations which is interconnected by the nature of its content, a quasi-causal relation between representational states.[31] Despite her emphasis on Kant's response to Hume's views on personal identity, Kitcher ascribes to Kant a variant of the bundle theory in which the Humean constraint of existential independence is relaxed. Where Hume maintained that all representations are ultimately completely disconnected from one another, Kitcher rightly has Kant insist that there are connections between representations. But, since such connections have no intrinsic connection to a self for Kitcher, she faces a problem that besets Hume's conception of the self. If the self is a construct out of a collection of representations, why then are my representations in fact mine, that is, on what basis do we think that a given set of representations belongs to the same self to begin with?[32]

The status of mental unity in Sellars's functionalist interpretation of the self is somewhat more difficult to assess. Sellars denies that persons are logical constructs out of mental or physical events. He thinks that persons have a kind of unity to them that Kant would attribute to the spontaneous activities of the self. Sellars rightly notes that, for Kant, perception is not purely passive, and that we also engage in other activities of thought that are more properly thought of as active or "spontaneous" in Kant's vocabulary. I think a sympathetic reading of Sellars would take him to be acknowledging that, whereas "thought taken by itself is merely logical function, hence pure spontaneity of connection of the manifold of a merely possible intuition" (B 429), inner experience, and hence an understanding of the whole panoply of differ-ent human representational states, is "no more mere spontaneity of thought, but also receptivity of intuition, that is, thought of myself applied to empirical intuition of that same subject" (B 430). In other words, it is through the concept-ladenness of sensible experience that the representational states belonging to such experience can themselves be understood in terms of the functional roles that properly belong to concepts and, more specifically, to logical concepts. Logical concepts are basic because they spell out the most basic forms of conceptual role in judgment and inference.

For Sellars, the passivity or affectedness of the mind displays itself in the fact that the states of the empirical self belong to a deterministic system of events that cannot be understood independently of interacting material substances.[33] The activity of the mind is displayed in its ability to reason and understand, capacities that are tied up with pure apper-ception. Sellars notes that Kant's theoretical philosophy does not pro-vide a compelling reason for assuming that the mind should be regarded as anything but relatively spontaneous, that is, as able to have a take on objects, but one which is activated by causes outside of it. However, Sellars does note that Kant takes his notion of the autonomy of practical reason to require a form of spontaneity that goes beyond the relative spontaneity required by theoretical reason. And, indeed, the passage that I have quoted from the Paralogisms concludes with the remark that in the moral law "a spontaneity would be found through which our reality would be determinable without requiring the conditions of em-pirical intuition" (B 430–431).

I have already indicated a good deal of sympathy with Sellars's interpretation of apperception and its transcendental subject. Here are some caveats. While Sellars acknowledges the primacy of the transcen-dental self in the order of knowledge and in practical deliberation about how we are to live our lives, and even insists that the self so understood plays a constitutive role in the manifest image of everyday experience, he also wishes to argue that the transcendental self is, in a certain sense, eliminable in the more fundamental scientific image of nature. While the thinking self is not simply a congery of physical events, it has no existence that is independent of certain configurations of physical events. As such, the self is a form of necessary illusion generated by the first-person point of view. We can dissolve the illusion by shifting to the objective point of view belonging to the scientific image of human beings. It would be unfair to say that, since the transcendental or thinking self is not a part of the objective point of view for Sellars, it simply drops out of any account of objectivity. But it is fair to say that Sellars does not really develop the sense in which one can regard the transcendental self as a basic epistemic condition of experience and it is unclear how the transcendental self can function as a basic epistemic condition while also having no fundamental ontological role to play in experience.[34]

In contrast to the Sellarsian account, I wish to show how Kant carries out the task of developing objective constraints on experience from the relation of different representations to the transcendental or impersonal representation of self that we have in self-consciousness. In the next chapter, I take up Kant's argument to the necessary representation of numerical identity from the need to be able to associate representations in order to be able to have any experience at all. First I show how one can argue with Kant that any discriminatory awareness involves the capacity to connect different representations in time. I then develop his argument that we can only make sense of the capacity to link different representations in time by appeal to our ability to associate items in experience. The key argument is, however, based on the claim that we can only make sense of this capacity for association by appeal to the concept of objects that are distinct from our immediate experiences. Since Kant maintains that the concept of an object requires the possibility of linking together what we represent from the impersonal standpoint of transcendental self-consciousness, this leads Kant to argue that such self-consciousness is a necessary condition for any coherent experience at all. This, then, is the ultimate basis of Kant's claim that apperception can prove its identity with respect to different representations and that such representations are therefore subject to functions of judgment.

CHAPTER 3

Concepts, laws, and the recognition of objects

I claimed in chapter two that Kant's notion of transcendental apperception involves a necessary representation of the numerical identity of the
self. I also claimed that transcendental apperception is a capacity that
Kant links to the conditions under which we could recognize any object
of a representation. I want now to turn to Kant's argument to the
conclusion that a necessary representation of numerical identity is
required if we are to be able to recognize objects that are distinct from
our representations. Kant not only argues that transcendental apperception and recognition of objects go together, he also argues that
recognition of objects must be possible if we are to make sense of even
the most minimal kind of discriminatory awareness. In this way, the
argument becomes crucial not only to a defense of objectivity, but also
to an understanding of the dependence of subjective on objective
experience.

In the first section of this chapter, I take up Kant's so-called threefold
synthesis of apprehension, reproduction, and recognition. Here, Kant
first argues that any discriminatory awareness of what we experience
involves the capacity to connect different temporal perspectives together. He then argues that this requires the ability to associate items
that we experience at one time with items that we experience at another
time. Such associations in turn require the existence of objects that are
distinct from what we experience from the vantage-point of any given
temporal perspective.

In the next section, I take up Kant's claim that we can only make
sense of objects that underwrite associations if we think of such objects
as represented by us in the standpoint-independent way that is made
possible by our ability to use concepts. Our ability to use concepts, as
Kant understands them, depends on our capacity to represent things in
the same way from any standpoint that is intelligible to us regardless of
what that standpoint might be. I argue that Kant regards concepts as

representations that are underwritten by a normative commitment to laws linking the properties represented by those concepts. It is these laws that then underwrite our capacity to associate items in experience.

Kant argues that we can only distinguish objects in our experience that underwrite associations to the extent that representations are linked together by necessary connections provided by laws. These laws are then the basis for our knowledge of objects. But we can only know them because they derive their lawlikeness from our ability to represent them as expressions of our numerical identity in any arbitrary situation. From this, Kant concludes that cognition is nothing but the unification of different representations in the impersonal point of view of transcendental apperception.

Perhaps the key claim in Kant's argument is that a necessary consciousness of one's numerical identity as a self goes together with our concept of an object of experience. This leads him to claim that we must be able to represent ourselves as numerically identical if our experiences are to have the kind of associability in virtue of which they may be said to belong to one experience. Kant draws interesting and far-reaching conclusions from his claim that experience must be conceptualizable if it is to be an experience of objects at all. Nature must be such that we are necessarily able to associate our different experiences of nature guided by concepts of the objects that we experience. And this means that nature must be regarded as uniform with respect to the concepts that we have, where this uniformity can only mean that we are able to provide a systematic description of nature in terms of the laws that our concepts purport to express.

FROM APPREHENSION TO RECOGNITION

Kant distinguishes between a synthesis of apprehension, of reproduction, and of recognition, corresponding to a capacity to distinguish different contents of consciousness, to associate different contents of consciousness, and to recognize different contents of consciousness by means of concepts. Ultimately, Kant wishes to argue that the categories are the a priori concepts required for the necessary connections required by the synthesis of recognition. Such recognition is itself an enabling condition for the apprehension and reproduction of items in experience. In this way, he hopes to show that categories must function as a priori constraints on recognition if we are to be able to apprehend items at all.

Now, in arguing for the need for a synthesis of apprehension, Kant insists that what we experience may be inherently complex, but it is only characterizable as complex, indeed as what it is, insofar as we are able to distinguish "time in the successive sequence of impressions" (A 99). To distinguish different times, and hence also the contents of different times, we must be able to connect the contents of our different experiences together in time. In this way, we come to grasp time as a whole of time, and also space as a whole of space. For intuition, through which we immediately experience items in time and space, "presents a manifold, but cannot give rise to this manifold as such and indeed *in one representation* without a thereby occurring synthesis" (A 99). The synthesis of apprehension is concerned with the basic preconceptual level at which we distinguish temporal perspectives and different items in perceptual experience.

It has sometimes been suggested that the synthesis of apprehension already involves transcendental apperception, and that no conceptual factor is required in order to account for the possibility of self-consciousness of the anticipations and retentions that go into the kind of discrimination involved in apprehension.[1] But this is not the way Kant himself argues. Kant argues that transcendental self-consciousness is required for conceptual recognition. To be able to recognize things by means of concepts, we must be able to represent ourselves as having the numerically same point of view in different experiences. This necessary representation of numerical identity is a transcendental consciousness of self, that is, it is a representation of self as an enabling condition of experience. Our ability to apprehend and reproduce what we experience is much less directly tied to transcendental self-consciousness than is our capacity to recognize objects by means of concepts. We can only apprehend and reproduce items in our experience because we are able to experience objects of the kind that make the associative processes involved in reproduction possible. But we can only make sense of the existence of such objects by means of concepts. And these concepts, in turn, depend for their existence on our capacity to represent ourselves as having the same point of view in different experiences.

Kant insists that all apprehension of items at a time requires processes of association, that is, a synthesis of reproduction, through which immediately past experience is retained in the present (A 102), and this synthesis of reproduction ultimately turns out to presuppose the synthesis of recognition, through which we recognize objects that are independent of our momentary experiences. Finally, such recognition of objects involves a kind of necessity that depends on transcendental apperception. Thus, the syntheses of apprehension, reproduction, and recognition are distinct, but mutually dependent processes of coming to terms with perceptual information that are supposed to be guided by the possibility of self-consciousness with respect to the experiences that involve them.

If even the states of our immediate past are not available to us at any given moment, then we will fail to distinguish anything from anything else, for we will have already lost the awareness of the item from which the second item is to be distinguished. On the other hand, such items need to be distinguished from each other through apprehension and recognized as identical or distinct through recognition. And Kant claims that this requires transcendental self-consciousness.

Kant follows Locke, Hume, Tetens, and many other empiricists in deriving our ability to connect a present state of consciousness with some past state of consciousness from a habit of associating the one state with the other state. Reproduction thus depends on empirical patterns of association. Like Locke, Berkeley, and Hume, Kant assumes that the items that we perceive and associate are appearances, that is, things as they appear to the mind. But Kant rejects the British empiricist project of understanding the unity of things as bundles of representations. Even Locke, who is committed to the existence of physical objects, accounts for our knowledge of such objects in terms of the bundling of sensations:

The mind being, as I have declared, furnished with a great number of the simple ideas, conveyed in by the senses as they are found in external things, or by reflection on its own operations, takes notice also that a certain number of these simple ideas go constantly together; which being presumed to belong to one thing, and words being suited to common apprehension, and made use of for quick dispatch, are called, so united in one subject, by one name; which, by inadvertency, we are apt afterward to talk of and consider as one simple idea, which indeed is a complication of many ideas together; because, as I have said, not imagining how these simple ideas *can* subsist by themselves, we accustom ourselves to suppose some *substratum* wherein they do subsist, and from which they do result, which therefore we call *substance*. (*Essay Concerning Human Understanding*, Book II, chapter xxiii, p. 1)

Against the associationist bundle theory, Kant insists that association would be completely arbitrary if there were no regularities in the world underlying the co-occurrence of our experiences. Such regularities explain why we associate one set of representations with another set of representations. A certain amount of regularity must be assumed in experience in order for us to come to associate different items of experience. Although things remain relatively constant in experience:

If cinnabar were first red, then black, first light, then heavy, a human being were to be changed first into this, then into that animal form, if on the longest day the land were to be covered first with fruit, then with ice and snow, then my empirical imagination would not even have the opportunity to think of heavy cinnabar when representing a red color. (A 101)

The kind of regularity required is complex. For, even if objects persist over time, they are also subject to change. Cinnabar turns from red to black when oxidized, and human beings take on different animal forms when they dress up as animals. Associations are only of interest in grasping regularities in experience if they are based on some significant shared feature of the items associated. Everything is similar to everything else in some sense or other. So there must be some basis for picking out one set of similarities as relevant to a set of experiences as opposed to another set. It might seem that relevance could be randomly determined. But a random relation between cognitive contents would be "a blind play of representations, less even than a dream" (A 112). Even dreams involve rather sophisticated forms of regularity that would be absent from a random collection of mental states.

Kant does not argue for his key and quite astounding claim that to account for the associability of our perceptions we must appeal to *a priori* connections between what we perceive (A 101). The more plausible view is that we directly perceive objects the co-occurrence of which accounts for our dispositions to associate certain things with certain other things. If we directly perceive objects that exist independently of us, then the recurrence of those objects can be invoked to explain our ability to associate items in our experience in non-arbitrary ways. Thus some form of direct realist theory of perception would be the more obvious solution to the problem of association than an appeal to a priori connection.

Fortunately, Kant's account of the synthesis of recognition attempts to show that a direct realist theory of perception presupposes a priori connections between the items that one experiences. His theory of recognition thus promises to supply the rationale for an appeal to a priori synthesis that is missing from his account of association. Kant does not deny the claim that we directly perceive objects such as tables and chairs that provide the basis for the associations in terms of which we connect diverse experiences. However, the problem with such

perceptual objects is that they are not the sort of things that are subject
to laws. When one bases associations on perceptual objects, one bases
the process of association on objects that are themselves, at best, only the
way that physical objects appear to observers under standard circumstances. For perceptual objects are characterized in terms of sensible
qualities that do not belong to the objective nature of things:

Colors are not properties of the bodies to whose intuition they belong, rather
mere modifications of our sense of sight, which is affected in a certain way by
light. Taste and color are not necessary conditions under which objects can
alone become objects of the senses. They are only connected to appearance as
contingently added effects of [our] particular organization. (A 28-29; see also B
44)

Now association requires not only repetition of patterns, but also
significant regularities. These regularities are provided by perceptual
objects. But there is some question as to whether the kinds of significant
regularities of co-occurrence provided by perceptual objects must not
themselves be underwritten by the kinds of laws governing physical
objects, that is, governing empirical objects as they are in themselves. To
say that an object is thus and such is to commit ourselves to the fact that
the object must be representable in that way from all standpoints, even if
it is a contingent fact that it has those standpoint-independent properties. The object is what Kant refers to in the Transcendental Aesthetic as
the physical or empirical (as opposed to the transcendental) notion of a
thing in itself: "what in universal experience amongst all the different
positions relative to the senses, is still thus and not otherwise determined" (A 46/B 63). The empirical notion of an object is just the notion
of something in our experience that is what it is independently of my
subjective manner of representing it; the object is thus determined for
absolutely all of us in one way rather than another way. The laws
governing the way such an object presents itself to any arbitrary observer would support the counterfactuals needed to spell out the circumstances under which something appears thus and such to standard and
non-standard observers, and hence explain why certain patterns recur
and others do not.

CONCEPTUAL RECOGNITION AND LAWS

Kant introduces recognition as an adjunct to reproduction. Recognition
is the consciousness that the data retained from past experience in one's

present consciousness is in fact the same data as that previously experienced. Without recognition, there would be no experience or memory in the sense with which we are generally familiar. Memory involves not only the ability to call up past data, but also the ability to recognize such data as derived from past experience. Kant notes that retention of past facts and the recognition of those past as what they are, are distinguishable capacities.[2]

The recognition of something as something, for instance, of a past fact as a past fact, has a normative dimension to it. Recognition can be successful or unsuccessful. Kant argues that recognition depends on our ability to use concepts. These concepts supply the norms governing the distinction between successful and unsuccessful recognition of a certain object. Concepts serve as rules for organizing the data of intuition by providing us with the capacity to recognize items in different situations (A 106).[3] Kant does not just think of a concept as "according to its form always something universal, and that serves as a rule," he also argues that "it can only be a rule of intuitions by: representing the necessary reproduction of the manifold with respect to given appearances, that is, the synthetic unity in their consciousness" (A 106). This means that someone who recognizes something as an instance of a certain concept will necessarily connect the possession of certain properties by that object with the possession of other properties. For, to fall under a concept, an object must have certain features for all persons who are competent with respect to that concept. The necessity relation extends not only to the relations between the object and the properties that are represented by a given concept, but also to the relation between the concept and the object itself. If the object does not fall under the concept with necessity, but merely accidentally, then, on Kant's view, the concept is not one that governs our understanding of that object.

By ascribing universality and necessity to concepts in the way that he does, Kant thinks of concepts as laws. For he thinks of concepts as rules that associate contents of representation in a necessary way, and he notes that "rules insofar as they are objective (hence necessarily attach to the cognition of an object) are called laws" (A 126). There are two obvious objections to the view of conceptual recognition that Kant defends in this context. One obvious problem is that the view seems to entail that all concepts are a priori, for Kant maintains that "necessity and strict generality are certain indications of cognition a priori, and also belong indivisibly together" (B 3). The other related problem is that taking necessity and strict generality to be marks of a concept does not seem to do justice to the difficulties in defining concepts to which Kant is otherwise quite sensitive: "One uses certain marks only so long as they are sufficient to distinguish; new remarks take some away and add some, the concept therefore never stands within certain limits" (A 728/ B 756).

The concepts that we have purport to represent kinds, but they may not. Concept formation is however guided by the regulative ideal of representing the world in terms of natural and artificial kinds that must have the same properties for all observers who succeed in identifying them. Kant wants to argue that our knowledge of such kinds is only possible to the extent that we are committed to the existence of a priori laws that make it possible for us to seek and identify kinds of objects. While he wishes to argue that the lawlikeness of the connection between the properties belonging to objects of individual kinds is not intelligible independently of a priori laws, he also wishes to claim that what natural and even artificial kinds there are is a matter of empirical discovery. Since laws are not mere regularities for Kant, but necessary and strictly general or universal principles, they cannot be known by induction on past experiences alone. They thus presuppose some a priori principle that allows us to know that they apply in every situation and with necessity. This view is not now popular; however, it does have in its favor that there are significant difficulties with inductive generalizations, especially if we are unable to appeal to a principle of the uniformity of nature that cannot be justified from past experience, for what is at issue is whether future experience must be like past experience.

CONCEPTUAL RECOGNITION AND TRUTH

Kant links his account of conceptual recognition to an account of the conditions under which cognition of an object is possible. He interprets the notion of a concept in terms not only of a necessary rule for recognizing items in different experiences, but also of the notion of a cognition or knowledge of an object (*Erkenntnis eines Gegenstandes*).[4] According to his more inclusive definition of cognition or knowledge (*Erkenntnis*) in the ladder of different representations in the Transcendental Dialectic, any representation of an object is a cognition. Thus, not only judgments, but even intuitions and concepts are instances of cognition, since they are "objective perceptions" (A 320/B 377), that is, representations of objects. Even this expansive usage leaves a distinction to be drawn between a representation that is and a representation that only seems to be true of an object. For we do not want to say that representations must be true of their purported objects. Thus, we still have room for the idea that in recognition we can either get our recognition right or not.

Unfortunately, we have no direct way of comparing our concept with its purported object. We could use another representation, but then the question would arise again with respect to the new representation. We need some non-contingent or necessary relation of correspondence between a representation and its object to support cognition because the only access we have to the necessary connection between a putative cognition and its object is through our beliefs about how objects are connected. Now we can appeal to the way the object must appear to everyone as a basis for claiming that the object is truly thus and such. But we can only determine how the object must appear to everyone to the extent that we have some way of comparing and contrasting the beliefs that we have about the object with the beliefs that other persons in other situations have about it. Kant argues that our only ultimate grip on the purported correspondence of our cognitions with their objects is based on the coherence relations between those cognitions themselves. Moreover, these coherence relations consist in nothing but our ability to connect those cognitions together in "formal unity of consciousness" provided by our capacity to represent the numerical identity of the self through the changes in representational content involved in represen- ting these different cognitions.

To distinguish an object distinct from our particular perceptions, we need the kind of "objective unity" provided by concepts of space and time. These concepts allow us to connect inherently perspectival per- ceptions together in a representation of space and time that is shared, public, and standpoint-independent. But this shared and standpoint- independent representation of space and time is nothing but a unity of consciousness that is necessary in the sense that it must potentially include all of our possible representations in it. It is on the basis of this potential unity of consciousness that empirical concepts then have objective reality, their purchase on objects of experience (A 109).

In appealing to an underlying necessary connection between the items that one experiences, Kant is responding to a skeptical dilemma concerning truth that he posed in the Introduction to the Transcen- dental Logic (A 57ff./B 82ff.). After noting that the skeptic can accept the nominal definition of truth as correspondence of knowledge to its object, Kant points out that this does nothing to resolve the famous skeptical problem of the criterion of truth. It does not seem to be possible to provide a criterion of truth in a completely general form, since one would then have to abstract from all content. A logical criterion of truth, at best, is a necessary condition for non-logical truth. Thinking that logic alone is sufficient to establish substantive truths leads to (dialectical) illusions of the kind that make a critique of pure reason necessary. Despite the tendency of reason to make substantive claims that it cannot substantiate, Kant thinks that this tendency can be curbed by limiting cognitive claims to experience and its preconditions. The Transcendental Analytic (i.e. the Transcendental Deduction and the Principle of Pure Understanding) constitutes a "logic of truth" in contrast to the "logic of semblance" provided by the Transcendental Dialectic. The Analytic provides a set of substantive necessary criteria (where a criterion is a canon or measuring stick) for empirical truth, but not for objects in general (A 62–63/ B 87–88). Our beliefs can be determined to be true or false depending on whether they can be connected together in one consistent account of experience. The connectability of our beliefs gives us a coherence criterion of truth. As Kant notes in the Appendix to the Transcendental Dialectic, without a "use of the understanding" that "hangs together" (*zusammenhängenden Verstandesgebrauch*) "we would have no sufficient mark of empirical truth" (A 651/B 679). But we cannot determine the truth of claims that go beyond what we can experience.

While the combination of a coherence criterion of truth with a correspondence definition of truth has much to be said for it, it is far less obvious why the connections between our perceptions, or beliefs in general involved in the establishment of coherence, must be necessary and strictly general. The reason to make such a demand lies in the idea of a general criterion of truth. If a criterion of truth is to tell us what beliefs are true or false, then it must pick out all beliefs that are true. This leads Kant to conclude that our beliefs must not only have necessary connections amongst themselves if they are to have the necessary connection to an object that he believes characteristic of knowledge, these necessary connections must also be based on a priori rules.

In arguing that conceptual recognition is required if we are to be able to make sense of experience, Kant is most interested in the status of non-empirical concepts. For it is the task of the Deduction to show that a certain set of such concepts, the categories, or pure concepts of the understanding, are legitimate concepts that pick out bona fide objects. To do this, Kant wants to show that these a priori concepts are necessary if we are to be able to recognize objects:

Real experience, which consists in apprehension, in association (reproduction), finally in recognition of appearances, contains in the last and highest (of the merely empirical elements of experience) concepts that make possible the formal unity of experience, and with it, the objective validity (truth) of empirical cognition. Now these grounds for recognition of the manifold, insofar as they concern *merely the form of experience in general*, are *those categories*. (A 125)

It is clear from the above passage that Kant thinks of the categories as the conditions that make it possible for us to distinguish a successful from an unsuccessful recognition of an object, that is, to distinguish a true from a false judgment about an object. How do they allow us to draw the distinction in question? They allow us to distinguish a unity of experience for me, from a unity of experience for everyone by establishing constraints on what counts as the form of experience in general. The key thing for Kant is that in order for there to be a successful conceptual cognition there must be necessary reproduction, that is, association according to an a priori rule (A 105). The a priori rule in question cannot itself be the concept through which we recognize what we have associated together in the mind, for then all concepts and all cognition would be a priori. The idea is rather that, in order for one to be able to apply even empirical concepts to experience, there must be necessary and strictly general connections between items of experience. It is this metarule that must be a priori. The metarule fixes the relations of potential data for knowledge a priori in such a way that empirical or non-empirical rules can be found that are capable of supplying us with knowledge.

Ultimately, Kant wants to argue that even the metarules, or categories of the pure understanding, that provide necessary and strictly general connections between items of experience derive their normativity from the unity of apperception itself:

The unity of apperception is the transcendental ground for the necessary lawlikeness of all appearances in one experience. And this very unity of apperception in respect to a manifold of representations is the rule (namely to determine it [the manifold] out of one [representation]) and the faculty of these rules is the understanding. (A 127)

APPERCEPTION AND TRANSCENDENTAL AFFINITY

In arguing that association requires laws governing physical objects that are independent of our immediate experience of those objects, Kant is interested in the nature of the similarities and uniformity required for associative processes of the kind postulated by Hume to get off the ground. He wants to show that lawlike regularities underwrite the mechanisms of association that Hume regarded as "the cement of the universe."

Hume admits that appearances cannot suggest rules for projecting predicates, unless there are constant conjunctions of appearances in our experience. Without such constant conjunctions, associative processes could not be initiated. For Hume, such patterns of association are based on innate dispositions to associate recurrent sets of appearances with one another. But even these innate dispositions must be triggered by similarities in what is perceived. Hume's effort to base causal connection on constant conjunctions is thus sensitive to the conditions under which events are to be regarded as similar. Consonant with his empiricism, Hume attempts to derive the principle that every event has a cause from the principle of like cause–like effect. Since he eschews a priori knowledge, Hume must treat the universal causal principle as a consequence of our custom of treating nature as uniform. The uniformity of nature in turn falls out of our habit of associating similar causes with similar effects.

Kant wants to argue for the thesis that "the order and regularity in the appearances, which we entitle *nature*, we ourselves introduce. We could never find them in appearances, had not we ourselves, or the nature of our mind, originally set them there" (A 125). Although the idea that we somehow produce the order of nature is controversial to say the least, there is nothing in this general idea that a Humean would have to reject. Kant does, however, soon give the thesis that we impose order on nature an interpretation which Hume could not accept: "For this unity of nature has to be a necessary one, that is, has to be an *a priori* certain unity of the connection of appearances" (A 125).

We must think of nature as a whole as conforming to the conditions under which we can make nature intelligible to ourselves. This is what gives nature its unity for us. But then, the only access to nature we have is through what we represent of it. Since nature is accessible to us only insofar as it conforms to the conditions under which we can make sense of nature, the nature which is accessible to us is nature as it must appear to us. Nature which appears to us is subjective only in the sense that it is construed as dependent on the conditions under which we can make sense of it. These same conditions, however, also serve to underwrite the objectivity and accessibility of our claims concerning nature for other persons. Kant refers to the unity and uniformity of nature as nature's affinity. He distinguishes between an empirical and a transcendental affinity of nature. In other words, there is thus supposed to be an empirical and a non-empirical dimension to the uniformity of nature. The empirical affinity of nature consists in the uniformity that we discover in nature based on the kinds of associations that we make between different items of experience based on repeated experience. Transcendental affinity, by contrast, is supposed to be the underlying uniformity of nature that makes it possible for us to associate items together in a meaningful manner in the first place. Kant's claim is that uniformity of nature, in the transcendental sense, is based on our capacity to connect different representations together in (transcendental) self-consciousness.

Kant starts with the empiricist notion that we become conscious of, and indeed construct, bodies and selves through the manner in which we associate representations, or rather simple sensations. Then he notes that association of representations means forming some kind of connection between those representations in consciousness. He then argues that any connection that might hold between individual representations in a particular consciousness must be such that it is consistent with the unifiability of those representations in self-consciousness. The move from an empirical affinity or associability of representations in an individual empirical consciousness to the idea that empirical associations are governed by a priori principles of associability is based on the idea that any perceptions that can be connected in any particular consciousness must conform to the conditions under which they can be associated with other representations in an arbitrary consciousness. The idea of the universal associability of representations in one possible self-consciousness is then all that an object that exists independently of my particular associations could be.

Henry Allison has criticized Kant's argument for taking a tack similar to Berkeley's notorious argument to the incoherence ("repugnance") of the notion of unperceived matter.[5] On this reconstruction, Kant argues as follows: things that appear to me, such as cinnabar, tables, chairs, etc., exhibit regularities that support associations connecting them together in various ways. These regularities are necessary. For only if appearances can be connected together in consciousness, and hence can be associated, do they exist at all. Something represented by me that cannot be a possible object of consciousness would be nothing at all. Therefore all appearances must be necessarily associable. The argument involves a fallacious shift between two different meanings of "appearance," corresponding to different senses in which consciousness can be unitary. An appearance in the subjective sense, an appearance$_1$, is an internal accusative of consciousness (a represented *qua* represented). It would be nothing at all, if it could not be represented. An appearance in the objective sense, an appearance$_2$, or a phenomenon in Kant's technical vocabulary, is an intersubjectively accessible object. This is an object that is independent of any particular mind or spatiotemporal perspective. If one thinks that appearances$_1$ are necessarily associable, then we may infer the existence of appearances$_2$ that underlie appearances$_1$. But what reason does one have to think that appearances$_1$ must be representable together by a subject?

Representations are entities that play a role in understanding the behavior of animals and human beings. If such entities are assigned a role that makes them cognitively meaningless, then there is no reason to assume their existence at all. The key claim however is that, in order for such representations to be cognitively significant, they must have differential relations to other representations that we can represent to ourselves. Appearances$_2$ must provide some ground for the association of appearances$_1$. This is what it is for them to be in themselves associable and thus susceptible to conceptual interpretation. Without this objective basis for associability, one would not be able to conceptualize the episodes in question and thus one would not be able to represent oneself as a numerically identical subject through these different experiences. It is only if those experiences allow for the application of concepts to them that it is possible to represent oneself as the numerically same subject with respect to them.

Similarity relations between concepts are themselves to be understood in terms of their systematic relation to other concepts and representations in a possible self-consciousness. Not all differences in representational content can come from experience itself, since there must be some way of thinking of the relations between representations that is independent of any particular experience, if we are to be able to represent their similarity relations as such at all. We must think of our experience, both representations and their objects (what is represented by them), as conforming on the whole to the conditions under which we can apply such concepts to experience, since this is the only way we have of making sense of experience, and giving any determinate content to our representations or thinking of ourselves as using concepts and forming judgments:

All error into which the human understanding can fall is only *partial* and in every erroneous judgment there must be something true. For a *total* error would be a complete contradiction *against* the laws of the understanding and reason. How could it arise as such in any way from the understanding, and insofar as it is a judgment, be held for a product of the understanding! (*Logic*, ed. Jäsche, Ak. IX, p. 54)

We can be mistaken in particular beliefs or representations of objects, but the very conditions under which we can make sense of the content of our representations precludes us from being completely wrong in all of our beliefs. The content of our representations (our beliefs) is linked to what is intelligible for us. In this way global skepticism is rejected.

THE UNIFORMITY AND THE SYSTEMATIC UNITY OF NATURE

Kant's argument to the transcendental affinity of nature suggests that nature must be uniform in every respect if there is to be self-consciousness. He wants to claim that there is sufficient uniformity in cinnabar with respect to its properties for us to have the notion of how cinnabar looks to standard observers under standard circumstances. Deviation from standard conditions will be made sense of in terms of a change in causal conditions. He assumes the validity of the prediction that, if cinnabar was red in the past, then it will be red in the future, since the future resembles the past. But, of course, this can mean at best that cinnabar has the dispositional property of appearing as red to standard observers under standard conditions. Such conditions will be determined in causal terms. Cinnabar is a difficult case because it may be observed to be both red and black depending on other causal factors such as oxidation. Its redness and blackness are dispositional properties connected both to the absence or presence of oxygen and to the manner in which our eyes process radiation of a certain wavelength.

One could take nature to be uniform with respect to some Goodman-type predicate such as the "brackness" of cinnabar. If something has the property of brackness then it will be red before 1800 and black after that date. It would be contradictory to say that nature is uniform with respect to both of these properties. Nature cannot be uniform in respect to every concept either. If nature is uniform with respect to the concept "red," we will not be able to think of it as uniform with respect to the concept "gred" and vice versa, where the latter concept is to be understood as "being red prior to 1787 and being green thereafter." For, if we take the predicate "gred" as basic, we may then define "red" as "gred before

1787 and redd afterwards," where redd would be a predicate defined in the red vocabulary as "red after 1787." Since mutually inconsistent universal conditional hypotheses involving both normal predicates and Goodman predicates can be formulated which are equally supported by available evidence, nature cannot be taken to be uniform in every respect. Some constraints are needed which will allow one to distinguish legitimate from pseudo-lawlike judgments. Even if experience exhibits regularity with respect to some concept or other, this is not enough to guarantee regularity under laws. More needs to be said about the kinds of regularity to be allowed.

Predicates are projectible, if they allow projection from observed to unobserved cases. Redness rather than brackness belongs to the group of predicates that we hold to be projectible on intuitive grounds. Redness is more deeply entrenched in our belief system. Projectible predicates are predicates that figure in generalizations expressing lawlike connections between events rather than merely accidental regularities of co-occurrence. Such predicates allow the universal conditional hypotheses containing them to be confirmed by positive instances. This means that the truth of singular empirical judgments that are instantiations of those hypotheses increase their credibility. Projectible will need to be distinguishable from non-projectible predicates. The uniformity of nature will also have to be restricted to projectible predicates. Otherwise there will be no fact of the matter about whether there is a change in state of some substance from time t_1 to t_2.

If cinnabar is brack, then the change from redness to blackness at $t=1800$ will not be a true change, since it is not a change in the brackness of that substance, whereas the persistence of the color red after that date would actually require further explanation, since it would involve a loss of brackness. It is certainly tempting to exclude Goodman predicates based on the Kantian demand for temporal neutrality. But, as the reference to causation and change suggests, the demand works both ways. From the point of view of the vocabulary using brackness, redness would itself need to be defined in temporal terms, i.e. as the having of the property of brackness prior to 1800 and of another property which may be called wreckness after that date.

In order to respond to the challenge of Goodman predicates, Kant must establish some basis for a priori constraints on which concepts can serve as concepts of a possible experience. Only in this way will he be able to isolate the causal conditions governing particular experiences in any plausible way. Kant, in fact, has the sketch of an a priori answer to this kind of problem.[6] He demands systematic unification of concepts as a regulative principle governing universal conditional hypotheses of the kind which play a role in theories. Systematic unification should exclude Goodman predicates by restricting the range of acceptable predicates to projectible predicates. Our choice of projectible predicates must be justified by reference to the best background theory that we have available to us. Our background theory will have to be not only strongly supported by available evidence, but also constrained by regulative principles governing the best way of systematically unifying the information gleaned from this evidence in a theory.

Non-natural Goodman-type predicates cannot be ruled out on an individual basis. But, if we think of our concepts as possessing constitutive systematic relations to each other, then it is plausible to assume that they must confront experience as a systematic totality, rather than on a one-by-one basis as Humeans are inclined to believe. Hume's account of induction is not, in fact, up to drawing plausible distinctions between natural and non-natural predicates. The problem is that Hume would have such predicates depend for their support on present experience of constant conjunctions of perceptions. But there will always be non-natural predicates that can find experiential support equal to that to be had for so-called natural predicates. These non-natural predicates can only be excluded by rejecting a molecularist account of concept application. The problem with non-natural predicates is that they cannot be systematically deployed and still maintain their non-natural meaning. One can find non-natural predicates corresponding to any given set of natural predicates, but one cannot construe all concepts as having such non-natural meaning.

Concepts are systematically related to each other in a manner that is both parasitic on the numerical identity of the self and a condition for its possibility. Thus, if self-consciousness is possible in experience, then one must conceive of experience as subject to concepts whose content is systematically interrelatable and relatable to that self-consciousness. This connection between the systematic unity of concepts and the identity of self-consciousness lies behind Kant's interpretation of the differences between concepts on the model of differences in the content of what is represented by a spectator from different standpoints:

One can regard every concept as a point, which, as the standpoint of a spectator, has its horizon, that is, a set of things, that can be represented and as it were surveyed from it. But to the different horizons, that is, kinds, that are determined by that same number of concepts, one can think of a shared horizon from which one observes them all from a point in the middle which is the higher kind, until finally the highest kind is the universal and true horizon which is determined from the standpoint of the highest concept, and contains all the manifold under it as kinds, species, and subspecies. (A 658/B 686)

Our representations and, more directly, our concepts figure in a systematic unity that relates our concepts to each other systematically. Systematic unifiability is an a priori constraint on experience. From Kant's point of view, inquiry is guided by the assumption that nature is characterized by a transcendental affinity among its concepts. Nature is transcendentally affinite with respect to concepts insofar as nature allows itself to be understood in terms of a system of concepts. We must think of nature as conceptualizable in terms of a system of concepts which could, in principle, be articulated by us in some systematic way to the extent that we think of nature as something that we can represent in terms of a self-consciousness that is basically impersonal.

While the transcendental affinity of nature is, in many ways, the linch-pin of Kant's argument for the a priori validity of the categories, it seems to be describable with equal justification as a transcendental deduction of the synthetic a priori maxims of unity, multiplicity, and relatedness or affinity. These ideas of reason provide the transcendental justification for the assumption that the complex conceptual hierarchies to be found in highly articulated theories are indeed applicable to nature. The hierarchical organization of concepts in a theory allows every event to be brought under not only a true generalization, but also a generalization that will be helpful in making predictions about other events. In fact, the problem of uniformity under concepts and laws reveals the close connection that must be demanded between understanding and reason.

The A-Deduction requires the uniformity of nature and, indeed, the lawlikeness of nature for any understanding or recognition of the world as what it is. But by the time one reaches the Transcendental Dialectic (A 644/B 672), it becomes apparent that any attempt to formulate the unity and laws of nature is necessarily hypothetical. The attempt to formulate an abstract conception of nature that is uniform with respect to all conceivable concepts generates antinomies. We do have to think of nature as conceptualizable by us, and hence as organized into a system of natural kinds that we can understand. But we cannot know a priori what that system must be like in its particulars, since there are a number of equally plausible, but mutually exclusive, alternatives. This does not mean that there must be mutually exclusive empirically adequate systematic characterizations of nature. For we do not have sufficient evidence to do more than provide a projection of what an empiricaly adequate system of the world would be like.

In the Appendix to the Transcendental Dialectic, Kant regards the notion of affinity primarily as a property of concepts rather than as a property of their objects (that is, of the manifold itself), as he does in the Deduction. But the notion of affinity developed in the Appendix has transcendental rather than purely logical force. It expresses a transcendental assumption to the effect that nature is susceptible to explanation in terms of the hypothesis of conceptual relatedness. Thus, the affinity in question is first of all constituted by a set of similarity relations between concepts, but these similarity relations between concepts must also be relevant to the objects that are interpreted in terms of those concepts, and hence to what Kant calls the manifold. This is brought home forcefully in the following passage:

> If there were such a great difference among appearances, I do not want to say of form (for in this respect they may be similar to each other), but with respect to content, i.e. with respect to the multiplicity < *Mannigfaltigkeit* > of existing beings, that the sharpest human understanding could not find the least similarity between them by comparing the one with the other (a case which is conceivable), then the logical law of kinds would not take place at all, nor even a concept of a kind, or any general concept of any kind, indeed there would not even be understanding which only has to do with such. The logical principle of kinds presupposes therefore a transcendental one, if it should be applied to nature (by which I understand only objects that are given to us). (A 653–654/B 681–682)

The transcendental principle of similarity between kinds seems to be precisely what Kant needs in order to be able to claim that association is based on some principle which makes occurrences associable in themselves. This transcendental principle of similarity seems to have its ultimate source in the fact that we must regard all representations as potential candidates for self-consciousness.

The systematic interest of reason in its pursuit of unification is limited in its empirical significance to the conditions governing the legitimate acquisition and application of empirical concepts. But even Kant thinks that the attempt to come up with precise a priori constraints on which concepts can function as concepts of empirical objects overtaxes both the understanding and reason. Each attempt to provide a specific understanding of the affinity of nature is necessarily hypothetical. It must be based on a projected unity of nature that transcends what we know through experience even though it is subject to revision in the face of recalcitrant experience.[7] The hypothetical character of any unity of nature demotes the synthetic principles a priori that function as criteria for the truth of our empirical judgments to the status of regulative rather than constitutive principles of experience. This is true even though we are unable to apply concepts without the background assumption about experience with which they provide us. Kant insists, to be sure, that the law of reason, that one must look for unity in nature according to principles of reason, is itself necessary:

> Without it [the law of reason] we would have no reason, without reason no coherent use of the understanding, and without that no sufficient condition of empirical truth, so that in respect to the latter we must presuppose the systematic unity of nature indeed as objectively valid and necessary. (A 651/B 679)

A proof of the transcendental affinity of nature is involved in Kant's justification of the validity of the categories. For these categories are supposed to provide a general notion of the lawlikeness of nature and its susceptibility to interpretation by means of empirical concepts. But, even were this project completely successful, there would still be room for the use of the organizational powers of reason and its ideas in attempting to formulate more specific models of objective affinity and specific laws of nature. It is these models that then guide the inductive enterprise of science. The principles that reason formulates are indeed synthetic and a priori, but they do not determine the character which objects of experience must have. They cannot tell us how individual objects of experience must be, but principles of reason do have an objective validity that transcends mere thought-economy. They allow us (provisionally) to determine whether our representations are true of the objects of which they seem to be true. In regulating our search for empirically adequate lawlike connections between natural objects as well as between natural objects and their properties (A 663/B 691), principles of reason provide substantive constraints on which of our representations can be true. Principles of reason are thus crucial in providing the necessary connectedness among our experiences that Kant takes to guarantee the correspondence of our representations with their object, that is with an empirical reality that is distinct from those representations (A 105).

CHAPTER 4

Self-consciousness and the demands of judgment in the B-Deduction

Kant's most sophisticated treatment of how self-consciousness constrains the character of experience is to be found in the B-Deduction. In the A-Deduction, in which the notion of judgment is only mentioned once in describing the powers of the understanding (A 126), Kant's argument turned on the enabling conditions of recognition. The B-Deduction establishes objectivity by way of a more explicit appeal to the normative demands placed on experience by the possibility of forming judgments about what is experienced. Kant first argues that any cognitively significant content is a potential candidate for representation in a consciousness of self that potentially includes all representations whatsoever. He then argues that whatever is a candidate for self-consciousness is also something to which we can apply concepts and hence a candidate for judgment.

Judgments make an implicit claim to objectivity by making a truth claim. In forming a judgment, we commit ourselves to the truth of the proposition that is asserted by the judgment. It might be thought that this truth could merely be a truth for me or for someone else. In this case, the truth would be merely subjective. However, such a subject-relative conception of truth would not do the job that we assign to the notion of truth, namely to capture the way things are independently of an individual point of view or take on the way the world is. For this reason, Kant accepts the nominal definition of truth as correspondence with an object even though there is no way to determine whether a judgment corresponds to an object independently of whether that judgment coheres with other judgments.

The claim to truth made by judgment, and with it the presumption that the proposition asserted by the judgment corresponds with an object, is the ground for the normative claim made by a judgment. This normative ground of judgment ultimately has its source in the possibility of representing the content asserted by a judgment in an impersonal

way. The possibility of representing the contents of judgment impersonally, in turn, is based on the fact that consciousness of one's particular
point of view as a representer is parasitic on the possibility of representing oneself in an impersonal manner.

"I THINK" IN THE B-DEDUCTION

Kant introduces the idea that the unity of self-consciousness is the
normative source of all content that can have any cognitive significance
for us in a passage that is as famous and controversial as any in his whole
corpus:

The *I think* must be *able* to accompany all my representations; for otherwise
something would be represented in me which could not be thought at all, which
would mean as much as that this representation would either be impossible or
at least nothing for me. That representation which can be given prior to all
thought is intuition. Therefore all the manifold of intuition has a necessary
relation to the: *I think* in the same subject in which this manifold is to be
encountered. (B 132)

Kant's initial aim in this passage is to show that I can think all my
representations. He apparently means that all my representations, taken
collectively, as well as distributively, are ascribable by me to me. To
establish the initial conclusion, Kant assumes for the sake of argument
that it is not the case that all my representations are thinkable by me.
From this, he claims that it would follow that something would be
represented in me that could not be thought at all. In other words, he
assumes that, if something in me is to be represented by anyone, it must
be represented by me. From this, he concludes that, if I cannot think a
representation in me, then no one else can either. Although he initially
seems to reject the possibility of representations in me that cannot be
thought, he then goes on to concede that there might be such representations, although they would be nothing for me.

The existence of thoughts in me that are not thinkable would certainly
entail a contradiction. A thought that could not be thought would be an
impossible representation. But it is not so obvious that I must be able to
think of all thoughts in me as my thoughts. Now Kant does not initially
argue for the claim that all thoughts must be potential candidates for
self-consciousness. One might argue that to have a thought of something
is to judge or at least entertain the possibility that something is the case. It
seems plausible to maintain that one cannot have thoughts in this sense
without being somehow aware that one is having them. However, Kant

has a less direct and ultimately more persuasive argument linking all (discursive) thought to self-consciousness. The argument for that claim comes later. For the time being, I will simply assume that an argument for the claim that all thoughts are potential I thoughts is forthcoming.

Now one can see that Kant's principle that the "I think" must be able to accompany all my representations would be established if there could not be representations in me that are nothing for me. It is reasonable to assume that, if a representation in me is to be something for me, it must be something that I can think of as mine. If only such representations were possible, it would seem that all representations in me would have to be thinkable by me. But Kant's suggestion that there might be representations in me that are nothing for me seems to throw a monkey-wrench in the argument. In restricting representations that are mine to those that are thinkable by me, one leaves open the possibility of representations other than thoughts in me, i.e. intuitions, that are not thinkable at all. The point to note here is that the existence of representations that are nothing for me, representations of which I am not conscious, is consistent with the principle that I can think all my representations so long as one restricts the meaning of mine to those representations in me that are something for me. The validity of Kant's argument thus depends on the assumption that representations in me that would be nothing for me cannot be mine at all.

Robert Howell worries with Paul Guyer that Kant falsely infers that I can become conscious of each representation that happens to be mine from the fact that I can become conscious of a representation as mine, if I represent it as mine.[1] But the point to note here is that Kant understands mineness in a restrictive sense. What is mine is something for me, as opposed to something of which I might be an owner in a sense that is cognitively inaccessible to me. I may own something, even though I do not know that I own it. I might even own something that contingent circumstances prevent me from ever recognizing as my own. But if I do not know that I own something, there must at least be some evidential base for a possible claim to ownership by me. There might be a misplaced deed or a long-forgotten relative to support my entitlement. I could appeal to these sources of evidence for my ownership if I were aware of them. The same general principle of entitlement that applies to property applies to the ownership of representations or mental states. If a representation is mine in principle, I must be able to recognize it as such, even if a representation can be mine without my being conscious at that time that it is mine.

I have interpreted Kant's argument as turning on a distinction between a weak notion of existence in my consciousness and a stronger notion of being mine. By contrast, Henry Allison suggests that there can be representations that are mine yet are nothing for me. He then argues that one can take the "I think" principle to be restricted to a subset of my representations, namely, those that function as representations through which I represent something to myself.[2] While Allison insists that representations could be mine in some sense without being something for me, Kant's argument depends on the assumption that, if a representation is mine, it is something for me. Kant allows for the logical possibility of representations *in me* that are nothing for me. He claims implicitly that such representations would not affect the validity of the claim that the "I think" can accompany all my representations. But he cannot allow for representations that are mine, but nothing for me.

Kant clearly does assume that representations which happen to be in me, but that I cannot think of as mine, are without cognitive significance. For, without such an assumption, his argument, establishing the claim that even representations in me that can be given prior to all thought must be potential contents of I thoughts, would be invalid. For, after implicitly distinguishing possible representations in me that are nothing for me from my representations, and arguing that all my representations are thinkable by me, Kant notes that intuitions are representations that are independent of thought. Surprisingly, he goes on to conclude that all contents of intuition *in me* must be thinkable by me, where one would have expected him to conclude that only all the contents of *my* intuition must be thinkable by me. The initial phase of Kant's argument seems to be free of the conflation of two different senses of ownership: ownership in the sense of what can be ascribed by me to me, and ownership in the weaker sense of what merely exists in me. But it is at this juncture in the argument that Henrich's worry, that Kant falls victim to an ambiguity in the notion of mineness in extending mineness to all representations that may be represented in me, seems to have considerable force.[3] However, I think a charitable reading of Kant's argument would be that he wishes to understand intuitions in me as restricted to those that are mine, that is, those that are something for me. Henrich would also acknowledge that this reading is the one most consonant with Kant's aim in this part of the Deduction, although he worries that Kant may have been taken in by the potential for confusion involved in the distinction between a representation being in me and being something for me.

Now a number of examples have been adduced to show that we are sometimes incapable of being self-conscious of a certain representation that occurs in us. This has often been adduced as evidence that Kant fails to establish that all my representations are self-ascribable. The most obvious point to make here is that Kant implicitly distinguishes representations occurring in us from representations that are ours in the sense of representations that have some cognitive significance for us. However, the examples in question might suggest that representations may have cognitive significance and yet not be self-ascribable. It is this possibility that I wish to address in discussing examples of states of consciousness that do not seem to be potential states of self-consciousness.

Let me start with Guyer's example in which another person infers that I have been dreaming from my rapid eye movements.[4] I do not remember my dream. Therefore the other person's inferential evidence is better than my own introspective knowledge. That person can therefore find representations in me that I do not find. In fact, it is almost definitive of a dream state that it is a state of consciousness that is not also a state of self-consciousness. Hector-Neri Castañeda makes the same point by appeal to the phenomenon of blind-sight.[5] In blind-sight one perceives things without having the capacity directly to be conscious of them, so that one can only learn by indirect inference from one's own behavior what one has perceived. We might also mention examples in which the corpus callosum of the brain has been bisected. Such bisection raises particular problems for the unity of consciousness, since each of the two hemispheres of the brain is capable of functioning independently of the other.[6] Terence Wilkerson notes the more familiar examples of babies and comatose individuals. They have representations, but they are not self-conscious or even, strictly speaking, capable of self-consciousness.[7] From examples such as these, it is reasonable to infer that there is consciousness without self-consciousness.

Manfred Baum attempts to respond to the possibility of unconscious representations that might never become conscious to me by arguing that the only access to my representations is a first-person access. He infers from the privileged access that each of us has to our own representations that there cannot be representations that cannot become conscious to the person who has them.[8] Yet, even if Baum is correct that I have no direct experience of other individuals' mental states, I may be in a better position than they to determine what their mental states are. So privileged access does not rule out the existence of states that can never become conscious to the person that has them. My inferences based on indirect evidence of their mental states may be less subject to error than their ascriptions of representations to themselves based on the immediate data of their experience. Introspection needs correction and amplification from the third-person point of view. On the other hand, we may grant the assumption that behavior such as rapid eye movements provides a good inferential basis for the belief that a person is dreaming, and thus experiencing a certain representation, without granting the very strong asymmetry between self-ascription and other-ascription to which Guyer, for one, is committed. If you can have inferential knowledge that I am dreaming through observation of my rapid eye movements, there is no principled reason why I cannot also come to have inferential knowledge of this as well. I might see myself later on film and conclude that I was dreaming.

Kant allows for representations of which we are not directly conscious:

To have representations and not *to be conscious of them*, seems to contain a contradiction; for how can we know that we have them if we are not conscious of them? *Locke* already made this objection and therefore also rejected the existence of this kind of representation. – But we can become conscious of a representation *indirectly* [*mittelbar*], although we are not immediately aware of it. Such representations are called obscure . . . Thus the field of obscure representations is the largest in human beings. (*Anthro*, Ak. vii, pp. 135–136)

While Kant denies Locke's thesis that all representations involve consciousness and even self-consciousness, he does assert that there is an indirect connection between representation and consciousness. We can know of a representation not only directly, but also indirectly in virtue of its role in explaining overt verbal and other behavior. Since Kant does not require that all consciousness involve self-consciousness, there is no reason to think that he would not concede that I may sometimes become conscious of a representation as mine only after the fact. And this suggests that even babies and comatose individuals could become conscious after the fact of representational states that they were in while in a state of unconsciousness. However, unless they were able to become conscious of their present or past experiences as babies or comatose individuals, those representations would have no cognitive significance for them.

Unlike the A-Deduction, the B-Deduction seems to allow for the possibility of representations in me or in someone else that have no cognitive significance for anyone. Such representations would be nothing for anyone. While we would have no reason to assume the existence of such representations, Kant now seems to rightly eschew the verificationist thesis with respect to representation that he advocates in those passages in the A-Deduction that rule out the very existence of representations that are nothing for me or anyone else.

PURE APPERCEPTION AND CONSCIOUSNESS OF SELF-IDENTITY

Kant refers to the self-consciousness of the "I think" as pure or original apperception, a notion he explicitly contrasts with empirical appercep-tion (section 16, B 132). This pure apperception is said to be original since it is the source of the representation "I think". This "I think" represents a logically basic subject of representation, since it refers to whoever may be the ultimate bearer of that representation. As a "spontaneous" representation (B 132), the occurrence of the representation "I think" cannot be understood solely in terms of the causal history of the person who has it. Thus in *thinking* about my representations, I must be repre-senting those representations of mine in a way which is underdeter-mined by any empirical facts about myself. I could have had the same thought in a whole range of different causal circumstances. So far, it would seem that the spontaneity of the "I think" might merely mark the fact that my I thoughts are independent of the particular causal circum-stances in which I have such thoughts. But Kant goes on to make stronger and more interesting claims. He links the spontaneity of thought, its originality, to a consciousness of self that is context-indepen-dent. The "I think" is supposed to be "one and the same in all consciousness" (B 132). It must therefore also be the same in the different states of consciousness that characterize different persons. This context-independence of the "I think" reflects its independence from any particular facts about the causal history of particular agents.

Perhaps the most important feature of the "I think" is that it is "one and the same in all consciousness." This identity of the "I think" in different psychological contexts has implications for an understanding of the notion of mineness that is linked to cognitive significance for an I thinker. The content of *my* representational states is determined by conditions which make it possible for those representations to co-occur in a single consciousness of self. The representations would not other-wise be my representations. But such mineness is, in a certain sense, general. It is true of each and every individual; as such it is subject to whatever general conditions apply to all consciousness in virtue of the dependence of such consciousness on a self-consciousness that has the same general self-referential structure for each individual instance of self-consciousness. The possibility of my becoming self-conscious of my representations puts constraints on whatever is represented by me that turns out to be general in the same way that the "I think" is general:

[A]s my representations (although I may not be conscious of them right away) they [my representations] must necessarily accord with the condition under which they *can* alone stand together in one universal < *in einem allgemeinen* > self-consciousness because they would not otherwise belong to me through all transitions < *durchgängig* >. (section 16, B 132-133)

Minimally a *general* ("allgemeines") self-consciousness must involve a consciousness that the members of a set of representations belong to oneself. However, since Kant also maintains immediately prior to this claim that the self-consciousness in question is transcendental because it is the basis for a priori knowledge (that is, universal and necessary knowledge), he must mean that the self-consciousness in question is an absolutely general, or *universal*, consciousness that different representations can necessarily belong together. So Kant is not just claiming that one's ability to become conscious of a group of representations is a constitutive feature of what makes them one's own; he is also claiming that, because such representation is possible for each of us who can become self-conscious, we must be able to think of all of these possible contents of self-consciousness belonging to different possible individuals as belonging to one possible global self-consciousness. This is a consciousness that any representation which is of any cognitive relevance to any person can belong to any other representation that is of cognitive relevance to that person. The representation in question may then be represented by that person as a representation of that very person. This very abstract notion of ownership can only be the capacity to say "I think" with respect to any arbitrary set of representations that one might have.

Kant links ownership of representations to a potential consciousness of one's self-identity. One is supposed to be able to become conscious of the diverse states of consciousness that belong to one. The capacity to say "I think" with respect to diverse possible representations that I could regard as mine is the basis for our consciousness of self-identity. But the self-identity in question is, first of all, that of any subject in general. It is only on the basis of that general representation of self-identity that we are then able to represent our individual self-identity.

Kant's account of the kind of self-identity that we attain through self-consciousness has anti-Humean implications, although he agrees with Hume that individual states of empirical consciousness give one no consciousness of self-identity. Individual disconnected representations, Hume's perceptions, do not even have the resources to express beliefs or any form of recognitional awareness, since this requires a distinction and, hence, also a connection between subject and predicate. The capacity to connect representations in one self-consciousness is what makes consciousness of the connection between representations poss-ible. And the same capacity for self-consciousness is the basis of all consciousness of identity.

Kant's concern with self-identity, as in the A-Deduction, is with the enabling role that a representation of self-identity plays in our ability to understand and use concepts. Self-consciousness is of crucial import-ance in concept formation and, hence, in all thought. There is a unity to the way in which what we represent is connected for us (a synthetic unity in Kant's terminology). This synthetic unity logically precedes the formation of any concepts:

A representation that is to be thought as common to *different* ones, is thought as belonging to ones that have apart from it something *different* in them, therefore they must previously be thought to be in synthetic unity with others (if only possible representations) before I can think the analytic unity of consciousness that makes them into conceptus communis [common concepts] in them. And thus the synthetic unity of apperception is the highest point on which I must support all use of the understanding, even the whole of logic, and after it, transcendental philosophy, yes, this faculty is the understanding itself. (B 134n)

In order to represent anything in terms of a sortal or attributive concept I must grasp what it is that distinguishes the class of objects to which that concept applies from other possible classes. I must therefore be able to compare and contrast different items that are represented by me. In his logic lectures, Kant divides the procedure of concept forma-tion into three steps: (1) comparison, through which I compare represen-tations to one another in a single consciousness, (2) reflection, in which I reflect on how to grasp different representations in terms of a certain unity of consciousness provided by the features that those representa-tions have in common, and (3) abstraction, in which I abstract from all of the features that those representations do not have in common (*Logic*, ed. Jäsche, Ak. IX, p. 94).

The important point in the present context is that, in order to be able to engage in the procedure of comparison, reflection, and abstraction, I need not only a consciousness in which those items are compared and contrasted, but also the capacity to represent myself as being the same subject of representations that represents the one as that which represents the other items. From such observations, Kant can legitimately conclude that the analytic unity of any conceptual consciousness, any ability to grasp what is represented by me in terms of a one over many, such as a sortal or attributive term, requires a synthetic unity of self-consciousness, that is, a capacity to represent the contents of representations together as my representations (B 134). It is this synthetic unity which is a condition for the formation of concepts and at the same time the condition for their applicability to objects of experience. It is important to notice that the synthetic unity in question is one that connects different items represented in a universal self-consciousness. It is then our capacity to represent ourselves as one and the same subject with respect to all the diverse representations of such a universal self-consciousness that allows us to represent things in the universal and standpoint-neutral way demanded by Kant's conception of a concept.

Kant commits himself more explicitly to a link between the standpoint-neutral identity of the I that serves as subject of self-consciousness, and the kind of standpoint neutrality involved in having a concept, in his lectures on *Anthropology*:

[E]xperience is empirical cognition, but cognition requires reflection (reflexio), and hence consciousness of the activity in putting together the manifold of a representation according to a rule of unity for that manifold, that is, *a concept* and thought in general (distinct from intuition). The I of reflection contains no manifold in itself and is always one and the same in all judgment, since it is merely this formality of consciousness. (Ak. VII, p. 141)

As universal representations, concepts involve consciousness of features common to a possible plurality of particulars (A 320/B 377). They are representations that can be contained in a number of numerically distinct individual representations or intuitions (*Logic*, ed. Jäsche, Ak. IX, section 1, p. 91). But what makes such representations universal is that they represent things in a standpoint-neutral way. This is possible because, as I thinkers, we can think of ourselves and other things in a way that is completely independent of any particular facts about us or the world.

SYNTHESIS AND SELF-CONSCIOUSNESS

At this point, I need to say something more about the nature of synthetic unity. Kant is careful to note that the need for synthesis is a feature of representations that are mine in the sense that they are cognitively significant for me. This is true regardless of whether we combine what we are representing under a concept, or combine it in one spatio-temporal experience (intuition). Indeed, Kant is committed to our capacity to conceptually represent any perceptual (intuitive) contents, since concepts are involved in all thought, and he has already claimed that the only intuitions that are of any cognitive significance for us are ones that we can think of potentially as our own. In order for a representation to have cognitive significance for us, we must be able to distinguish its different contents. But in order to be able to distinguish those contents, we must already be able to connect. For Kant, analysis always presupposes synthesis (section 15, B 130). Representing something as connected, regardless of whether there is anything already complexly characterizable there to begin with, involves an activity that one can refer to as a self-activity. For it is through the activity of connecting and distinguishing information that the subject establishes the connected-ness of the object *for itself*:

[W]e cannot represent anything *as* connected in the object unless we have previously connected it ourselves and among all representations *connection* is the only one which is not given through objects, but can only be performed by the subject itself, since it is an act of its self-activity. (section 15, B 130)

The different bits of information that we experience are only accessible to us as what they are insofar as we can compare them with each other. But to compare them we must connect them to each other. It is this fact about us that makes us discursive intellects. Indeed, although Kant introduces the notion of a purely intuitive intellect (a God's eye point of view) by way of contrast with our discursive intellect, he argues that we cannot even make sense of such an intellect, so that the theocentric perspective on the world that has been popular with rationalist philos-ophers is not even really coherent for him:

That understanding through whose self-consciousness a manifold of intuition would be given, an understanding through whose representation the objects of this representation would also exist, would not require a particular act of synthesis of the manifold for the unity of consciousness, needed by human understanding which merely thinks and does not intuit. But it is the first principle for human understanding, so that it cannot form the least concept of an other possible understanding, either one that *itself* intuits or even of a sensible intuition, but of another kind than the one grounded in space and time. (section 17, B 138–139)

For a being with a discursive intelligence, there is a fundamental distinction to be drawn between the way objects are given to it (receptivity); and the way it represents those objects as given to it (spontaneity). An intuitive or non-discursive understanding would not, according to Kant, require a connection or synthesis that is distinguishable from the way objects are given to it. In the *Critique*, Kant accuses the philosophical tradition of conflating understanding and intuition. So he cannot take the idea that ours is a discursive intellect in his sense as uncontested, for otherwise his philosophical critics can accept the conclusion that he draws from what is required for experience by a discursive understanding and simply deny that ours is a discursive intellect.

Although the *Critique* as a whole can be regarded as a defense of the claim that ours is a discursive intellect, at B 130 Kant adduces the fact about us that he thinks directly supports the claim that ours is a discursive intellect. This synthetic fact links cognitive significance for us to our being able to make cognitive connections for ourselves. A representation is cognitively significant for me only if I can think of that representation as a representation that could be mine in the sense that it is connectible to other representations that I ascribe to it myself. Kant can then appeal to the claim that it is analytic to all representations that are mine that they are ascribable by me to me. This mineness of representations gives even intuitions, including those of space and time as a whole, their unity (B 136n).

Now the A-Deduction maintains that there is a synthetic a priori connection between all empirical consciousness and a possible self-consciousness (A 117n). There Kant is concerned with the implications of self-consciousness for the empirical content of thought. He argues that an empirical consciousness is only consciousness of an object insofar as it can be connected to other contents of consciousness in one possible self-consciousness. In the B-Deduction, Kant takes the need for synthesis to be analytic to self-consciousness. There is, however, an important distinction between the A-Deduction and the B-Deduction. For the B-Deduction claim concerns the need for synthesis relative to representations that are mine:

(1) The thought: these representations given in intuition all belong *to me* means as much as I connect them in one self-consciousness, or can at least connect them there, and even if it is not itself the consciousness of the *synthesis* of representations, it presupposes the possibility of the latter, that is, only insofar as I can grasp that manifold in one consciousness, do I call all those representations *my* representations; for otherwise I would have such a multicolored different self, as I have representations of which I am conscious . . . now this principle of the necessary unity of apperception is identical and hence an analytic proposition, but explains a synthesis of the manifold that is given in one intuition as necessary without which that pervasive identity of self-consciousness could not be thought. (section 16, B 135)

It is analytic of a representation being my representation that it is one that I can ascribe to the identity of my self-consciousness. But I can think of different representations as belonging to my self-consciousness only insofar as I can think of them as ones that are linked together by my consciousness of self. This might suggest that these representations must therefore have a content that is purely subjective. But Kant rightly resists this conclusion. To think of representations as my representations is to think of them as representations that belong together in a certain distinctive unity of consciousness, that is, in a certain history. But they can only belong to a certain distinctive unity of consciousness, in a certain history, to the extent that they could be connected together with the representations belonging to other distinctive unities of consciousness, that is, to other distinctive histories, histories that are yours, his, hers, and its. Moreover, representations can only be regarded as belonging to these distinctive unities of consciousness, or points of view, insofar as they can be taken to have cognitive significance for me and my thought. It is my capacity for such I thoughts that allows me to represent things from different possible points of view. I can do this precisely because I thoughts have a conceptual content that is independent of any particular point of view.

(2) The synthetic unity of consciousness is therefore an objective condition of all cognition, not which I merely require in order to know an object, but under which any intuition must stand *in order for it to become an object for me*, because in any other way and without this synthesis this manifold would *not* become unified in consciousness. The last proposition is, as was said, itself analytic, although it makes synthetic unity the condition of all thought; for it says nothing more than that all *my* representations in any given intuition must stand under the condition that I can alone ascribe them as *my* representations to an identical self, and therefore can grasp them together synthetically connected in one apperception by means of the universal expression *I think*. (section 17, B 138)

APPERCEPTION AND CONCEPTS OF OBJECTS

After arguing that self-consciousness places impersonal constraints on all my representations, Kant moves to the claim that these impersonal constraints are the basis for concepts of objects. These concepts of objects are then interpreted as ones that we use to form judgments and to articulate cognition or knowledge in judgments. Initially, we expect to see Kant derive the conditions for concept use, judgment, and knowledge from the conditions governing self-consciousness; he seems instead merely to shift from talking about conditions on self-consciousness to talk of conditions on conceptual cognition and judgment without clarifying how concepts or judgment depend on self-consciousness.[9] It seems as if, instead of arguing from the a priori enabling conditions for the unity of self-consciousness to the a priori enabling conditions for concepts and for knowledge of objects, he argues from the a priori conditions governing concepts and knowledge of objects to the a priori enabling conditions for the unity of self-consciousness.

An argument to a priori enabling conditions for self-consciousness based on the existence of knowledge will only be convincing to the reader who is already prepared to accept the existence of knowledge as a given. Initial appearances to the contrary, Kant really wants to argue that enabling conditions for the unity of self-consciousness are enabling conditions for judgment and knowledge. His line of thought in arguing for the idea that the unifiability of representations in self-consciousness is a necessary condition for cognition may be reconstructed as follows: knowledge involves judgment. Judgment involves the possibility of agreement or disagreement between different persons about some purported state of affairs. As such, judgment involves an implicit commitment to the idea that there is some normative ground that allows one to determine whether the judgment is right or wrong, whether it is true or false. But such a normative basis for agreement or disagreement is only present where there is at least the possibility of a standpoint that is outside of the standpoints of those who articulate judgments that either agree or disagree. It is this standpoint that is implicitly presupposed when we interpret a certain object in terms of certain concepts. Such a standpoint is precisely that provided by Kant's idea that different representations must be unifiable in a possible self-consciousness that is able to abstract from any particular point of view within experience.

Without self-consciousness, I do not have a consciousness of myself as one person among others. I am thus unable to represent my point of view as one which is either distinguishable or indistinguishable with respect to some subject-matter from that available to some other being. But if I have self-consciousness, then I also have the capacity to represent myself in a way that is indistinguishable from the way any other self-conscious being represents itself or the world. I exercise this capacity when I represent myself in abstraction from what distinguishes my point of view from other points of view and when I represent things in a manner that is, in principle, available to anyone. Concepts represent contents in terms of representations that can be had in altogether different circumstances in experience.

Kant captures the implicit objective commitments of subjective experience, the implicit universal intelligibility of even subjective experience, by characterizing his notion of object in terms of representations that are unified under concepts: "Object is that in the concept of which a given manifold is unified" (section 17, B 137). Since concepts are representations of items in a standpoint-independent or universal manner, the concept of an object is something the content of which is represented in a way that does not depend on a standpoint. If concepts are to be applicable to experiences, and if those experiences are to become an object for me, then those experiences must be unifiable in consciousness under concepts. But the consciousness in question must have universal significance if we are to think of it as a consciousness that could be right or wrong about what it is representing.

Failure to pay attention to Kant's somewhat technical conception of a concept can lead one to think that he simply shifts from a notion of unifiability in consciousness that applies to anything that can be an experience in any sense at all to a notion of unifiability that is restricted to representations that have objective validity. For Kant moves directly from his definition of an object to the claim that representations unified in that way in consciousness have objective validity and count as cognition or knowledge (section 17, B 137).

As in the A-Deduction, Kant introduces the concept of an object in a context in which he is also willing to talk of cognition (knowledge) of an object that has objective validity. The idea seems to be that we only have a bona fide concept of an object if we are able correctly to use the concept in judgments that provide us with knowledge of an object. Indeed, Kant is not satisfied with the assertion that cognition has unity of consciousness as its necessary condition; he claims that unity of consciousness is sufficient for cognition.[10] The important thing to note here is that the unity of consciousness is sufficient for cognition only when it includes both empirical and a priori conditions for the unity of self-consciousness. Kant does not suggest that the a priori conditions are themselves independently sufficient, nor does he suggest that empirical conditions on the unity of consciousness would be sufficient.

Allison tries to fill the apparent gap in the argument generated by Kant's shift from treating the unity of consciousness as a necessary condition for knowledge to treating it as a sufficient condition for knowledge by weakening the notion of object involved here to that of a purely logical notion.[11] This is tempting, but it will not work, since Kant does not restrict cognition (*Erkenntnis*) to logical knowledge in the first part of the B-Deduction as Allison maintains. Kant defines knowledge as the determination of representation in relation to an object (section 17, B 137). In his summary of the argument in the first part of the Deduction, Kant claims that unitary *empirical* intuition is determined with respect to the forms of judgment (section 20, B 143). He thus takes himself to be showing in the first part of the B-Deduction that we have knowledge of objects belonging to experience as well as purely formal objects.

Treatment of the unity of consciousness as sufficient for cognition is licensed by a further premise, that something is a cognition if and only if it involves the unification of empirical representations under concepts. Kant's definition of a cognition as the determinate relation of given representations to an object supplies this missing premise. He does not officially introduce the notion of judgment until section 19, but he does think of cognition as involving judgment. So the determinate relation in question is a relation for judgment, since judgment is "the representation of the unity of consciousness of different representations or the representation of their relationship insofar as they constitute a concept" (*Logic*, Ak. IX, section 17, p. 101). Judgment represents items in a way that commits one to those items being the same for everyone, that is to their unifiability in an "I think p" that could be anyone's. This capacity to abstract from what is the case for me as a particular individual and to take things as they would be represented by anyone else is what is expressed by the "is" of assertion:

[A] judgment is nothing but the way given cognitions are brought to the objective unity of apperception. That is the target of the little relational word "is" in them [judgments] to distinguish the objective unity of given representations from the subjective. (section 19, B 141–142)

The universal commitments of judgment and claims to knowledge expressed in judgment are already implicit in the concepts involved in judgment. But in judgment concepts are related to each other in such a way that a claim is made that can be either true or false. The unity of consciousness in a judgment thus makes the relation of representations to each other determinate in a way that makes agreement or disagreement possible.

Kant finally makes the distinction between the objective unity to be found in shareable self-consciousness and the merely subjective unity of consciousness we are accustomed to in our introspective self-consciousness explicit in section 18. He identifies empirical apperception in section 18 (B 140) with an associative connection between representations that is valid for me or for you, in contrast with an objective unity of consciousness that is universally valid. In general, how I happen to connect different words or other representations with objects in my consciousness is a contingent matter that depends on the circumstances under which I have come to connect those words with those objects. Such accidental connection by association is not sufficient for an objective unity of consciousness, that is, for a consciousness of what we represent that can be the same for all of us. Kant identifies this objective unity of consciousness with the transcendental unity of apperception (B 139).

Kant's reference to transcendental apperception as having an objective unity to what it represents provides indirect support for the way I have been reading his claim that representations must be able to belong together in a self-consciousness. The universality of the unity of transcendental self-consciousness that Kant invokes in the second paragraph of section 16 cannot be restricted to the representations in my individual consciousness alone, for then it could not support the objective validity that he identifies with transcendental apperception in section 18.

To be sure, the very introduction of a notion of "empirical apperception" (B 140) in contrast to the transcendental unity of apperception seems at first to wreak havoc with the argument. It is tempting to take the view that consciousness of self-identity should then be possible without the more ambitious conception of transcendental apperception. Another response is to reject the notion that empirical apperception really is a form of self-consciousness. On either of these interpretations, the role of transcendental self-consciousness as enabling condition for empirical self-consciousness drops out. Kant's suggestion is crucial that empirical apperception which is only subjectively valid is derived from transcendental and objective apperception "under specific conditions in

concreto" (section 18, B 140). Empirical self-consciousness is characterized by a unity of the contents of consciousness that depends for its
character on the spatio-temporal context of a particular individual.
Such subjective unity of spatio-temporal experience is derived from an
objective unity based on facts about spatio-temporal objects that hold
for any arbitrary observer. Empirical apperception may be subject to
the unity required by transcendental self-consciousness without directly
displaying that unity.

ALLISON ON APPERCEPTION AND SUBJECTIVE UNITY

Henry Allison identifies apperception with the narrowly logical powers of
understanding and with the role of judgment in the making of objective
claims.[12] He worries that by assigning subjective validity to empirical
apperception Kant contradicts the principle that empirical consciousness
is subject to the transcendental conditions of unity. As a consequence of
Allison's assimilation of self-consciousness to judgments with objective
import, self-consciousness threatens to drop out of subjective experience,
and subjective experience threatens to disappear altogether.

Allison insists that a subjective unity in consciousness is not something
through which even subjective states could be represented since it is not
something through which anything could be represented at all: "There
is in fact only one thing that could count as a subjective unity in the
Kantian sense: a unity or connection of representations through which
nothing is represented, not even our subjective states."[13] Since Allison
does not think that what Kant calls a subjective unity of consciousness
can be a bona fide unity of consciousness, he concludes that it cannot be
a fortiori a unity of self-consciousness either, although it can become the
topic of consciousness.[14] As objectified for self-conscious thought, the
subjective unity of my experience would be an object of judgment and
empirical knowledge. Thus on Allison's interpretation all (empirical)
consciousness of oneself as a particular individual is knowledge of
oneself as an object. And this knowledge is knowledge by a non-empirical self. The implication is that all *self*-consciousness is *knowledge* of the
self through transcendental self-consciousness.

Although Allison initially maintains that Kant "refers to the subjective unity as a unity of *consciousness* and to the objective unity as a unity of
self-consciousness," he soon is forced to concede that he also finds Kant
"treating the empirical unity of apperception as equivalent to the
subjective unity of consciousness. The problem is that Kant also seems

to regard empirical apperception as equivalent to empirical self-consciousness, that is, as the mode of consciousness through which we represent ourselves to ourselves as objects of inner sense."[15] As Allison admits, the view that a subjective unity of consciousness is not a unity of self-consciousness conflicts with Kant's reference to empirical apperception both as self-consciousness and as a subjective unity (B-Deduction: section 18, B 140). Allison concedes that, even though Kant notes that the original unity of consciousness that is based on the relation of intuition to one I think is "alone objectively valid," Kant also insists that "the empirical unity of apperception which we are not considering here and which is only derived from the former under given conditions *in concreto*, has only subjective validity" (B 140). Allison can find only confusion in this remark of Kant's because Allison's interpretation of the Kantian notion of apperception and self-consciousness only allows for a self-consciousness of objective states of affairs.

Allison's restriction of self-consciousness to objective states of affairs forces not only him to ascribe confusion to Kant, it also has a more devastating consequence. Our experience of ourselves as distinct individuals is based on what Kant calls inner sense. Allison argues plausibly that "Kant's theory of inner sense is best understood in terms of the account of the subjective unity of consciousness which we have already considered."[16] Because Allison's reading of inner sense and the subjective unity of consciousness makes it independent of self-consciousness, he argues that "Kant's account of inner sense explains how the mind can become aware of its own representations as 'subjective objects,' but it does not explain how it can represent *itself* as an object."[17] In contrast to spatial objects, that is, the objects of outer sense, Allison thinks that Kant is forced to adopt a "substratum" or "bare particular" theory of predication when he deals with judgments about inner states.[18] One might ask why the self cannot be experienced. Allison's answer is: "the important point is simply that, as non empirical, the I cannot know itself through the (empirical predicates) representations which it refers to itself in judgments in the same way in which it knows outer objects through the predicates which it attributes to such objects in judgments of outer experience."[19]

The self ceases to be something that we can experience at all in Allison's reconstruction of Kant's account of experience. For according to Allison the self can only be experienced as an object of judgment in which its character as a point of view is no longer in play. But worse, the self cannot even be experienced as an object of judgment, for then its character as self would elude us. This consequence of Allison's interpretation seems quite unappealing. In general, his failure to do justice to the Kantian account of empirical self-consciousness and to the fact that having self-consciousness involves having a particular point of view makes his account of transcendental self-consciousness irrelevant to the phenomenon of self-consciousness as it is generally understood. For most consciousness of self is not a consciousness of a proposition that has a truth value. To the extent that the self is something of which we can be conscious in being conscious of judgments that have objective validity, an account must be offered of how our own subjective take on things could be involved in a consciousness of something that on Allison's view must have a truth value.[20] We need to be able to understand how empirical self-consciousness could require transcendental self-consciousness. Allison's interpretation of transcendental self-consciousness precludes him from offering such an account.[21]

Now I wish to argue that, in the logical space of reasons opened up by transcendental apperception, transitions from one representation to another are governed not only by the kind of causal connections that underwrite habits of association, but by normative principles of rationality as well. Since the causal connections between representations involved in the empirical psychologist's description of the regularities in our individual representations themselves depend on our ability to make normative claims about what came before what and where and what caused what, these empirical connections are not really free standing. As the A-Deduction makes abundantly clear, our ability to make sense of associative patterns itself depends on our ability to form the concept of an object that is independent of the way it appears to us at any given moment, and this requires the possibility of a point of view that is able to abstract my own particular take on things.

THE OBJECTIVE VALIDITY OF JUDGMENT AND THE UNITY OF CONSCIOUSNESS

It is worthwhile to contrast the account of judgment in the B-Deduction with that of the *Prolegomena*. In the *Prolegomena*, Kant distinguishes between subjective judgments of perception that do not require the application of categories and necessarily intersubjective judgments of experience involving application of the categories. In the case of judgments of perception, no issue of disagreement or agreement can arise, since they merely express the subjective take that an individual has on his or her own experience, whereas in the case of judgments of experience agreement or disagreement between persons is necessarily possible:

[J]udgments are either merely subjective when representations are referred to a consciousness in one subject only, and are united in it, or they are objective when they are united in consciousness in general, that is necessarily. (*Prolegomena*, section 22, Ak. IV, pp. 304–5)

In a review of Ulrich's *Institutiones*, Johann Schultz argued that the theory of perceptual judgment in the *Prolegomena* was inconsistent with the claim in the first edition of the *Critique* that all perception is subject to the categories. Kant refers to the review in a famous footnote to the *Metaphysical Foundations* (Ak IV, p. 474n) near the date of the second edition of the *Critique*, so he clearly gave the problem some thought. Perceptual judgments in the *Prolegomena* are independent of any application of the categories. This is what distinguishes them from judgments of experience. The independence of perception from the categories is not something that Kant can advocate without giving up the universal scope of categories with respect to our experience, and that would be to give up the claim that the categories can make to being a priori enabling conditions of experience.

In the B-Deduction, Kant responds to this objection by restricting judgments to the objective states of affairs expressed by judgments of experience in the *Prolegomena*. Such judgments involve the use of categories. For categories are the basic concepts that underwrite claims to objectivity. In section 19 of the B-Deduction, the distinction between judgments of perception and of experience in the *Prolegomena* becomes a distinction between judgments of experience and associative connections between perceptions. There are now statements that seem prima facie to express judgments which turn out merely to express associations. Such statements are to be understood as a mere evocation of inner states, comparable to cries of pain. In the cases of such subjective statements, agreement or disagreement is inappropriate. It no more makes sense for me to call into question the associations that you have than it does for me to reject your pain. Judgments, by contrast, are now taken by Kant to make claims that presuppose the possibility of agreement or disagreement.

Judgments are based on what Kant calls the necessary unity of self-consciousness, that is, the unity that representations must have if they are to be able to belong together in any self-consciousness. By contrast, associative connections of the kind established by largely accidental causal circumstances are based on empirical self-consciousness (section 19, B 142). The fact that judgment involves an implicit commitment to the existence of necessary connections between what is represented by the concepts that one uses in the judgment seems at first to rule out any possibility of expressing a subjective standpoint. However, such a commitment is always taken on from a particular subjective standpoint. Thus, judgment is compatible with the existence of differences between persons in what they experience. The important part is how what is experienced is interpreted. A judgment should express relations between the objects and properties or relations attributed to those objects that purport to be true for anyone in the circumstances stated by the judgment.

The assimilation of objecthood to objectivity, and the idea that judgment expresses objectivity lead to several problems. The first problem concerns the relation between judgment and knowledge. Kant sometimes treats judgment as a relationship between concepts that is objectively valid (section 19, B 142). Of course, not all judgments are objectively valid even if they purport to be so. But, on the whole and in the same context, he implicitly concedes that judgments have the kind of objective unity that yields objective validity merely as their target.[22] Not every judgment is an instance of knowledge. Kant is interested in the fact that a judgment is a claim to knowledge. As a judgment it must purport to be true. He also treats all objects of experience as publicly accessible because he wants to deny that there are any private objects that are not available to us under some public description. Any object of which I can be conscious ought to be an object of which someone else could have indirect consciousness. Kant thus finds himself compelled to defend the view that all judgment purports to state objective facts. Restricting judgment to objective facts seems to leave no room for judgments concerning my inner states, at least insofar as these judgments are about those inner states as I experience them. Since knowledge or cognition requires judgment, the implication seems to be that there is no self-knowledge.

Kant tries to find a way of accommodating self-knowledge in the second step of the proof in the B-Deduction, which I will concern myself with in the next chapter. I will show how the second step of Kant's proof resolves the difficulties posed by his theory of objective judgment for his account of inner experience. In the process, I will try to throw some light on the manner in which subjective experience is dependent on objective experience.

CHAPTER 5

Self-consciousness and the unity of intuition: completing the B-Deduction

Kant develops and supports the claim to objectivity implicit in judgment by first arguing that all judgment that is dependent on a specific subject-matter dependent judgment derives its content from spatio-temporal experience and then by arguing that we can represent all objects in space and time together in a manner that is standpoint-neutral. This standpoint-neutral manner of representing objects in space and time is due to their relation to a possible self-consciousness. As contents of consciousness, objects in space and time are representable in a manner that depends on the spatio-temporal standpoint of the observing consciousness. However, this standpoint-dependent perspective is itself only intelligible relative to a possible standpoint-independent perspective from which the standpoint of the observer becomes cognitively accessible.

By appealing to the standpoint-neutral constraints on representing standpoint-dependent truths, it is possible to justify the objectivity claim made by judgment. Objectivity then consists in the way things must be represented in space and time so that they are the same for all observers at all spatio-temporal locations. Kant seeks to make it comprehensible how even subjective experiences can be regarded as subject to objectivity constraints. The key thesis here is that subjective experiences are inherently dependent on the way things present themselves to the spatio-temporal point of view of some consciousness. But this particular point of view is only intelligible as a specific perspective that one can take as a self. In self-consciousness one is then, in principle, able to combine the different possible spatio-temporal points of view in a single encompassing objective point of view. It is because the individual perspectives of diverse subjective experiences themselves presuppose a single comprehensive point of view of which they are the perspectives, that subjective experiences are subject to objectivity constraints.

THE PROBLEM OF THE PROOF STRUCTURE

Initially, Kant's argument for the objective validity and empirical reality of the categories seems to be complete by section 20 at the end of the first step in his two-step proof. Thus, his transcendental deduction seems to be complete. He takes himself to have shown that categories act as constraints on the empirical contents of judgments made by any possible self-consciousness. But he soon claims in section 21 that he has only just begun his proof. This has given rise to the much debated problem of the proof structure of the B-Deduction. The question of the proof structure is of some importance to my general argument. For I wish to argue against the leading interpretations that Kant does not need to appeal to an *ad hoc* assumption of spatial and temporal unity in order to support his argument from the self-ascribability of representations to their being subject to conceptual constraints that allow us to form judgments about them.

Kant summarizes what he takes himself already to have proven in the form of a syllogism (section 20, B 143). The major term of the syllogism and initial premise of the argument states that the content of intuition must be subject to the unity of self-consciousness, since this unity of self-consciousness makes the unity of what we sensibly experience possible. This is what he takes himself to have established by section 17. The middle term of the syllogism injects the idea that data are brought under self-consciousness in general through logical functions of judgment. This is supposed to be established in section 18–19. The notion of a logical function is not mentioned explicitly in section 19, but Kant has developed the idea that the objective import of judgment is based on its relation to impersonal self-consciousness, and he has already argued in the Metaphysical Deduction of the Categories that categories are derived from the logical functions underlying thought by applying such logical functions to objects. Assuming that the way objects may be given to us is through empirical intuition, he then concludes that anything given through a unitary empirical intuition is determined with respect to the forms of judgment. For it is through being determined in respect to the logical functions of judgment that contents are brought into a "consciousness in general" (*Bewusstsein überhaupt*) (section 20, B 143). The important thing to note here is that every cognitively significant (spatio-temporal) intuition is given to us as part of an intuition that is unitary in the sense that it can be represented by us as belonging to our own consciousness. But this need not yet involve a representation of how the object of such an intuition would figure in a consciousness in general, that is, in an impersonal consciousness. The task of showing what the objective position in consciousness and intuition is of such an object falls to the category:

A manifold that is contained in an intuition that I call mine is represented as belonging to the *necessary* unity of self-consciousness by means of the synthesis of the understanding, and this occurs by means of the category [B 144]. The basis for the proof depends on the represented *unity of intuition* through which an object is given that always includes a synthesis of the manifold given to an intuition and already contains the relations of the latter to the unity of apperception. (B 144n)

According to Kant's definition of the categories, categories are not just forms of judgment, but ways in which data are determined by thought to fit forms of judgment (section 13). Application of the category of substance to experience determines, for instance, whether information provided by sensibility is to be represented by a singular or an attributive term. Given that anything represented by us in a single empirical intuition is supposed to be subject to the categories, the conclusion of the argument must be that we have knowledge whenever we have a unitary empirical intuition, that belongs to a consciousness in general, that is, an empirical intuition that is the same for each of us. The initial conclusion in section 20 limits the domain of application that categories have to information in unitary empirical representations, thus seeming to allow for the possibility of non-unitary intuitions. But the final conclusion in section 20 seems to close off the possibility of non-unitary intuitions by lifting the restriction: "Therefore the manifold of a given intuition necessarily stands under categories" (B 143). The possibility of non-unitary intuitions is at any rate difficult to take very seriously in Kant's epistemology, since intuitions are defined as unitary and immediate representations.[1]

Although it is now generally agreed that the B-Deduction argument consists of a proof in two steps, with the argument from sections 15 to 19 as one step and the argument from sections 22 to 27 as the other, what is supposed to be shown in each step is very much a matter of debate. There are five different basic approaches that have been taken to the proof structure in the more recent literature: (1) according to the Henrich interpretation, the argument of the first step is synthetic, but is restricted to the applicability of categories to unitary intuitions, while in the second step the applicability of categories to all of our sensible intuitions is demonstrated.[2] (2) According to the interpretation first suggested by

Tenbruck and developed by Bernhard Thöle and Henry Allison, the first step shows that categories apply only to possible objects of intuition, relying on a second step for a proof that they apply to actual empirical objects. The first step is then analytic, while only the argument of the second is synthetic.[3] (3) The approach defended by Brouillet, Wagner, and, more recently, by Howell, takes the first step to show that categories apply to intuitions in general and the second to show that they apply to objects of our empirical intuition.[4] (4) According to Baum's interpretation, the second step of the proof is required in order to demonstrate that space and time are intuitions in the sense required by the first part.[5] (5) McCann argues that the first step of the Deduction is based on the analytic principle of apperception that all my representations can be represented by me as mine. The concept of an object in general and the a priori concepts that specify it are derived from the unity of this apperception. In the second step, Kant then purportedly argues that one cannot so much as think of oneself as an individual thinking thing without having determinate knowledge of oneself. From this it follows that the existence of a determinate self-consciousness entails the validity of categories that apply to objects of sensory experience.[6]

Henrich attributes some confusion to Kant about his own proof-intentions in an effort to explain away those passages (especially in section 16) in the first step which appear to claim that any manifold of our intuition belongs to a unitary self-consciousness (see B 132, B 135–136). Kant is supposed to slide from ascribing unity to any representation which is mine in some restricted sense to ascribing unity to all representations in me. But, if he is guilty of this error, why should he then attempt to prove the latter claim in an additional step? The principle of charity discourages one from accepting Henrich's proposal as a reconstruction of Kant's own intended purpose for the second half of his proof.[7] It is also difficult to see how an appeal to space and time would help to establish the fact that all intuitions must be unitary, if that unity depends, as Henrich claims that it does, on powers of synthesis by the understanding, the scope of which are themselves in doubt.

One can object to the second interpretation of the first step as an analytic argument that this makes it implausible to refer to the first step as a bona fide first step in a two-step proof, since the burden of proof has then been shifted to the second step.[8] The decisive difficulty for the second view seems to me however to be that Kant insists in his summary of the first step in section 20 that "any manifold insofar as it is given in one empirical intuition is *determined* in respect to one of the logical functions through which it is namely brought to one consciousness in general" (section 20, B 143). Kant thinks he has already established the possibility of empirical judgment and empirical knowledge in the first step. In fact, he introduces cognitions ("Erkenntnisse") into the first step in the B-Deduction through the claim that they "consist in the determinate relation of given representations to an object" (section 17, B 137). The specific contribution of the second step cannot therefore be a proof that categories are objectively real. The notion of determination is used by Kant to characterize a feature of the object of judgment which is precisely not determined by logic alone. For instance, which concept will serve as predicate and which as subject in a judgment will be determined by which concept is held to refer to a substance and which to its accident. This point is made in section 13 (B 128–129), a passage to which Kant himself refers in the next sentence of section 20. Kant must therefore believe himself already to have proven that the categories have not only objective, but also empirical reality by the time he has completed the first step of the proof. This objection also seems to be enough to reject the third interpretation. The conditional claim that the Baum interpretation ascribes to the first step in the proof is hard to identify in the text. It is also difficult to see why Kant would not think that the Aesthetic already simply supplies the antecedent premise that we have a priori knowledge of space and time to the conditional claim without an additional step in the proof.

McCann is certainly right that in the second step of the Deduction, Kant wants to show that all states of my empirical self are subject to the categories. However, a central point of Kant's is also that not all experiences that I have as a particular empirically knowable individual are instances of objective judgment or knowledge of the kind requiring the application of categories. How do the categories apply to such subjective experiences if they are constraints on objective judgment? McCann misses this important dimension of Kant's argument, and thus leaves the nature of subjective experience a mystery for Kant, because he conflates all empirical consciousness of self with empirical knowledge of the self. McCann argues that by making self-knowledge a necessary condition for consciousness of oneself as a thinking being one is able to meet a Cartesian skeptic who endorses the *cogito* argument, but rejects our possession of any knowledge of the content of our mental or physical states. But, curiously enough, McCann quotes a passage from the Refutation of Idealism in which Kant expressly disconnects the certainty of the cogito from any claims of self-knowledge:[9]

Certainly, the representation "I am," which expresses the consciousness that can accompany all thought, immediately includes in itself the existence of a subject; but it does not so include any knowledge of that subject, and therefore also no empirical knowledge, that is, no experience of it. (B 277)

Nothing in the Deduction does anything to undermine a Cartesian skeptic who accepts the existential claim embodied in the conditions governing the assertion of the proposition "I think," but rejects the existence of external bodies. However, section 24 of the Deduction does argue with the Refutation that knowledge of inner states is parasitic on knowledge of outer states.

It seems to be specifically the problem of self-knowledge that leads Kant to divide the argument of the B-Deduction into two steps. Since he defines knowledge in terms of judgment in the B-Deduction, and judgment has an objective force that the so-called perceptual judgments of the *Prolegomena* do not, the implication of Kant's new theory of judgment appears to be that no knowledge of inner states is possible. For inner states seem to be precisely states that are inherently subjective. This suggests that there is no such thing as self-knowledge and that there are no inner objects of judgment. Since categories are defined in terms of that with respect to which logical functions of judgments are determined, the implication is that categories do not apply to inner states. A whole dimension of experience appears to resist use of the categories. Kant needs to block this implication of his new theory of judgment, without undermining the link he has established between judgment, objectivity, and self-consciousness.

At the same time he must meet the serious objection that his theory of self-knowledge renders transcendental idealism as a whole incoherent. The clever critic Pistorius had argued in his 1784 review of the *Prolegomena* that transcendental idealism is incoherent because the thesis that things in themselves are unknowable cannot apply to self-knowledge without undermining the possibility of anything genuinely appearing at all. Pistorius could not:

convince himself that the sensations given in time would be merely phenomena just as the intuitions given in space, because he cannot help himself past the difficulty that because our inner sensations or representations would not then be things in themselves, but appearances, there would be nothing but mere illusion < *Schein* > and no real object would remain to which something would appear. How is one to think it possible that representations which one must after all presuppose as real [reell] or as things in themselves, if one wants to explain at all how appearing < *Scheinen* > is possible, can themselves be an illusion <*Schein*>, and what is it through which and in which this illusion <*Schein*> exists?[10]

Consciousness of oneself must be of a bearer that is not itself a mere appearance, if there is to be any representer to which inner and outer objects of any kind are to appear. Otherwise, appearance becomes total illusion. At the same time, self-knowledge and knowledge in general must be restricted to objects as they must appear to us spatially and temporally, if the categories are to apply necessarily to all the objects to which they do apply.

In contrast to the different reconstructions of the argument in the Deduction, I wish to argue that the first step attempts to show *that* all cognitively significant contents of our representations are candidates for judgments determined by categories. Cognitively significant contents are candidates for judgment, because they are potential candidates for the kind of impersonal self-consciousness expressed by the proposition "I think." One might worry that the restriction of the argument to cognitively significant representations would leave the argument in the first step incomplete. However, there is no reason to think of the argument for objectivity in the first step as essentially incomplete, since Kant has no need to be concerned with the status of representations that are completely beyond anyone's ken. Why then is a second step needed in Kant's proof? Kant needs to show *how* all sensible representational contents can be candidates for judgment requiring categories. In this way, Kant can sustain the claim of judgment to objectivity and still provide room for subjective experiences.

Before the second step, Kant claims to have abstracted the second step from the manner in which data belonging to an empirical intuition are given. He now wants to explain how it is possible for the categories to apply to all objects:

In what follows (section 26), it will be shown through the way that empirical intuition is given in sensibility that its unity is none other than that which the category prescribes according to the previous section 20 to a given intuition in general and by thus explaining their validity a priori with respect to all objects of our senses the Deduction will be attained for the first time. (section 21, B 145)

Since Kant has already concluded that any manifold given in an empirical intuition will have to be subject to the categories, in the second step, he can only be concerned with demonstrating how the validity of the categories with respect to all empirical objects is to be explained, that is, he wants to show how a priori knowledge of all objects of experience is possible. Thus in section 26 he notes that he first argued for the categories as a priori cognitions of objects belonging to an intuition in general (sections 20–21), and now wants to explain how categories can apply to all objects that may present themselves to our senses.

Kant thinks that an a priori claim must be necessarily true of all the objects of which it is true. And he thinks that this implies that the objects of which an a priori claim is true can only be objects as they must appear to us. This is why he invokes his conception of transcendental idealism to show that the categories must apply to all objects of experience and only to objects of experience. First, he argues that judgment and cognition, including mathematical knowledge, is restricted to the form of objects belonging to our experience (sections 22–23). He then argues that judgment and hence the categories that provide contentual constraints on judgment necessarily apply even to our inner experience, even though not every inner experience is *per se* an object of judgment (section 24). While inner states are necessarily subject to a pre-judgmental temporal synthesis that makes them candidates for judgment, the judging subject is conscious of itself in a way that is independent of such temporal synthesis (section 25). Kant concludes his argument by noting that any object of empirical consciousness in any sense, and hence all inner states, belong to space and time that have their unity in virtue of their cognitive significance for self-consciousness. Thus, even the subjective experiences that belong to my empirical self must be subject to the laws that allow one to form a single empirical space and time in which every object has a determinate position for an objective judgment.

SELF-CONSCIOUSNESS, SELF-KNOWLEDGE, AND OUTER OBJECTS

Kant does not just restrict the role of the transcendental self-consciousness expressed in the proposition "I think p" to concepts, judgments, and inferences. He argues that any representational content that is to have any cognitive significance for any one of us, must be a representational content that is a potential content of the proposition "I think p." The world is not simply a construction of the self. But the world is something which the self must construct *for* itself on the basis of information it receives. The self must be able to view information provided by receptivity as information for it. In order for the self to view information as its own, it must be able to interpret and hence to conceptualize experience. This means that even those representations that have a content that depends on our receiving information from the world must be potential contents of the proposition "I think p." Such representational contents are potential candidates for judgments of the form "I think p" because they are experienced by us in a manner that is already concept-laden. However, the representational contents provided by receptivity are not themselves concepts, judgments, or inferences. Rather they are contents that are concept-laden because they are potential candidates for the kind of self-consciousness expressed in the proposition "I think p."

The most fundamental distinction within our capacity for receiving information is that between information that is internal to our own particular point of view as particular individuals endowed with self-consciousness and that of information that is external to our own point of view as particular self-conscious beings. The distinction between what is external and what is internal to representation is not one that is entailed by thought in its most general sense. However, any finite rational being endowed with self-consciousness will have to be able to draw a distinction between what is internal to its own point of view and what is external to that point of view. Due to the nature of finite self-consciousness there must be objects that present themselves to a being that is conscious of itself in such a way that it represents them as internal to its point of view and in such a way that it represents others as external to its point of view. For without the distinction between the internal and the external, there is no determinate consciousness of oneself as a distinct individual at all. Such consciousness is implicitly contrastive. For there to be a contrast there must be some distinction between the way things are for me and the way they are externally to me.

Creatures that have a sense of self that they can articulate have the ability to attribute experiences to themselves and thereby to distinguish themselves from other objects and other selves. The ability to ascribe a multiplicity of different episodes belonging to experience to oneself as opposed to attributing it to some other individual, accounts for the general sense in which what is experienced by a self is inner to the self. In order for the self to be conscious of facts about itself as a distinctive individual, the self must be given to itself in a way which distinguishes it from other selves. The particular experience which distinguishes one individual self from another may be referred to as what is inner to that self. What is inner is juxtaposed to what is outer in experience. What is outer in experience is just what is outside of the self as representer while what is inner is what makes the representer's point of view what it is.

The distinction between the internal and the external would seem to lapse for a non-finite rational being, at least for a being that was non-finite in every respect. But unless a finite rational being can draw a distinction between the inner and the outer, it will not be able to distinguish the way things appear to it from its own point of view from the way they might appear to some other possible point of view. Such a being would have no grip on the idea that it itself has beliefs. Unless one can allow for the possibility that one's own beliefs might be different from those of someone else, one does not have the notion that one holds them for either the right or the wrong reasons. But then there is no reason to think that one is a (finite) rational being at all. Even a non-finite rational being would need to be able to represent things, but it would not need to regard its point of view as distinct from the point of view of the whole universe.

Now, even if the very notion of finite rationality requires some distinction between the inner and the outer, this does not give any indication how such a distinction must be drawn. Kant makes two rather controversial moves here. First, he argues that there is a form of inner and a form of outer experience, then he maintains that the only distinction we have between the inner and the outer is one we make in terms of time and space. He concludes that the form according to which we must order our inner states is time, while the form according to which we must order our outer states is space.

Kant insists that the difference between what is internal and what is external to a certain finite point of view is to be expressed in terms of the distinction between states that are essentially tied to a certain point of view and those that are, in principle, independent of a certain perspective. Past, present, and future are essentially dependent on a temporal point of view, while temporal properties or relations that are independent of a particular point of view seem to depend for their existence on spatial relations. From this, Kant concludes that time and space are the only forms in terms of which we can make sense of objects given to the self. He refers to these forms as the forms of receptivity and, more specifically, as the forms of *our* sensibility. He maintains, quite plausibly, that the content of our experience is essentially spatial and temporal because the faculty through which we receive information about the world represents the world to us spatially and temporally.

Kant argues for the claim that there must be a form of inner and outer sense in the following way: in order to be able to relate sensations to objects that are external to each other or internal to our point of view one must already have the disposition to represent objects as outside of or inside of our point of view in terms of correlated sensations. The way in which what is sensed is ordered is distinguishable from what is sensed. It is not a property of what is sensed in isolation but depends on the relations between what is sensed: "That in which sensations alone order themselves and can be put in a certain form cannot itself be in turn a sensation" (A 20/B 34).[11] The way in which sensations array themselves is a function in part of those sensations themselves. This suggests the idea that sensations might have positions relative to each other that would be sufficient to induce an order in inner and outer sense. However, sensations taken on their own lack intentionality, that is, they lack object-directedness. They are what Kant calls "subjective representations" that merely express the state of their bearer rather than representing an object. Since sensations do not represent objects, they do not represent outer or inner objects. To represent outer or inner objects we need a representation that does have intentionality, and this representation will have a content that is derived from sensation, but a form that is independent of such sensation. Here Kant distinguishes a form according to which we represent outer objects, and a form according to which we represent inner objects. The former is the form of outer sense, the latter is the form of inner sense.

The notion of outer sense is relatively straightforward, since we have a good rough-and-ready understanding of what it is for an object to be experienced as outside of our representations. It is somewhat more difficult to understand just what it means for an object to be internal to our representations and yet logically distinct from those representations. Thus, Karl Ameriks distinguishes three different theories of inner sense: (1) the reflection, (2) the independent stream, and (3) the act theory.[12] According to the reflection theory, inner sense consists only of reflection on past acts of consciousness. This theory seems to draw its support from earlier texts in which Kant did not distinguish between inner sense and self-conscious reflection. It has the difficulty that it fails to account for how representations are given to us in the first place which is one of the avowed tasks of Kant's conception of inner sense. According to the independent stream theory, there are two streams of consciousness, one representing spatial contents, and the other representing contents that may have no direct reference to spatial contents. This two-stream theory fails to do justice to the dependence of both spatial items and mental events on the (single) temporal stream of our successive representings. Finally, according to the act theory, anything that is a representing, rather than a represented, belongs to inner sense. The notion of an act suggests a process of taking that is not wholly appropriate to the way representations are immediately given to us in inner experience. I want to defend a modified version of the act theory according to which anything belongs to the form of inner sense in virtue of being something represented by a representing. Thus, on my interpretation, sensations belong to inner sense, although they do not have an object that is logically distinct from the sensing itself. But inner sense also includes the representations of all other objects insofar as they are potential objects of consciousness.

The identification of the form of inner sense with time and the form of outer sense with space raises obvious questions. For one thing, things outside of us seem to be as much in time as our inner states. And other creatures have distinctive experiences that are internal to their distinctive points of view, but external to each of our own. It is not an analytic truth about self-conscious beings in general that they must experience things temporally or spatially. Different temporal series of representings corresponding to different spatial standpoints do, however, distinguish different self-conscious beings for us. These different series are orderable in relation to each other in time and space, giving different empirical meanings to the notion of the inner and the outer. Now, in order for one to have a way of thinking of a certain set of representations as belonging to a certain point of view, there must be some further way of characterizing the relation of that point of view to another point of view. This function is performed by linking time as the form of inner sense to space as the form of outer sense.

Without an outer sense there would be no inner sense. Due to the diaphanous character of consciousness and its self, the feature that Kant refers to as the emptiness of consciousness, there would not be anything to be represented by an experiencer. If the self as a determinate self is essentially associated with a temporal point of view undergoing a successive shift, then that which is outside of the self must be thought of as not essentially temporal. We can make sense of the notion of a givenness to us that is not essentially temporal through the notion of spatiality. Space provides us with a way of organizing those items that we experience as outside of us in a system of differences common to different points of view. Time distinguishes different experiences that belong to the same individual, and thus also provides a way of attributing different mutually exclusive states to the same individual regardless of whether those states are themselves experiences or not. We then bring space and time together when we think of different individuals, each of which is outside of the other, as being in a sequence of different states.

Kant takes the plausible position that the inner experience which is essential to a distinctive notion of mineness does not have a content which is uniquely inner (section 24, B 154; section 3, B 67). The content of our representations of our inner states, inner experience, is derived from outer experience. This thesis is intimately connected to his argument against psychological idealism. In his Refutation of Idealism (B 274ff.), he argues that I could not have determinate mental states if there were no physical objects (no objects existing outside of my mind). The upshot of this is that there is no self as a particular empirically knowable individual that can exist independently of a certain body. The necessary relationship between determinate mental states and embodiment avoids the bare substratum view of the self that has sometimes been ascribed to Kant. By committing Kant to a form of externalism concerning the content of representations, the dependence of mental content on embodied experience also provides the self with a determinate point of view from within experience.[13] It is, however, true that the self is never itself directly present as an object of empirical inquiry. This is because the self is essentially the point of view from which any inquiry can take place. The self can thus be characterized as an object of knowledge only by objectifying the set of empirical representations that distinguish one point of view in the totality of all experience from another point of view. It is possible to derive a kind of no-ownership theory of the self from this view, as Allison does. But such a view fails to do justice to the fact that we are able to think of ourselves as a distinct individual, with a distinctive point of view, by identifying the point of view of the self in general with the history of a particular body. It is this body and its states that are then the appropriate objects of self-knowledge. They have the kind of accessibility to intersubjective scrutiny that Kant demands for bona fide judgments and cognitions. Once we have such self-knowledge or knowledge of others, then the spatio-temporal location and hence standpoint dependence of my self-consciousness accounts for the discrepancy between the merely subjective validity of what is given to self-consciousness empirically and the intersubjectivity possible on the basis of an impersonal self-consciousness. We can thus allow a place for subjective experience in our account of subjectivity without giving up on the claim that objective experience is a condition for the very intelligibility of subjective experience.

In section 24 Kant makes it clear that all non-empirical concepts have content only in respect to appearances which are given to us through our inner sense and outer sense, that is through our experience of objects in time and space. He specifically argues that self-knowledge requires a figural synthesis of transcendental imagination. The important thing about this synthesis of the sensible contents of experience is that it is contrasted with the kind of "intellectual synthesis" involved in applying categories to objects of an intuition in general. While it takes places "in accordance with the categories," and depends on the "original synthetic unity of apperception," it is independent of the actual application of the categories in the forming of judgments (B 151).

What Kant is concerned with here is a perceptual synthesis that is independent of actual perceptual *judgment*, but guided through its cognitive significance for us by the possibility of judgment. "Figural synthesis" or synthesis speciosa (B 151) is the construction of shapes and sizes in productive imagination. There is a double potential for paradox about the idea of figural synthesis. First, it is surprising to find our consciousness of our inner states and even self-knowledge linked to the construction of shapes, and, second, it is odder still to connect self-knowledge with *a priori* construction of shapes. Kant's motivation for these two claims has to do with his need to make a place for subjective experience in the kind of objective experience that we can have with respect to spatial objects.

The identification of the process through which we conceptualize perceptual information with the tracing of a priori structures in space points up the way empirical perceptions of particular shapes in space depend on a priori constraints on how spaces may be connected. This is relevant to self-knowledge because of the way in which our beliefs depend for their content on what we perceive outside of ourselves. Figural synthesis is involved even in our beliefs about our inner states, since Kant wishes to argue that all our beliefs are ultimately about external objects in space. Even the truths of logic and mathematics are truths only because they tell us about possibilities that constrain the existence of things in space. If, as Kant claims, the content of even our beliefs about our own inner states is parasitic on objects outside of us in space that are intersubjectively accessible, and if, as he also claims, our very ability to order those inner states in a determinate way is parasitic on the existence of a determinate order in objects that exist outside of us in space, then even objects that we represent in a subjective fashion will turn out to be available in objective terms. We will be able to have knowledge of our own inner states, albeit not under the description under which they immediately present themselves to our minds.

A subject of experience can only become a determinate object of knowledge insofar as it is able to grasp itself as something that is characterizable by more than the bare idea of having a temporal perspective. In order to provide an adequate characterization of oneself as an object of knowledge, one must also be able to characterize this temporal perspective from outside of it. One must grasp it as a standpoint within a certain system of standpoints. Thus, the only way we have of locating ourselves in time is parasitic on our ability to locate ourselves spatially. Space provides us with the only conception we have of the way in which individuals exist outside of each other. Our knowledge of the duration and temporal position of introspective objects depends on our knowledge of the changes in external objects (section 24, B 156). Indeed, Kant wants to argue that the very successiveness of inner episodes is based on our ability to connect different spaces together:

Motion, as an act of the subject (not as a determination of an object), hence the synthesis of the manifold in time, when we abstract from it [space], and merely pay attention to the act through which we determine inner sense according to its form, actually generates the concept of succession. (B 155)

Kant interprets the idea that self-knowledge is based on figural synthesis by means of the claim that self-affection is parasitic on outer affection. Self-affection is the way in which we affect ourselves when we have an experience of our inner states. Self-affection may also be described as the process of connecting the nows of consecutive awareness in a second-order consciousness of one's identity through those successive states (B 155). There is an obvious disanalogy between the outer affection that supplies us with information about external objects and self-affection.[14] Inner or self-affection is the way in which we connect bits of information that are already part of consciousness (inner sense). Self-affection allows us to interpret who we are as well as what the objects are that exist outside of us. By contrast, outer affection is supposed to be the source of information about as yet uninterpreted (undetermined) appearances (A 19–20/B 33–34), and self-affection is about the interpreting (determining) of these appearances. The analogy between inner and outer affection seems to depend on an equivocation in the notion of determination. Outer affection determines the content of our beliefs by providing us with specific information, while inner affection determines the content of our beliefs by interpreting that information in a specific way. The problem is less serious than it seems to be. Kant does not claim that we are to understand self-affection on the model of outer affection. These are, in fact, simply two different ways in which we are determined. There is indeed a connection between self-affection and outer affection. But this connection is based on the thesis that self-interpretation depends on the interpretation of what is outside of us. The interpretation of objects outside of us does depend on information about objects inside of us, as well, but the argument here is based on the relation between self-interpretation and interpretation of what is outside of us. Working from the assumption that outer affection is being affected by external objects that are mere appearances, Kant attempts to show that self-affection must concern objects merely as they appear to us to be. The content of what we experience when we have determinate representations of our inner states is based on our representations of what exists outside of us, and what exists outside of us is itself represented by us only as it must appear to us to be. From this he concludes that we have self-knowledge only of the way in which we must appear to ourselves. We do not have knowledge of how we really are.

To meet the worry about incoherence posed by his idealist interpretation of self-knowledge, in section 25 Kant attempts to establish a sense in which one can be conscious of oneself without knowing who one is. If I am conscious of myself then it is pragmatically necessary that I exist, whoever I might be. This existence is not restricted to how I appear to myself or to anyone. In thinking about myself I am thinking about someone and hence referring to a particular individual. However, I do not know who that individual is unless I know some further self-locating facts about myself. In self-consciousness I am conscious of someone who is a basic rather than a dependent particular, since I am conscious of whoever it is who is the bearer of that self-consciousness. Thus, in self-consciousness I am conscious of myself as a thing in itself in the transcendental sense, although any description I have of myself will apply only to the way I must appear to myself spatially and temporally.

THE PISTORIUS PROBLEM

It is now time to see how one can meet the objection raised by Pistorius by looking at a contemporary version of it articulated by Robert Howell. Howell argues that Kant gets trapped between the necessity claims he wants to make based on *de dicto* properties of self-consciousness and the need for self-knowledge to anchor those claims. One must be in a position to be conscious that this representation is a representation *of* (belonging to) the entity that one in fact is. According to Howell, Kant is then seduced into making conflicting demands on self-consciousness not only by the deceptive surface grammar of his claims, but because he runs together "the traditional theory of self-awareness" with a revision-ary theory of knowledge.[15] Kant's theory of knowledge commits him to restricting knowledge in general, and self-knowledge in particular, to appearances. A conception of knowledge which is restricted to appearances will not support the traditional conception of self-knowledge and self-awareness. It will not support knowledge of the subject *de re*.[16] On the other hand, such *de re* knowledge is needed, if self-ascriptions to particular selves are to have any purchase a priori. We need to know that we do in fact have knowledge, but "if we are to know ourselves really to have knowledge, then that entity – our self – to which all appearances appear must be known to be real."[17] But, according to Howell, we can only know this by violating the strictures on knowledge associated with Kant's claim that we can know only appearances.

Howell's worry is not compelling. For the bearer of representations that we know to have knowledge need not be known by us under the description under which it is the ultimate bearer of thought. We may know that the bearer of self-reference is real insofar as self-reference could not take place without something which is real. This does not imply that we have any knowledge of the specific character of that bearer. It does imply, according to Howell, that "one veridically grasps the fact that the self in itself really exists."[18] This conclusion is, however, premature. While it is true that there must be some bearer for one's representations, it simply does not follow that this bearer must be characterized in itself as a self.

SELF-KNOWLEDGE AND THE SUBJECT–OBJECT THEORY

Kant treats self-knowledge on the model of a subject that represents itself as an object: "I as intelligence and *thinking* subject know *myself* as *thought* object" (section 24, B 155). This has suggested to many interpreters that empirical self-consciousness or even transcendental self-consciousness is to be understood on the subject–object model, or the reflection theory as it is generally called.[19] According to the reflection theory, self-consciousness is capable of a reductive analysis into a two-termed relation between the subject of consciousness and the object of consciousness. It should be noted that Kant does not seem to use the term reflection to characterize the activity of self-consciousness in the way described by the reflection theory.[20] According to the section on the Amphiboly of Concepts of Reflection, reflection "is the consciousness of the relationship of our different sources of cognition through which alone their relationship to one another can be correctly determined" (A 261/B 316). Reflection thus refers to the capacity to distinguish and properly connect the contributions of the different faculties of representation. In order for one to be able to evaluate the contributions of the various faculties of cognition, one must be able to see them as contributions to cognition that one makes as the subject of cognition. But there is no obvious reason that reflection of this kind has to be construed as an identification of a subject of consciousness with an object of consciousness.

Those who have interpreted Kant as a defender of the subject–object model and reflection theory of self-consciousness have come to the conclusion that Kant's conception of either empirical or transcendental self-consciousness is incoherent. While I shall argue that Kant did not hold a subject–object or reflection theory of self-consciousness, I do think that he held a reflection theory of self-knowledge. The reflection theory of self-knowledge is defensible so long as it is based on a non-reductive theory of self-consciousness. The subject–object schema applies to self-knowledge because self-knowledge is constrained by criteria governing the recognition of oneself as an individual person distinct from other persons. The criteria for identifying and reidentifying persons are parasitic on the criteria for identifying and reidentifying material bodies, since the only way we have of identifying and reidentifying different times is in relation to material objects that occupy spaces. However, since self-knowledge requires *self*-identification, the object to be identified under a certain description must not only be identified in spatio-temporal terms but also be thought of as oneself. It is here that the subject-model needs supplementation if it is to provide a coherent account of self-knowledge.

If we try to extend the subject–object model to self-consciousness we get the following paradox. The self must be able to identify itself (subject = object) in order to be conscious of itself, but in order to identify itself it must already have some form of knowledge of itself as a thinking subject and object of that thinking subject's thought. Self-knowledge involves knowledge of the identity of the knower *qua* subject of self-consciousness and the known *qua* object of self-consciousness (and subject of the conscious state of which one is conscious in self-consciousness). But this knowledge of the identity of knower and the known actually presupposes an immediate reflexive awareness of self. The subject–object reflection theory already tacitly presupposes the self-conscious awareness it attempts to explain. This is a fatal flaw if the subject–object theory of self-knowledge is extended to include self-consciousness, or thought to be a stand-alone theory.

The subject cannot be thought of as its own object without already having some direct access to itself. Kant has two bases for such direct access. As thinkers, we have an immediate representation of an impersonal self, and, as sentient creatures, we have an immediate spatio-temporal representation of ourselves. Kant sometimes seems to suggest that there is no empirical subject or self at all. But he also carefully distinguishes the I which thinks from the I or self-consciousness which intuits itself (and therefore has data concerning) *itself* (section 24, B 155). The empirical aspect of the self does not reduce the self to a mere object of reflection. In fact, being an object of such reflection, the possibility of self-knowledge depends on the ability to refer to oneself as having a distinctive point of view. Empirical apperception must express a particular point of view with respect to experience from within experience without necessarily involving reflection on oneself as an object of knowledge. This is the force of the remark concerning self-intuition. Such self-presentation from a particular point of view within experience is what makes my representations mine, as opposed to yours. In this way, Kant can explain how one can represent oneself as object. The directly self-referential aspect of self-consciousness needs to be extended to include a self-descriptive aspect. Self-description requires experience. Although self-reference is possible without self-description, no self-description is possible without self-reference. This descriptive aspect distinguishing empirical self-consciousness is expressed in the Kantian doctrine of self-intuition and self-affection.

There are strong reasons to resist interpreting the direct access of the self as representer to the self as represented on the subject–object model. On the other hand, self-consciousness appears to presuppose a certain amount of self-knowledge. The knowledge that I (who am the subject of self-consciousness) am the subject of the consciousness I am ascribing to myself is presupposed in self-consciousness. Such self-knowledge might seem to preclude a sharp distinction between self-consciousness and self-knowledge. A question arises as to how the self can know or be conscious of itself, without already being conscious of the fact that it is of itself that it is conscious. Indeed, we must already think of our experiences as reflexively self-referential in order to make sense of the possibility of self-consciousness with respect to them. Reflexive self-referring to x involves not only the use of a term that actually refers to x, but reference to the referee doing the referring as internal to the act of referring.[21]

Ascription by me of representations to my own particular consciousness must conform to the conditions under which access to any self-consciousness is possible. But, in self-ascription to my consciousness, reference to the fact that I am thinking the proposition in question is an essential part of the statement. In such self-ascription of states, I claim that this is the way representations are connected in my consciousness, as opposed to someone else's consciousness. As Kant sees it, intersubjectivity and objectivity are attained when such self-reference is no longer relevant to the empirical truth of a statement. Then we have what he would call a judgment (or, more perspicuously, a judgment of experience). Looking at things in this way helps to resolve the paradoxical status of self-knowledge in the B-Deduction. Statements expressing one's own propositional attitudes cannot be instances of self-knowledge for Kant, because they involve an essential reference to the context in which they are formulated. It is, however, possible to form judgments concerning the having of such propositional attitudes. Such thoughts are judgments because there is no essential reference to the point of view of the empirical consciousness in which the thoughts in question occur.

We must therefore distinguish three different things: (1) consciousness of myself as the potential subject of any of a potential infinity of different representational contents, (2) empirical consciousness of inner states in which I associate one representation of mine with another, and (3) knowledge of myself as a particular empirical individual (based on evidence accessible to a third-person point of view). In pure apperception or consciousness of the self a priori, representations are ascribed to the self as subject of thought. Here I represent myself as the formal subject of thought. I can, however, enrich this formal notion of subject through introspection and more indirect empirical evidence (included in the general term "self-intuition"). This empirical self-consciousness differs from self-knowledge. The self is something of which one can and must have consciousness as a subject, i.e. from the first-person point of view. However, the self can only be *experienced* as an object, something which has been objectified, something which has become an object for consciousness. As an object, the representations of the self are, in principle, accessible to other points of view. Such experience of the self as an object of knowledge is based on consciousness of the self as subject of representation, since the self is only available through the possibility of a point of view.

After distinguishing self-knowledge from self-consciousness in section 25, Kant attempts in section 26 to establish that even perception must be subject to the a priori principles governing unification of representations in one self-consciousness and hence to the objective standards set by judgment. In this way, he bridges the gap between his thesis that perceptual statements are not judgments if they involve an essential reference to the person having them, and his thesis that self-knowledge is only possible through non-perspectival statements about inner states. The key to defending this position is the thesis that all mental states are also temporal states of human beings and thus have a position in a shared public time.

According to the received view, the conclusion of the B-Deduction comes through an appeal to the unity of space and time as a priori facts of which we have phenomenological evidence through our everyday experience. The implication of this view is that Kant has no real defense for the assumption that space and time must be unitary. According to Allison, the first step shows "merely that insofar as unity is introduced into the manifold of intuition by the understanding, that is, insofar as it is represented as *a* manifold, it must conform to the conditions of the unity of consciousness and, therefore, to the categories. This result leaves completely unsettled the question of whether data given in accordance with the forms of sensibility are capable of being unified in a single consciousness according to the categories."[22] Thus, the very unity of self-consciousness would be in jeopardy, if space and time were not unifiable in this way. On Allison's interpretation, the unity of space and time *qua* intuitions is somehow independent of the synthesis through which space and time are said, in the footnote to section 26 to be given in the first place. There is some question as to why the unifiability of intuitions should be an issue at all. Allison does not deny that the Aesthetic already treats space and time as unifiable.

But as I argued in *Kant's Transcendental Idealism*, we cannot infer the unity of time (or space) from the unity of consciousness because there is no logical contradiction in the thought of appearances being given in different times (or spaces). Consequently, we cannot argue directly from the unity of apperception to the applicability to appearances of the relational (or, indeed, any) categories. We can, however, reverse the process and argue from the unity of time to the necessary conditions of the consciousness of this unity. I take this to be the crucial move in the second part of the Deduction.[23]

Allison's point must be that objects can be given in the different spaces and times of different experiences. This claim is still ambiguous. Given the fact that the unity of spatial and temporal intuition, as Kant understands it, covers the unity of space and time as privately experienced, as publicly experienced, and as physically real, Allison might take the unity of consciousness to allow for the possibility of different disconnected private, public, or even physical times or spaces. But, given Allison's thesis that the unity of consciousness as developed in the first step of the B-Deduction is consistent with the existence of objects existing in different spaces and times, he must be claiming that a plurality of either public or private spaces and times is consistent with the unity of consciousness in either its subjective or objective form.

Contra Allison, it seems to me to be crucial to distinguish the weak unity of empirical and subjective consciousness from the strong unity of the consciousness in general that makes such subjective consciousness possible for Kant. Allison appears to be right that, taken in isolation, the subjective unity of consciousness is consistent with the disunity of time or space. However, against Allison, I have argued that the subjective unity of consciousness is itself parasitic on what Kant calls the objective unity of consciousness. Thus, if the objective unity of consciousness is inconsistent with the existence of multiple disconnected phenomenal times and spaces, then so is the subjective unity of consciousness. Of course, Allison implies that even the objective unity of consciousness is consistent with the existence of multiple disconnected times and spaces. To be sure, Allison does not wish to claim that there are, in fact, multiple disconnected times and spaces. Instead, he argues that such times and spaces are ruled out by the unity of our intuition of space and time.

The implication of Allison's interpretation is that the unity of space and time a priori is a brute given, or fact about the phenomenology of our experience that we discover through direct intuition. The unity of space and time gives our experience and self-consciousness their unity, and the task of the understanding is merely to represent to itself that unity.[24] Allison is clearly right that we do experience space and time at least as if they were each of them necessarily connected in an experiential whole. However, the unity of space and time is, at best, a phenomenological fact that needs explanation and defense. The problem with the Allisonian interpretation is that it offers no prospects for providing such a defense and thus makes Kant's claims for the unity and objectivity of experience ultimately depend on a seemingly *ad hoc* assumption that space and time are inherently unitary.

Henrich's interpretation seems to me to be closer to the mark here. He argues that Kant is able to include all representations within the scope of the apperception principle by appeal to the Aesthetic, since intuition contains all representations in it and now turns out to have unity due to the synthesis of the understanding.[25] Henrich seems to me to be right to emphasize the manner in which even the unity of intuition depends for its existence on a synthesis that Kant ascribes to the spontaneous powers of the mind. Given his thesis that the self-ascribability thesis needs to be supported by an appeal to intuition, Henrich needs to argue that this is a new premise. In fact, it is a mere application of the argument in the first step of the proof.

By section 17, Kant already takes himself to have established that space and time are unitary because they consist for us of representations that are cognitively significant for us. These representations are cognitively significant because they are my representations that are thus potential candidates for self-consciousness and objective judgment. The footnote to section 17 tells the reader that the synthetic unity of consciousness is contained in intuitions as singular representations. The unity of consciousness is characterized as original, thus clearly linking it with pure apperception. The claim that unity of our intuitions of space and time is parasitic on the unity of self-consciousness is made explicit in the summary of the argument in section 17 provided by section 20 (B 143):

The manifold given in a sensible intuition belongs necessarily under the original synthetic unity of apperception because [Henrich reads "weil" here as "insofar as"] through this unity the *unity* of intuition is alone possible (section 17). (B 143)

Here, Kant claims that the unity of intuition is only possible through the connectability of intuitions in one self-consciousness. This is a stronger claim than that the unity of intuition (i.e. space and time) is represented as such only through self-consciousness. It is the claim that unity of space and time is constituted by self-consciousness.[26] The reference to section 17 takes up his claim, at section 17, B 136n, that space and time as individual representeds have a distinctive synthetic unity of consciousness (where it must be insisted that all such connectedness derives from an activity of the self).

In section 26, Kant appeals to the assumption of the Aesthetic that we have a priori knowledge of space and time as a whole in order to justify the claim that all of our perceptions must be empirically connected in a manner that is compatible with the a priori laws imposed on representational content by the self (section 26, B 160). These a priori laws are themselves the laws that make it possible for us to make objective judgments about spatio-temporal episodes. It is important to note that Kant insists that the unity of connection involved in space and time "can be no other than that of the connection of a manifold of intuition of a given *intuition in general* in an original consciousness, according to the categories, only applied to our *sensible intuition*" (B 161). There can be little doubt that this original consciousness is, in fact, the synthetic unity of impersonal self-consciousness. Thus the unity of space and time is supposed to be the mere specification of a relation which holds between self-consciousness and any intuition to our (spatio-temporal) intuition.

Synthesis is always an activity of the self, and never simply received by us from objects, as Kant emphasizes at the very beginning of the Deduction in section 15 (B 130). In section 15, Kant also notes that the unity of synthesis is something that precedes all concepts and judgments (B 131). In section 16 it then becomes apparent that the unity that is higher than all concepts and judgments is the unity of self-consciousness. But now, in section 26, B 160n, the unity of space and time is supposed to be a result of synthesis by the understanding preceding all use of concepts, but displaying itself in perception. How are we to understand Kant's claim in section 26 that the very givenness of space and time as representeds depends on an activity of synthesis? How can space and time, which are supposed to be infinite wholes existing prior to their parts, be given through a process of synthesis? The notion of space and time as infinite given wholes suggests a notion of totality that Kant maintains must escape progressive synthesis by a finite intellect.

Kant can only avoid contradiction by construing the synthesis of space and time through which space and time are given as infinite wholes as an ongoing process of unification that never actually comes to an end. In effect, we must construe the unity of space and time as ideas of reason, rather than concepts of the understanding. The synthesis in question must be the pre-conceptual and hence pre-categorial synthesis of imagination and perception as opposed to the intellectual synthesis of judgment.[27] In introducing the distinction between imaginative (perceptual) and intellectual synthesis in section 24, Kant links the perceptual synthesis of imagination to the "original synthetic unity of apperception" (section 24, B 151). What this means is that imagination must be guided in its synthesis of perceptual information by the possibility of unification of those perceptions in an impersonal self-consciousness. In this way, it becomes possible for us to conceptualize what we perceive.[28]

At least part of the unity that Kant ascribes to space and time can be derived from reflection on what it is to have any consciousness of space and time as space and time and thus to be able to distinguish space and time from what is in space and time. The capacity to distinguish the structure of space and time from objects that occupy spatio-temporal positions is lacking in subhuman animals. They lack such ability because they lack the capacity for forming bona fide concepts. This capacity is linked to the possession of dispositional self-consciousness. Self-consciousness allows one to abstract from the current context so that one can explore alternative possibilities. This ability to conceive of space and time as abstract structures according to which data may be organized, may be characteristic of all self-conscious beings. But, even if all finite self-conscious beings were to represent the world spatio-temporally, further argument would still be required in order to justify the strong notion of spatio-temporal unity that Kant assumes. The capacity to order data spatio-temporally would seem to allow for a plurality of spatio-temporal orders of things. It does not seem to give the uniqueness of spatio-temporal order that Kant wants.

The apparent unity of space and time derives from the fact that we think of different spaces and times as being connectible in a single comprehensive point of view. This single comprehensive point of view is just the impersonal unity of self-consciousness. We need to distinguish two different aspects to the unity of space and time corresponding to the unity of experiences in transcendental and empirical self-consciousness. In empirical self-consciousness, experiences belong together in my or your individual mind. Different individual minds assign different spatio-temporal relations to different experiences. However, these different spatio-temporal configurations of experiences are themselves reflections of the different standpoints that different individuals can assign to each other within a shared space and time. This shared space and time is intelligible to different individuals because they can represent themselves as experiencing things in different ways systematically corresponding to these different alternative possible spatio-temporal positions. In doing so, they are forced to abstract from the particular context in which they actually find themselves and in which they happen to be experiencing what they are experiencing.

Based on considerations such as these, Kant seems to assume that there can be only one space and time. But it has been suggested that experience might, in fact, lead one to believe in multiple space-, or time-systems.[29] Random occurrences which seemed to violate the unity of space or time could always be explained away by auxiliary hypotheses which would not require the extreme measure of giving up on the unity of space or time. Kant would, in fact, argue that the occurrence of such events could only be confirmed or disconfirmed against the background of objects characterized by spatio-temporal continuity. If there were systematic appearances and disappearances of particulars at regular intervals, one might, however, be tempted to defend multiple spaces or times. Systematic appearances and disappearances of certain particulars could be accounted for by a reformulation of natural laws. Could there, then, ever be evidence which would lead us to opt for giving up the unity of space and time instead of reformulating the laws in terms of which we connect spatio-temporal particulars?

It seems that this is at least a real possibility. The thesis of spatio-temporal unity seems to rule out singularities in space and time of the kind postulated by contemporary theories of cosmology. Black hole physics postulates the existence of quantum tunnelling effects that provide a form of indirect coupling between disconnected spaces which gives empirical significance to disconnected spaces.[30] Such developments need not completely dismay the Kantian, since there may well be a way of accommodating such singularities in a continuous space and time.[31] But it is more plausible simply to concede that neither Kant's notion of a unity of intuition, nor his notion of the necessary unity of self-consciousness require that space and time be unique (quasi) individuals unless we accept his claim that space and time cannot be features or relations of things as they exist in themselves. To concede that claim is, however, to concede that we cannot legislate to nature except in a limited sense. We can show that all objects in space and time of which we can become conscious must belong to a unitary space and time, but we cannot show that the notion of a non-unitary physical space or time is inherently incoherent.

CHAPTER 6

Time-consciousness in the Analogies

So far, we have seen that an impersonal consciousness of self can be regarded as a necessary condition for experience in as much as an impersonal perspective is built into our ability to interpret the world in terms of concepts. And, in a very general way, Kant has connected the possibility of such impersonal self-consciousness with the existence of categories. The task of this chapter is to explain how the categories can serve as enabling conditions of experience. Carrying out this task involves an explanation of the link between self-consciousness and the kind of time-consciousness that is necessary to any experience that is intelligible to us. For the sake of brevity, I shall restrict my discussion to the arguments Kant develops in the Analogies of Experience for the enabling role in experience of the most significant set of categories: the relational categories of substance, causation, and interaction.

In contrast to the categories of quantity and quality, the so-called mathematical categories, Kant does not regard the dynamic categories in general, or the relational categories in particular, as constitutive of intuition. Kant insists that there cannot be intuitions that do not have some kind of extensive magnitude or metric, or some kind of intensive magnitude, or magnitude corresponding to the intensity of sensation involved in them. Nevertheless, he does regard the dynamic categories as constitutive of any concept that we might have of an object in experience:

In the transcendental analytic, we have distinguished amongst the principles of the understanding, between the *dynamic*, as merely regulative principles of *intuition*, and the *mathematical*, that are constitutive of the latter. Nevertheless, the dynamic laws in question are indeed constitutive of *experience* in that they make *concepts* possible a priori, without which no experience would take place. (A 664/B 692)

We might be able to have an immediate awareness of the contents of our perceptual field, even if the concepts of substance, cause, and interaction had no purchase in experience. But, Kant wants to argue, we would not have any concepts of objects. If it were not a necessary fact about experience that we are able to apply the concepts of substance, cause, and interaction to objects of experience, it might turn out that, in fact, objects of experience could not be identified and reidentified across different times and spaces. But, if we had no way of identifying and reidentifying those times and spaces themselves, Kant wants to argue, we would have no experience at all.

In this chapter, I want to argue that the so-called relational categories are involved in justifying our judgments about the temporal and less directly the spatial position of events and things because events present themselves to us in such a way that we are able to apply the concepts of substance, causation, and interaction to those events. Unlike commentators such as Melnick and Guyer, I wish to deny that every judgment concerning the occurrence of an event or a change in a thing involves the application of these categories to a judgment. Instead, I wish to argue that judgments concerning the occurrence or non-occurrence of events or changes involve an implicit commitment to the truth of principles (metaconceptual judgments), such as "every event is the change in the state of a substance" or "every event has a cause" in which such categories figure as concepts. We can make judgments about the temporal and spatial positions and relations of objects without applying the concept of substance, cause, or interaction to those objects. But in order to justify those judgments we need to appeal to the concepts of substance, cause, and interaction, as well as to the more specific laws governing substances, causes, and interactions.

The categories in general, and the concepts of substance, cause, and interaction, in particular, can play a role in justifying our judgments concerning experiences because perceptions and other inner states are already given to us in such a way that categories must be applicable to them. But, in contrast to interpreters such as Allison, I wish to argue that the categories apply to objective experience because they are indirect enabling conditions of subjective experience. I wish to reject the idea that any experience at all must present itself to us in a way that already involves the actual application of the categories of substance, causation, and interaction.

Inner states are given to us in time, and have content in virtue of belonging to a possible self-consciousness. Outer states are given to us not only temporally, but also spatially. The concepts of substance, cause, and interaction are required if we are to connect different inner episodes, especially perceptions, together in a global representation of time that is capable of supporting an impersonal and standpoint-neutral representation of self: "The general principle of the three Analogies rests on the necessary *unity* of apperception, in respect of all possible empirical consciousness, that is, of all perception, *at all times*" (A 177/B 220). In linking the inner states of different individuals together in time, the concepts of substance, cause, and interaction link those inner states to outer states that are accessible to different observers. In the process, they help to constitute a single unified time and space for all observers.

Now any representational content must be connectable to any other representational content in one possible encompassing consciousness of different representations belonging to different persons with different spatio-temporal positions. For all representations that are intelligible to us directly represent temporal objects, and at least indirectly, represent spatial objects, and representations of spatial and temporal objects are only distinguishable from one another in virtue of the different contributions that they make to experience. Thus, the differential contributions that different representations make to experience must be sufficient to yield a way of distinguishing one space and time from another. Absent any empirical content to distinguish one space and time from another, spaces and times may be distinct, in that they have different relations to each other, but they are indistinguishable, since there is nothing that allows one to pick out one term of a spatial or temporal relation from another.

In the First Analogy, Kant argues that we must postulate substances as substrates relative to which all change occurs. These permanent objects with changing accidents make it possible to determine whether a change has or has not occurred. Substances make it possible for us to ascertain the truth value of judgments about change by making it possible for us to set up a time-series in which changes are determinable. But they make it possible for us to distinguish different clock-times in a time-series by providing us with something at those different times that allows us to distinguish one clock-time from another.

Even if substances are necessary for setting up a time-series, they are not sufficient for ordering times or events. Our knowledge of substances does not tell us which times or events are earlier, later, and simultaneous with which other times or events. In the Second Analogy, Kant argues that causal connections are needed if we are to order episodes in objectively valid temporal relations of earlier and later. The Third Analogy then argues that interactions between substances are required in order to establish objectively valid relations of simultaneity. It thus extends the general analysis of causal relations provided in the Second Analogy from the temporal relations of earlier. and later to relations of simultaneity.

In accordance with Kant's claim that subjective experience is parasitic on objective experience, the objective relations of earlier, later, and simultaneous underwrite our ability even to make judgments about a subjective temporal order to events. It is not that we cannot directly perceive changes in our mental states or their objects. But, in forming judgments about even the subjective order of our inner states, we take on a normative commitment to be able to justify claims about the order of our inner episodes. Even claims about the subjective order of our inner episodes can only be sustained by recourse to the way in which the subjective temporal order of our inner episodes depends on the objective temporal order of outer episodes. For without a distinction between my subjective take on what I am experiencing and what I am (subjectively) experiencing, it does not even make sense to say that I am formulating a judgment about my inner experience. I do not even have a basis for thinking of myself as having inner experience.

Now, even the relational categories are not enough to elicit an objective spatio-temporal order from experience; we must also rely on higher-order principles of reason that guide inquiry in the search for specific empirical concepts of objects and laws. In the concluding section of this chapter, I attempt to do this fact justice in a discussion of the nature of the connection between the general principle that there are identifiable substances, causes, and interactions, and the existence and recognition of specific concepts of substance, causation, and interaction.

SUBSTANCE

Given the fact that space and time are the forms according to which anything real must be represented, regardless of whether it is represented as existing externally or internally to our points of view, any substantive notion of a subject will have to be expressed in terms of the numerical identity of a spatio-temporal point of view. For, taken in abstraction from the experience of spatio-temporal particulars, the concept of substance collapses into the purely logical relation of subject to predicate.[1] It seems at first that the subject in question would also have to be a spatio-temporal continuant in order to capture the distinction between different possible temporal points of view. But identity in point of view across different temporal experiences does not entail that the bearer of that identical point of view is the same individual through those changes in point of view.

Instead of arguing that the self must be a persistent individual over time, Kant argues that the self must experience persistent individuals in order for it to be in a position to represent even its identity as a temporal point of view. The self *per se* is only a form of experience. The self can only identify and reidentify an individual across different spaces and times if the individual is actually in space and time and hence distinguishable from the first-person point of view that the self must take on all of its experience. Without locating itself in space and time, there is no distinction for the self between a true or false judgment about its persistence across time and space. But, in order to locate itself in space and time, the self must be able to locate itself relative to other events in space and time. Kant argues that, in order to be able to locate events relative to other events, we need to have an experience of an object that persists over different events and changes.

Since Kant's argument for substance, and indeed for causation and interaction, is limited to the way we must experience the world if we are to have the kind of self-consciousness that is constitutive of being a finite rational creature, the argument is limited in its validity to the way objects must appear to us in experience and hence to phenomenal (spatio-temporal) substance and its states. The argument for phenomenal substance is synthetic. There must be something that one takes to be the bearer of properties in order for one to have a thought of an object at all. However, the characterization of the subject of a judgment as a persistent object is a synthetic claim. It is only relative to the fact of temporal experience that it makes sense to identify persistence or even permanence as the criterion for being the kind of object properly regarded as a bearer of properties. For it is clear that the general notion of a bearer of properties does not require that the bearer persist over time. The synthetic character of the argument is emphasized in a note of Kant's:

Between substance and *accidens* the logical relation is synthetic. The subject is itself a predicate (for one can think of everything only through predicates with the exception of I), but it is consequently only called a subject which is not a predicate of anything further: 1, since no subject is thought with it; 2, since it is the presupposition and *substratum* of the other. This latter can only be inferred from duration while the other is replaced. Therefore it belongs to the essence < *Wesen* > of a substance that it is persistent. If one supposes that substance ceases to exist, then the cessation proves that it is not a substance, and since therefore no *substratum* is thought of as belonging to this appearance, there are predicates without a subject, therefore no judgments and no thoughts. (Refl. 5297, Ak. XVIII, p. 146)

Here Kant argues that the only thing that picks out a substance in experience is something persistent. What makes the substance an appropriate object to be represented by a logical subject, as opposed to a logical predicate, is that it involves something that persists which then serves as the real subject or bearer of change. There is nothing in the meaning of a subject that requires one to think of subjects as things that persist. Yet, once the notion of substance is interpreted as a spatio-temporal bearer of properties, then persistence over time is analytic to the enriched notion of substance that only properly applies to objects of experience (A 184/B 227).

In arguing that experience requires the notion of a permanent substance, the First Analogy takes the passage of time that displays itself in the successiveness of our experiences as a datum. It then attempts to explain how our experience of passage is possible by appeal to the existence of permanent substances. The passage of time is marked by the persistence of temporal order through the shifting successive nows of apprehension. This allows Kant to argue that time as form of intuition serves as a persistent substrate for the representation of coexistence and succession which are determinations of time. Kant insists that time as the form of experience itself cannot undergo succession (A 183/B 226). Time cannot come to be or pass away, for that would require some further temporal series relative to which it would make sense to say that time had come to be or passed away. Insofar as time is the order of things relative to which change occurs, time cannot be thought to change on pain of an infinite regress. If time were to change, a further time would always be required relative to which that time could be said to change. We must think of the temporal order relative to which change occurs as a tenseless ordering of events according to relations of earlier, later, and simultaneous. For only such an order is not subject to succession, since it does not involve a distinction between past, present, and future.

Since tenseless temporal relations are independent of the shifting perspective of the present or now, they are not subject to succession. However, in addition to tenseless temporal relations that are independent of temporal perspective, there are also inherently perspectival temporal episodes. There are also the different nows of apprehension that replace each other successively. These nows of apprehension are inherently perspectival, because each state of consciousness picks out its own distinctive now and that now is the only now that is now for it. Kant's initially puzzling remark that time "as the permanent form of inner intuition" is the "substrate in which alone simultaneity and succession can be represented" (B 224) can be explained. The permanence of temporal order is the way in which the (now independent) tenseless order of time manifests itself in the successiveness of the now-series of apprehension.

Kant assumes that we can only perceive objects of experience and their properties, and not times (or spaces for that matter) themselves. Times and spaces are only observable by us in terms of the changes in temporal or spatial position of objects that occupy time and space. From the fact that time and space are not directly observable, but only observable through changes in the position of objects in space and time, Kant concludes that there must be something persistent in the objects of perception (empirical objects) that allows time (and space) to be represented, if they are to be represented at all. This persistent something must survive the successive replacement of the individual nows of perceptual apprehension. Replacement and coexistence is perceptible only through the relation of objects of experience to this persistent object of experience.

We perceive objects. In order, however, to be able to perceive change or coexistence it must be relative to some perceptible object. Substance is the persistent substrate of all objects of experience. Substance is not itself perceptible, but it is that in virtue of which the persistence and change of perceptible objects can be determined. It is that in those objects of experience that always remains the same and unchanged.

According to Paul Guyer, there is no compelling reason why permanence in something that is not itself perceptible must be represented by permanence in something perceptible. After all, Kant distinguishes between the representation of something permanent and a permanent representation (B XLIII) in the context of articulating his argument against idealism. The fact that there is no general principle that properties of what is represented must mirror those of what represents them would pose a problem were it not for the fact that Kant does not argue directly from the fact that time is permanent to the permanence of the substrate that represents it. Instead, Kant argues for the existence of something in objects of experience that allows one to determine whether two objects of experience coexist or exist one after the other. This also explains why the detour through the permanence of substance is required despite the fact that our knowledge that substances are permanent or even persistent in some weaker sense is not immediate, but inferential. The point is not about the need for a permanent representation to represent something permanent. It turns on how the relations of something can be known that is not itself perceptible. Guyer's second objection is that Kant shifts from treating substance as something that serves to represent the permanence of time to something that is the bearer of properties. But the point of Kant's argument is that time must be represented through objects of experience by something that allows one to determine what the temporal relations between objects are empirically, and this is whatever it is that counts as the bearer of properties.[2]

If something comes to be, a point in time must precede it in which it did not exist. Again, if something passes out of existence, it must pass out of existence at a certain time. To determine that something has come to be or passed away we must be able to say when such a coming to be or passing away occurred. We need a procedure for assigning a certain time to the event immediately before or after a putative coming to be or passing away. But, if all changes were becomings and passings away, in other words, if all changes were existence-changes, rather than the replacement of accidents that themselves belong to persistent substances, we could not perceive or empirically determine that a change has occurred at all.

We can assume for the sake of argument that a change is a bona fide case of the coming into being of something out of nothing, or the passing out of existence of something. What problem arises in this case? If there is no object that persists through a change, if the change is a genuine case of coming to be or passing away, that is, a case of something that comes to be out of nothing or passes away into nothing, rather than a change in the state of something that continues to persist, it seems to be impossible to determine whether a change of any kind has occurred at all.

A basic assumption of the argument is that all changes must be empirically determinable. The assumption depends on a principle of empirical significance that is not universally accepted. It is just not obvious that in order for there to be a certain change that change must be empirically knowable. This is an assumption that a metaphysical or transcendental realist will simply reject. Kant thinks that all non-logical meaning derives from experience, and from this principle he infers the principle that all cognitively significant claims must have empirical significance, but his ultimate reason for accepting the principle of empirical significance is his transcendental idealism. In respect to appearances, one can show that all changes must be changes in the state of something that persists, for appearances themselves have existence only relative to the possibility of being recognized to be thus and such by us. Such an argument will not go through for things in general. For we cannot infer with respect to any thing at all that its change must be observable, unless, as Kant argues, the only things that can undergo changes are things that undergo changes that are necessarily determinable by us.

There is no reason why the changes of things in general must be within our ken unless the very notion of change is tied to time and the structure of time turns out to be somehow necessarily mind-dependent, as Kant argues in the Transcendental Aesthetic. Kant's assumption that we need to appeal to the fact that time is a structure of the human mind is why he thinks that all "dogmatic" attempts to argue for the necessity that there are substances are doomed to failure (A 184/B 228). Absent transcendental idealist assumptions, there is no contradiction in the general idea of an unobservable change. It is arguable, however, that there is a contradiction in thinking of an object of experience as something that undergoes unobservable changes. And we can defend the determinability of changes in objects belonging to experience even if we reject the further Kantian claim that there are no changes at all that could occur independently of experience.

Even if one grants Kant's assumption that changes in objects of experience must be determinable, the argument is still open to an objection that may seem to be fatal. It proves, at best, that there must be things that persist through some interval; it does not prove that there are any things that must endure forever. Most of the spatio-temporal continuants with which one is familiar in everyday life and even in the most arcane domains of natural science are particulars of finite duration that come and go against a background of relatively persistent objects. Such continuants suggest the idea of permanence to us only because of their relative longevity. Not only animal bodies, trees, tables, and chairs, but also mountains, continents, and electrons are only relatively permanent. All of these things undergo change or transformation over time. Eventually they disappear altogether. This raises the question of whether anything lasts forever at all. Relative persistence seems to be possible without permanence or absolute persistence.

Kant implies that recognizable changes must be construed as changes in the accidents of substances. But additional argument is needed to show that some kind of replacement could not be perceived or otherwise observed to occur in the same perceptual fields as substances (of finite or infinite duration) without that replacement itself being a change in state of a substance that endures. Strawson makes the prima-facie compelling objection that changes could be observable against the background of persistent objects of which they are not themselves the states. Each of the objects could then persist through some time without persisting through all of time.[3] This would allow for the possibility of objects coming into being and passing out of being, while also providing for the possibility that objects persist over restricted stretches of time. The problem with Strawson's objection is that it assumes that we already have some way of determining which states of things coexist in the same space at the same time. Appealing to relatively persistent things in the surrounding space will only help us in determining whether a change has occurred or not if we already know which states of those things are simultaneous with a putative change in state of some other thing. But the spatial relations between things and their states are no more observable independently of the things that occupy a certain position in space, than are the temporal relations between things and their states. In order to relate one event to another event in space we must already be able to link the one space with the other space at one time or at another time. But we can only do this if there is something that empirically distinguishes the one space and time from the other space and time. But empirical content to distinguish different spaces and times is only helpful to us to the extent that such content also links spatial and temporal positions together in such a way that we can actually distinguish them from each other.

It seems at first rather easy to dismiss the worry about how to determine the spatial or temporal position of objects or of their states. We do, after all, simultaneously perceive things in space. But there will always be a further question as to whether the things that we observe as simultaneous are indeed simultaneous and in the position in which we perceive them. We can only resolve this question if we know what their objective position in time and space is. But we can only determine that position if we are able empirically to distinguish one time and space from another, and relate those individual times and spaces to public space and time as a whole. If relatively persistent objects come to be and pass away, there will be nothing that distinguishes the spatio-temporal point at which they come to be or pass away and hence no way of linking them determinately to other objects that come to be and pass away. This is a powerful argument so long as one accepts the idea that spaces and times must be precisely distinguishable. But, plausible as the assumption is that spaces and times are always empirically precisely distinguishable, it is an assumption one could reject. And, in fact, it is an assumption rejected by quantum mechanics. But, even if it is not true that we can assign a completely determinate spatial or temporal position to all objects, it does seem plausible to argue that most of the objects that we experience must be such that we can precisely determine their spatial and temporal position.

Now Kant does not just wish to argue that spaces and times are empirically distinguishable, he also wants to claim that empirically distinguishable spaces and times all belong to one space and time. But if some substances were to come to be and others were to pass away, then the empirical unity of space and time would be disrupted. Space and time would break up into different parallel and partially, or perhaps even wholly, disconnected spatial and temporal series. Kant makes the point explicitly with respect to time:

Substances (in appearance) are the substrates of all time-determination. The coming to be of some and the passing of others of these [substances in appearance] would eliminate the sole condition of the empirical unity of time and the appearances would then relate to two different times in which existence would flow on; which is absurd. For there is *only One* time in which all different times must be positioned, not contemporaneously, but after each other. (A 188–189/B 231–232)

We give empirical significance to temporal sequence by means of objects that occupy different times. In coming to be, a new substance gives rise to a new sequence of events in time. In passing away, it ends a sequence of temporal events. But, if there is nothing in experience that allows one to justify a judgment to the effect that one sequence of events is temporally (and spatially) connected to another sequence of events in a certain way, then the commitment to be able to justify the judgments that one makes will not be satisfiable with respect to such temporal sequences. One will have no reason to think that we are experiencing objects that belong to the same time at all. We will then have the apparent "absurdity" that time is not inherently unitary.

The reason Kant seems to think this is absurd is that he is convinced that no empirical evidence could be sufficiently compelling to force us to give up our ability to make determinate statements about whether an object existed in a time during which it was not directly observed.[4] Kant assumes that we would not be able to make out the laws governing interaction between the two time-systems. This would make it impossible to confirm or disconfirm claims about objects outside of one's direct perceptual field. Kant seems to be right that changes in the intersubjectively available perceptual objects of our experience must, in principle, be subject to confirmation and disconfirmation. Such perceptual objects must therefore be thought of as states of objects that persist throughout time. This makes it tempting to think of the objects of physical science as sempiternal particulars. Now, even if the objects of physical science are sempiternal particulars, such as quantities of energy, we could still make sense of the notion of different disconnected physical times, if we could formulate laws linking physically discontinuous times.

The existence of singularities in space and time would seem to call into question the strong claims that Kant wishes to make about the unity of physical space and time. Such singularities are not only generally accepted to be empirically verifiable. There is also widespread belief among astrophysicists and astronomers that we have sufficient evidence to warrant the assumption that they do, in fact, exist. But the possibility of independent time-systems need not undermine the assumption that there are persistent substances. For it might be argued from Kantian premises that the empirical knowability of different time-systems must itself presuppose the existence of substances that persist through changes from one time-system to another. This may also be given the alternative formulation that every empirically significant event must have a cause that is, in principle, knowable. Our ability to identify causal laws operating between different time-systems, and hence to provide a sufficiently rich notion of the relation of our own time-system to another time-system to warrant its acceptance as an empirical possibility, presupposes something that persists through the change from one time-system to the other. One will have to give up the assumption of spatio-temporal continuity. But whatever comes into being in one time-system will have to be numerically identical with what has passed out of being in the other time-system. Without this numerical identity, there is no empirical basis for the assumption that there are two distinct time-systems. Thus, one might be able to defend Kant's claim that there must be an empirical unity to time, without also accepting his claim that time is a single unique whole. Alternative time-systems depend for their empirical significance on something that can be taken to be a numerically identical particular. The particular in question must be both distinct from self-consciousness and systematically representable in such a manner that the conditions governing self-ascription of representations are satisfied. Thus, even if the uniqueness of the one space and time with which we are familiar in our experience does support the notion of permanent substance, the notion of permanent substance seems to allow for more recondite versions of spatio-temporal unity than Kant believed to be possible.

The argument for the persistence of substance involves several distinct ideas. The first idea is that every time and every space is distinguishable from every other because of the fact that it is occupied by something that fills it. There is also the idea that these spaces and times are connected by means of particulars that must be numerically identical over all time. Kant expresses these ideas in the following passage: "Now time cannot be perceived on its own. Therefore the substrate that represents time in general, and on which all change or contemporaneousness can be perceived through the relationship of the appearances to it [the substrate] in apprehension must be encountered in the objects of perception, that is, the appearances" (B 225). In the second edition of the *Critique*, Kant tries to link the idea that there are numerically identical particulars to the conservation of whatever it is that makes these particulars what they are. He insists that the "quantum" of whatever serves as the real substrate of change cannot be "increased or diminished" (B 225). The conclusion that some quantity must be conserved in nature has been repeatedly excoriated for importing a conservation principle of Newtonian mechanics into a discussion of transcendental conditions on the possibility of experience.[5] While I think that this criticism misses the mark, his argument for the conservation of the quantity of matter in the universe must ultimately be regarded as a failure.

In the *Critique* no argument is articulated for the conservation of the number of substances; Kant simply concludes that the number (quantum) of substances must remain constant in the universe from the assumption that substance does not undergo replacement change. However, an argument which moves from the premise that phenomenal substance cannot undergo replacement to the conservation of the quantum of that phenomenal substance is to be found in the *Metaphysical Foundations* written between the first and second editions of the *Critique*. Presumably, Kant's reflection on arguments concerned specifically with the conservation of matter motivated his decision to include the new claim in the revised edition of the First Analogy. Appealing to the arguments in the *Metaphysical Foundations*, many interpreters have now found the argument for the conservation of the quantity of substances more promising.[6]

Kant maintains that the only thing that can strictly satisfy the demand for numerical and qualitative identity in experience is material substance. This is because material substance is the only thing that has wholly external relations to its parts and to all other things. It is also the only thing that is subject to quantifiable and lawlike relations according to the preface of the *Metaphysical Foundations* (Ak IV, p. 471). Kant is attracted to the idea that in a material substance all differences in intensive magnitude would reduce to differences in extensive magnitude and, indeed, to the number of substantial material units of which a thing is composed. According to the *Metaphysical Foundations* (Ak. IV, p. 542), if substance is construed as what is movable in space, then quantity of substance will be the number of substances in that space. The quantity of something that is purely spatial will depend only on the number of parts it has, all of which are related to each other externally and spatially. But, if these parts are to be real parts, they must be movable parts, and, if they are movable parts, they may be said to be corporeal substances. Kant concludes that if substance is conserved, and the movable in space is substance, then the quantity of the movable in space must also be preserved. If the quantity of substance (insofar as it is the movable in space) were either to diminish or increase, then the substances which make up what is real in space would have either to come to be or pass away. Such becoming is precluded by the general argument for the conservation of substance.

Kant thinks that the conservation argument will not go through with respect to everything that undergoes change. The intensity or magnitude of consciousness is not dependent on the quantity of mental substances of which that consciousness is composed. Consciousness can increase or decrease in magnitude without the coming to be or passing away of constituent substances.[7] After arguing that the increase or decrease in intensity of consciousness is compatible with the persistence of substance, he goes on to suggest that consciousness could disappear altogether through continuous diminution:

It is logically possible for something to exist up to and at a given period of time and from that moment on *not* to exist. It ceases to be and begins not to be in the same moment. There is no contradiction in supposing a simple substance to be annihilated. (*Metaphysical Foundations*, Ak. IV, p. 93)

The supposed contrast between the status of the mental and the physical *vis à vis* conservation principles raises a worry about whether even material substance can be conserved. Kant uses his distinction between extensive and intensive magnitudes to argue that material substances are conserved while there is no conservation principle for mental substances. But, given his own premises, the preservation of the quantum of substance needs to be understood as the preservation of both the extensive and the intensive quantity of substances rather than of extensive quantity alone.

There is a crippling difficulty for Kant's attempt to base a conservation principle on material atomism.[8] As he formulates the conservation principle for phenomenal substance, it concerns the quantum of substance. In the *Metaphysical Foundations*, he clarifies this notion of a quantum as a collection of units. The number of units of matter in a collection of matter would have to remain constant, if the quantum of substance is to be conserved. In order for it to make sense to say that the quantum of substance is a function of the number of units which make it up, one must assume that the number of units is finite. If the number of units in any quantum of substance is infinite, the quantum of any particular substance could not be a function of the number of units of which it is composed. For one could take away or add units to that quantum without affecting the quantum. But Kant is committed to the idea that space is infinitely divisible. He maintains that the infinite divisibility of space entails the infinite divisibility of matter. The infinite divisibility of matter and the external nature of all relations between parts of matter leads to the idea of a potential infinity of atoms. This prevents us from claiming that each material object is composed of a certain definite number of material atoms and that the number of such material atoms is conserved in any closed system. There just will not be a fact of the matter concerning the number of units of which an atom is composed.

Kant is aware of the difficulty, and opts to measure quantity of matter by means of quantity of motion (Ak. IV, pp. 537–538). Motion and matter itself are, in turn, traced back to dynamical forces of attraction and repulsion. The dynamical construction of matter in the *Metaphysical Foundations* does indeed provide a way out of this dilemma. Instead of thinking of conservation in terms of bits of matter, one can move to the forces or energy which distinguish matter from space. This allows one to circumvent problems concerning atomism and the continuum. Something that is a continuous quantity in one sense can be a discrete quantity in another sense. This is true of bits of matter. As bits of space and time, matter is infinitely divisible and continuous. As a physical quantity resulting from the existence of a certain quantity of force, matter is discrete. It consists of grains with a determinate metric:

Infinite divisibility refers only to appearance as quantum continuum and is indivisible from the filling of space; since the basis for the infinite divisibility of space lies in that [filling of space]. But as soon as something is assumed to be a discrete quantity: the number <*Menge*> of units is determinate in it; hence always equal to a number. (A 527/B 555)

Spatio-temporal continuity is consistent with the existence of discrete atoms endowed with determinate number as physical quantities. But the argument cannot depend on the fact that matter is an extensive magnitude. So, to the extent Kant wants to argue that material substance rather than mind is the only thing that could be conserved, he must appeal to the anomalousness of the mental rather than to its lack of physical extension.[9] In conclusion, we may observe that Kant's argument in favor of an Aristotelian conception of substance, as a substrate of change, is relatively successful, since he has shown that we need substances to the extent that changes are to be determinate. However, his own theoretical assumptions raise major reservations about his effort to privilege matter (in the narrow sense) as substance.

CAUSATION AND PERCEPTUAL ISOMORPHISM

Kant uses the perception of an event as the starting-point for his discussion of causation. After arguing that we can only determine whether an event occurs by regarding such events as changes in things that persist, Kant attempts to establish that we need to appeal to causal relations in order to be able to determine the objective order of events in time.We cannot simply read off the objective sequence in which two phases of an event or set of events occurred from the order of our perceptions of those events. There are two important reasons for this. (1) We apprehend things successively (A 189/B 234). Succession arises from the flow or elapse of different states of consciousness, and the changes in these states may not always reflect changes in the things observed by consciousness. The problem is not that we cannot have introspective awareness of succession.[10] But we may be mistaken about the order in which we perceived what we perceived. For what we have is at best a short-term memory of the order in which we perceived the two states. We need some criterion for distinguishing a (veridical instance of) memory from a false memory of the sequence. (2) Even if the order in which we judge ourselves to have perceived a state x followed by a state y is, in fact, the correct order of those representations, we cannot be sure that the order of our perceptions of states x and y corresponds to the order in which they actually occurred. The distinction between the order in which we perceive a set of states and the order in which those states occurred in the object of which they are states is crucial to the proper understanding of the argument from the irreversibility of a certain perceptual order to the existence of an underlying causal covering law.

When we (veridically) perceive an objective change, or an event, the sequence of percepts in that perceptual sequence corresponds to the sequence of changes in its object. Following Van Cleve, I shall refer to the circumstance in which the order in which we perceive a change corresponds to the order of the states in the change itself as "perceptual isomorphism."[11] Perceptual isomorphism is analytic to what it means to perceive an event, where an event is to be understood as an objective change. Now Kant distinguishes the successive apprehension of an event (of an objective change in state) from the successive apprehension of an unchanging object. He uses the apprehension of a ship going downstream, and of the coexisting parts of a house, as examples of perceptions of changing and unchanging objects, respectively. In both of these examples, a change of perceptual states is involved, since we represent the items successively and our spatio-temporal perspective undergoes a change. But only in the case of the ship going downstream is the object in a state of change that is isomorphic to that of our perceptions. The order of our perceptions is said to be "tied down" in apprehension in the case of the perception (or rather apprehension) of an event (A 192/B 237).[12]

The perception of a(n objective) change differs from a mere (subjective) change in our perceptions. When I perceive the event of a ship going downstream, the order of my perceptions cannot be reversed. I cannot see the ship downstream first and then perceive the ship upstream. This would be the perception of a different event, i.e. it would be the perception of a ship going upstream. Irreversibility of the sequence in which an event is perceived is analytic to the perception of an event in the sense that the order of our perceptions must correspond to the order of objective change. The ship might go downstream again after going upstream. It is quite improbable that the ship could return to precisely the same type of state on any understanding of what it is to be an event. And, if event identity is tied to the relations of that event to other events, it will be quite impossible for strict recurrence to occur. For if A–B are different then A in the change A B will have to be different in content from A in the sequence B–A for they will be involved with other events that will make them different. And, even if the two A event-tokens in the sequence A B A were type identical, the change from A to B and B to A would nevertheless be different. The sequence A to B and B to A would be irreversible with respect to event-tokens, if not with respect to event-types.

The irreversibility of sequence that Kant imputes to perceptions of changes has sometimes been thought to be the basis for his assertion that those changes in the state of objects are themselves objective.[13] By identifying the order of objective sequence with the order in the subjective sequence of perceptions, he would come into conflict not only with Special Relativity, but also with the way the distinction between subjective and objective sequence operates in Newtonian (and Leibnizian) mechanics. For even here the motions in terms of which spatial and temporal intervals are measured are dependent on the frames of reference that different observers have. The identification of subjective and objective sequence is incompatible even with our experience of such phenomena as lightning and thunder. Under normal circumstances our perception of thunder follows our perception of lightning, although the lightning and thunder actually occur simultaneously. We also perceive states of stars as simultaneous with us, many of which may have long ago ceased to exist. Moreover, if a star lies one light-year from us, we will perceive the light it emits earlier than the light emitted from a star that is 5 light-years away, even when the light from the star that is five light-years away was transmitted almost four years earlier than the light from the nearer star.

Counterexamples against perceptual isomorphism of this kind are based on the misunderstanding that irreversibility in perception is supposed to function as the criterion of temporal and causal sequence. But knowledge of an irreversible order in perception is supposed to presuppose knowledge of an objective irreversibility of succession. Thus, in discussing the example of my perceiving a ship going downstream, Kant notes: "In our case, I will therefore have to derive the subjective sequence of apprehension from the objective sequence of appearances, since otherwise the latter is completely indeterminate and does not distinguish any appearance from any other" (A 193/B 238). Kant is not claiming, to be sure, that we cannot have any beliefs about the temporal order of our perceptions without knowing the objective sequence of the objects of which they are perceptions. But we can only know that a given sequence of states in which we perceive something is irreversible, that is, must occur in a certain order, if we know the object perceived.

We only become aware of changes in our beliefs and desires by virtue of the way they represent changes in what we represent outside of ourselves. Once we have some perception of changes in things outside of us, then we can assign some order to our representations. For, without the possible perspective of an outside observer to draw on, I have no sense that I or my representations are really in time at all (A 362). From a purely first-person perspective, the temporal order of my representations is indistinguishable from my present take on the temporal order of those representations. It is not until I see that my present take might be false, by thinking that another person might assign a different temporal order to my representations, that I am really able to form judgments about the temporal order of my inner episodes. That order will then only be knowledge properly so-called to the extent that we are able to derive the subjective ordering of time-sequences from an objective ordering of changes in spatial objects by reference to the standpoint of perception. If A is the first stage of some event and B is the stage which follows it, then, given the isomorphism definitive of event perception, there will be perceptual states A′ and B′ corresponding to A and B. The order of the occurrence of A′ and B′ is subject to this irreversibility rule that is definitive of the concept of event perception.

So far, all we know is that if we perceive an event, then the irreversibility rule applies to perceptions. This does not tell us how we know what the order of change from state A to state B is. Assuming that one is perceiving an event, the order of what is perceived is fixed. The act of perceiving A′ will be followed by the act of perceiving B′, just as the event A will be followed by the event B. We have not yet explained, however, how it is that, given an act of perceiving A′ followed by an act of perceiving B′, we are then able to determine that an objective change from A to B has occurred. For it always seems possible that the order of our representations A′ . . . N′ may not correspond to the order of changes in things A . . . N that are independent of our particular standpoint. There must be some connection between A and B such that we can know that if A occurs then B occurs. Once we know what this connection is, we are then in a position to determine whether we are correct in our belief that A precedes B. We can determine whether the order of A' and B' according to which we perceive A and B corresponds to the actual order of A and B. And only if we are in possession of such facts are we able to challenge even our belief that A' preceded B'.

Whenever we perceive what appears to be a change in state, we are presented with opposite states that are perceived sequentially. Perception alone does not tell us the objective relation between two successive states of objects perceived, although we are conscious of the fact that the one state precedes the other in our consciousness. Now, two temporal states constitute an event only if they are opposites. It thus appears to be sufficient to know that they are opposites in order to know that, if they are parts of an event, they are non-identical parts of an event or sequence of events. For, if they are opposites, they cannot be simultaneous states of the same thing.[14] If we perceive a state B and we know we have immediately previously perceived a state A that is opposite to B and we know that B is at the same spatial location as A, then we know that A cannot have occurred at the same time as B. If we know that two states are opposites and states of the same thing, then we know that the two states must belong to that thing at different times. And from the existence of opposite states at different times we can conclude that a change has occurred. However, we can only determine which of the two states is earlier if there is something about the opposite states such that the one could only exist after the other.

Kant infers that there is a necessary connection between an occurrence (an event) and something that precedes it from the rule determinedness of the perceptual sequence in an event perception:

According to such a rule there must therefore lie in that which precedes an occurrence in general a condition for a rule according to which this occurrence always and necessarily follows. Thus since it is something that follows, therefore I must necessarily relate it to something else in general which precedes it and which it follows according to a rule, i.e. necessarily, so that the occurrence as that which is conditioned gives certain indication of some condition, and this determines the occurrence. (A 193/B 238)

Kant does not directly argue for the claim that objective succession according to a necessary and strictly general rule is identical with our notion of causation. One might wonder why succession according to a necessary and strictly general rule would have to be construed as causation. This is ultimately a matter of the appropriateness of terminology. Nominal definitions can be as arbitrary as one likes, but a real definition must be adequate to the explanatory tasks that a concept is to fulfill. The term "causation" is generally taken to mean that which necessitates a change from some event-type A to some event-type B. Objective succession that is determined by a necessary and strictly general rule gives us the regularity of sequence that is generally required for a conception of causation. It also expresses the idea that a certain occurrence generates another occurrence. The one occurrence had to occur given the assumption that a certain other occurrence preceded it.

What then is the basis for the postulated necessary connection between events? It is tempting to trace the necessity in question back to the concept of an event perception. But the analytic principle involved in perceptual isomorphism, based on the concept of what it is to perceive a perception, cannot itself provide the basis for the categorical necessity that Kant must justify.[15] Since he regards causal connection as synthetic and a priori, he does not intend the mere analysis of the meaning of event perception to be the key premise in his argument.[16] How can the claim that there is a necessary connection between individual tokens of certain event-types be justified? Part of Kant's answer is that the existence of an earlier time is a sufficient condition for the existence of a later time. Time is supposed to have a direction that is represented a priori (A 194/B 239; A 199/B 244). This leads to the idea that it is a necessary law that earlier times determine later times.

Kant takes the direction of causation to be an expression of temporal direction. However, temporal direction is not simply causal direction or reducible to causal direction in any interesting sense. Nor is causal direction just temporal direction. The notion of cause, based as it is in the non-material conditional and its ability to support counterfactuals, is irreducible to the direction of time. In this respect, it must be distinguished from the essentially temporal notion of causal direction. This allows for a conception of causal action that is not essentially temporal in character, since it does not involve causal direction. Now, despite the manner in which Kant wishes to link causal connection to the direction of time, his notion of temporal causation is consistent with the possibility of the backward causation postulated in some recent physical theories. He nowhere indicates that the direction of time and the direction of causation are directly linked in a manner that precludes causal vectors from traveling from the future to the past. In fact, his theory of action, which provides the model for his more general conception of teleology, involves the idea that action is caused by the agent's anticipation of a certain outcome from that action. The agent's beliefs concerning the outcome of a certain action gives rise to a desire or aversion in anticipation of the feeling of pleasure or displeasure that the outcome would bring.

It seems to be a necessary feature of a finite temporal consciousness that it experience changes in a direction that is irreversible in the order of succession. But this does not rule out the possibility that the laws or *de facto* regularities governing objective change give rise to reversals in the order of temporal changes. Some objective sequences, such as the motion of a ship, and perhaps even all objective sequences, may turn out to be in some sense time-order reversible. The laws of Newtonian mechanics are, for instance, invariant under time reversal. From the point of view of the physics of Kant's time, all processes are, in principle, reversible. This seems to be true for the fundamental laws of contemporary physics as well. There are phenomenological laws such as the second law of thermodynamics that are not time-order invariant, but these laws are based on other statistical laws that are time-order invariant. It seems quite possible for there to be spatial and temporal regions in which there is a constant increase in negentropy rather than entropy. This reverse order of change to our own would not appear to observers in that part of the universe to be time-order reversed, although our part of the universe would appear that way to them and theirs to us.

The synthetic a priori necessity that later events follow earlier events is part of Kant's reason for thinking that there are necessary (causal) connections between events. But perhaps a more fundamental reason is to be found in the idea that changes must be determinable. The necessity that changes be empirically determinable provides the key premise in Kant's argument that every event *must* have a cause and that tokens of a certain event-type *must* be connectable to tokens of some other event-type according to laws that fix the order of their occurrence in objective time.[17] Now, the transcendental or metaphysical realist simply accepts the possibility that there may be changes that we cannot explain and that there may therefore be events that have no cause. But, for Kant, a judgment that a change has or has not occurred must, in principle, be justifiable by us. Transcendental idealism not only demands that the subjective conditions under which evidence is available to individual observers be subject to constraints that apply to all observers regardless of their standpoint, it also limits empirical judgments to claims that can, in principle, be supported by evidence. Transcendental idealism limits change to what, in principle, is determinable by us or at least by a being with finite powers of understanding. This is why Kant thinks that "if appearances were things in themselves, then no human being would be able to figure out how the manifold is connected in the object from the succession of representations of that manifold" (A 190/B 235).

The distinction between the subjective order of representeds and their objective order amounts, for Kant, to a distinction between contingent and necessary connections between those representeds. Representations are true of an object, if and only if they cohere "necessarily" amongst themselves. Here the object is just whatever all of our beliefs correspond to when they are internally coherent. The necessity that the object transmits to those representeds is itself nothing but the necessary connectedness of those representations (A 197/B 242). This aspect of the argument is a direct application of the recognition argument in the A-Deduction, where Kant ultimately based the possibility of conceptual recognition on the possibility of an impersonal self-consciousness of diverse representations. Only such an impersonal self-consciousness is capable of supporting the normative claim implicit in conceptual recognition that one is representing or rather judging the item in question as anyone ought to do so.

The idea that what makes for objective relations between items that we experience is that such items must be connectable in self-consciousness in a way that allows conceptual recognition, has an immediate relevance to the problem of how temporal episodes may be ordered in time. The only way of assigning a determinate temporal position to what is experienced is relative to all other items of experience: "the appearances must determine for one another their position in time, and make their time-order a necessary order" (A 200/B 245). A necessary order is invariant with respect to changes in observers and their spatio-temporal positions. In this invariant spatial and temporal order, a position is provided for all possible empirical consciousness. By "carrying the time-order over into appearances and their existence" (A 200/B 245), we get the notion of an object that is independent of any particular standpoint, and at the same time a sequence of percepts that corresponds to the a priori structure of intuition. We must identify different times relative to different events that occupy them because this is the only way we have of identifying different times. "For only in appearance can we empirically know this continuity in the connection of times" (A 199/B 244). Our perceptions are true of their objects just in case they are connected in a lawlike way to those objects. To order perceived events in time in a way that corresponds to the objective order of those events, we must identify the causal laws that connect those events to other events.

When we perceive an event, we take it to be something that necessarily follows something else. We assume that if we perceive the set of circumstances that ought to bring about a certain event and the event does not occur, we are merely imagining or dreaming that the appropriate circumstances are on hand (A 202/B 247). The information link between those perceptions and their object is then deviant. To be sure, in order to determine that an information link is deviant, we would have to have knowledge of all of the relevant conditions governing a succession from one state to another. This is unattainable by us, since the number of *ceteris paribus* clauses that may be relevant to the occurrence of events is potentially infinite. We rely on knowledge of the most relevant conditions. Determining which conditions are most relevant is itself a matter of skill in judgment, and is inherently interest-relative.

Now, in contrast to the holistic account of time-determination that I have been defending, Allison insists that the argument in the Second Analogy is concerned only with the succession of one state to another that makes up an event, rather than with a sequence of different events.[18] His distinction between the sequence of states in an individual event and in a series of events tends to be undermined by the nature of the identity conditions for events. Allison admits that an event is to be construed as a succession of states. Individual momentary states do not involve either replacement change or changes in state. They cannot therefore constitute an event, as Kant understands the notion of event. And, given the Kantian assumption that time is continuous, there will be a further momentary state between any two momentary states. This is an explicit part of Kant's general defense of the continuous character of change and causal influence: "Between two moments <*Augenblicke*> there is always a time, and between any two states in the two moments there is always a difference which has magnitude" (A 208/B 253). Since all temporally extended states are themselves divisible into further temporally extended states, there is no fundamental distinction between *an* event such as the melting of a piece of ice, or a ship sailing downstream, and an event comprising almost the whole time-series.

The example of a ship sailing downstream consists of a sequence of events, and both the A and B edition formulae for the principle of causation explicitly cover all changes, not just changes from one momentary state to another (A 189/B 232). In the *Critique of Judgment*, Kant does maintain that the condition for subsumption (the schema) under the category of cause is that of "the succession of the determinations of one and the same thing" (Ak. v, p. 183). First we may note that bona fide things are supposed to be substances that last forever. Moreover, Kant certainly does not think that the relation between cause and effect is restricted to the states of one thing. Knowing what caused a change from one state of one thing to another allows us to order those states in an objective temporal order. However, even though the change is from one state of the same thing to another, the cause of that change is often to be sought in some other thing.

Thinking of causation in terms of the successive determinations of one thing seems to run together the order of causation with the temporal order of events. However, we do not wish to argue *post hoc, ergo propter hoc*. Today may indeed follow yesterday and tomorrow follow today with necessity. But, as Reid argued against Hume, and Schopenhauer later argued against Kant, this does not yet establish anything about the manner in which yesterday's events are connected to today's or tomorrow's events. One event may precede another event without being its cause. Kant avoids the fallacious conclusion by arguing that when something succeeds something else there is some cause of the change from A to B, but that will have to be sought in some further state, or rather set of states, C, that precedes and is non-identical with A. In the example of a ship going downstream, the objective change involves different states of a ship and water. Neither the ship nor the water is, strictly speaking, a physical substance, although they are dependent particulars supervening on the states of such basic particulars. The changes which the water and the ship undergo are changes which we can only understand by reference to causation. However, the ship being upstream is not the cause of it being downstream, rather this change is to be understood in terms of underlying causal conditions. This means that, in a sequence of states which is isomorphic to the perceived order of those states, the earlier state A cannot generally be said to be the cause of the later state B. Thus, not every necessary succession from one state to another state involves a causal connection between those two states. In most instances, the lawlike change from A to B is itself the effect of a set of causal conditions whose most prominent member is some event other than A or B that we can then refer to as an event of type C.

INTERACTION

The Third Analogy argues for interaction between all substances as the basis for objective determination of simultaneity. In Kant's argument for interaction, the order-indifference of the perceptual sequence of contemporaneous states plays a role strictly analogous to that played by the irreversible order of event perception in the Second Analogy. Again the strategy is to assume the order-indifference of perception as definitive of simultaneity, but presupposing perceptual isomorphism. Although Kant initially implies that order-indifference is a necessary but not a sufficient condition for determining the simultaneity of two states, it is not really even a necessary condition. Deviant causal chains can give rise to non-order-indifferent sequences of perceptions of simultaneous states. This complicates the situation somewhat, but does not have a crucial effect on the main argument. The crucial test of simultaneity is not the order-indifference of the sequence of our perceptions, but rather the dynamic interaction upon which our perception is based. Kant rightly stresses the need for a causal medium to transmit information from objects to our senses in order to determine relations of simultaneity:

It is easy to note in our experiences that only continuous influences through all positions of space can guide our sense from one object to the other, that the light which plays between our eye and the heavenly bodies effects an indirect community between us and them and through it proves the contemporaneousness of them, that we cannot change any place empirically (cannot perceive this change) without matter making the perception of our position possible everywhere, and it can only demonstrate its contemporaneousness through its reciprocal influence and through it its coexistence with the most distant objects (although only indirectly). (A 213/B 260)

Schopenhauer argues that there cannot be a play of light *between* the eye and the distant star, and hence there cannot be interaction, as Kant claims. But this ignores the fact that some light will generally be reflected back by the eye to its source, although there will be a considerable time-lag between reflection and incidence. Schopenhauer also argues that Kant's use of light from a distant star as a signal for determining simultaneity is empirically false, since light takes time to travel from the star to us.[19] However, there is no textual evidence that Kant endorses the empirically false assumption that light travels at an infinite velocity. Kant was in a position to know to a fairly close approximation what the actual velocity is that light travels at. So the assumption that he thinks that light travels infinitely fast depends on the assumption that he confuses the optical perception of simultaneity with objective simultaneity. While we may perceive two events as simultaneous, it does not follow from the fact that we perceive them at the same time that they are, in fact, simultaneous. Again Kant was in a position to draw the distinction in question, although he does not explicitly do so. Schopenhauer's objection is based on the tendentious assumption that Kant takes there to be instantaneous causal transmission between states across space, rather than indirect evidence of simultaneity relations on the basis of states that are already in the causal past of the object to which they are transmitted. Kant does not explicitly commit himself to the existence of instantaneous causal transmission across finite distances, although gravitational force in Newtonian mechanics does depend on instantaneous action at a distance. Immediate transmission of causal influence between contemporaneous states of substances at different spatial locations is consistent with his account of simultaneity in the Third Analogy. But the Third Analogy does not entail the existence of unmediated or superluminal causal transmission.

Kant was not in a position to draw all the distinctions with respect to simultaneity that we would now want drawn. Special Relativity introduces a failure of transitivity with respect to objective relations of simultaneity that Kant did not anticipate. There is no reason in classical mechanics to assume that events that are perceived subjectively as simultaneous with each other must be objectively simultaneous with each other. However, if an event e_1 is objectively simultaneous with an event e_2 and the event e_2 is objectively simultaneous with an event e_3, then e_1 will be identical with e_3. This no longer holds in Special Relativity. We cannot simply assume simultaneity to be a transitive relation. If an event e_1 is simultaneous with an event e_2, then this by no means entails that if e_2 is simultaneous with a third event e_3, then e_1 must also be simultaneous with e_3. Kant probably assumes that objective simultaneity relations are transitive. But this does not significantly affect his account of simultaneity, since it is concerned with the conditions under which objective relations of simultaneity may be distinguished from subjective relations of simultaneity.

Kant does not formulate his notion of interaction and simultaneity as a relation between events, but as a relation between substances. The First Analogy requires that substances are sempiternal. Such substances can interact with each other even if there is no instantaneous action at a distance or superluminal velocities of transmission. For such substances, simultaneity of states is indirectly definable by appeal to states of the same substance that are in the causal past or future of those states. His conception of substances as sempiternal persistents re-establishes the validity of the assumption that substances observed to be contemporaneous with the percipient must also be in causal interaction and hence contemporaneous with one another. But it is important to note that this by no means establishes that *states* of two substances that appear to be contemporaneous with one another need also be in causal interaction with one another. Only substances that can neither be created nor destroyed must interact. Even if such substances are infinitely distant from each other and the forces connecting them can operate only at finite velocities, in the infinite length of time during which they exist, they will eventually interact.

In this chapter, I have looked at the role of substance, causation, and interaction, in establishing not just an objective, but also even a subjective order of episodes in time and space. I have argued that some notion of substance, cause, and interaction is needed if we are to be able to make judgments about public objects or even to be able to make judgments about private experiences. These notions turn out to be conditions under which we can be conscious of distinct spaces and times, and hence of distinctions between different representations.

In the next chapter, I want to look at the manner in which we come to formulate laws governing substances, and their causal interaction. For it is these laws that Kant takes to underwrite our ability to form empirical concepts of objects and with them to understand the associations involved in even the most minimal notion of experience.

CHAPTER 7

Causal laws

In the last chapter, I developed the argument in the Analogies of Experience for the principle of substance, and for the general causal principle and principle of interaction. In this chapter, I discuss the relation of the general causal principle, the general principle of interaction, and the general substance principle to the existence of specific laws governing causes, interactions, and substances. First I discuss the relation of specific causal laws to the general causal principle. I argue that the general causal principle entails the existence of specific causal laws, but does not entail any particular causal law.

Then I take up the question of the extent to which our knowledge of specific causal laws depends on a priori knowledge. I argue that Kant thinks of the causal necessity of particular causal laws as parasitic on a universality and necessity that cannot be derived from experience. But I reject the view that Kant wants actually to derive individual causal laws a priori. I then argue that even probabilistic laws exhibit the kind of necessity and universality that Kant requires of a causal law.

The existence of probabilistic causal laws governing human action leaves room for indeterministic causal explanation of human behavior. However, I argue that Kant insists on the regulative ideal of deterministic causal explanation for human behavior. When this regulative ideal is taken to be a constitutive principle of experience, a conflict arises with the assumption that individuals are capable of free action. Kant resolves the problem by noting that a complete causal explanation of human behavior is never actually possible for us even in principle, even though it is a regulative ideal in our explanation of human behavior. The first-person perspective of self-consciousness involves a kind of independence from causal determination that Kant refers to as spontaneity. This spontaneity turns out to be only relative to antecedent causes when taken from the second- and third-person perspective that we must take in order to observe and understand the behavior of others.

CAUSAL LAWS AND THE GENERAL CAUSAL PRINCIPLE

The general causal principle defended by the Second Analogy and the general principle of interaction defended by the Third Analogy tell us that, wherever there is a change, there must be something that causes the change to occur. They do not tell us what occurs at the same time as what, or what follows upon what in objective time. But Kant takes the existence of the general causal principle and the general principle of interaction also to involve the existence of a specific set of causal covering laws that explain the change from tokens of a certain event-type to tokens of another event-type. Thus, Kant maintains that "in conformity with such a rule there must lie in that which precedes an event the condition of a rule according to which this event invariably and necessarily follows" (A 193/B 238-9). Kant implicitly distinguishes a first- and a second-order rule. The second-order rule would have to be the general causal principle that everything has a cause or, rather, that everything that happens presupposes something upon which it follows according to a rule. The second necessary and strictly general rule is just a specific causal law. Given the assumption that the event is repeatable, Kant is obviously treating the event covered by the law as an event-type rather than an event-token. The causal principle is thus a condition on succession that underwrites the existence of universal and necessary rules governing the occurrence of specific event-types.[1]

In the last chapter, I argued that, while we can have an immediate consciousness of a sequence of perceptions, we cannot make a bona fide judgment about the order in which those perceptions occur without it being, in principle, possible for us to show that a claim that our perceptions occur in a certain order is correct or incorrect. Some recent interpreters have made a much stronger claim. Melnick and Guyer maintain that we cannot even form a judgment to the effect that a sequence of representations has occurred without knowing the causal laws to which that sequence is subject, since not even the subjective order of our representations is ever directly given to us.[2] They appeal to Kant's commitment to the inherent successiveness of all of our representations to justify the ascription of this claim to Kant. However, the successiveness of representations does not preclude us from having a direct experience of succession, so long as we take such a direct experience of succession itself to involve a succession of representations.

Quite apart from the correct interpretation of Kant, it is quite implausible to claim that, before lawlike correlations in experience had been discovered, individuals had no awareness of the successiveness of their experiences. A worry also arises about circularity. In order to form judgments about succession, we need to know causal laws, but it is hard to see how one could come to know causal laws without being able to recognize regularities of succession. There is no evidence that Kant ever thought that we could only assume that one of our mental states preceded another if we also thought that we knew all of the relevant causal laws governing the change from one represented to the other. To require knowledge of all the relevant causal laws in order to perceive experiences in a determinate temporal order would quickly lead to extreme skepticism. Not only would it undermine our ability to ascribe a temporal order to our states, but also given Kant's assumptions about the dependence of content ascription on our ability to assign a temporal order to our experiences, it would force us to deny that we were able to self-ascribe inner states, as well as outer states.

A weaker claim seems to be in order. While there is no reason that we cannot directly experience change and temporal succession, in forming judgments about change and succession we take on epistemic commitments that, in principle, must be redeemable by us if they are to be valid commitments. The claims we make in judgments concerning the temporal relations between our inner as well as our outer states are to be justified by appeal to the idea of a projected order of nature in which a causal explanation of this succession, in principle, is possible. But it is important to distinguish what is involved in an immediate representation of a sequence of subjective states and what is involved in the justification of a claim that this is the sequence in which one perceived what one perceived.

Gerd Buchdahl and Henry Allison have gone to the other extreme of the position staked out by Melnick and Guyer. The former philosophers note that Kant thinks that the temporal positions of phases of an event are determined by means of the general causal principle. But they argue that there need not be a specific causal covering law that allows us to have knowledge of an objective change.[3] They even maintain that we do not have to believe that there are causal laws together with other causal conditions that are sufficient to explain the occurrence of a given event in order to take ourselves to have knowledge of an objective succession.[4]

Buchdahl maintains that the Second Analogy "does not show that nature is lawlike, but only that the *concept* of law is built into our notion of each objective element of nature."[5] Part of the reason that Buchdahl denies that the Second Analogy demonstrates the lawlikeness of nature is that he seems to identify lawlikeness with repetition, at least this would be a sympathetic reading of his idea that the causal principle does not give "Hume–Mill-like support to the special laws of science."[6] Buchdahl maintains that "the transcendental proof *depends* [his emphasis] on regarding [a statement expressing a change from] A–B as an absolutely contingent empirical, indeed, singular statement."[7] The singular causal view advocated by Buchdahl does not seem to do justice to Kant's view that causal connection is always succession of states according to some law (i.e. a specific rule endowed with necessity). For Kant, causal connection is always connection that is covered by some law. It is succession according to a necessary rule:

> It is crucial to show by example that we never attribute succession (of an event in which something is happening that did not occur before) to an object and distinguish it from the subjective one of our apprehension, unless a rule is presupposed that compels us to observe this order of perceptions rather than another, yes, this compulsion is what it is that properly makes a representation of succession in the object possible. (A 196–197/B 247)

The only way in which a particular order for perceived events is going to be necessitated is if we are able to distinguish some particular kind of causal law. Kant's notion of compulsion here might be understood, in a psychologistic way, as a kind of Humean subjective necessity. But, in talking of the temporal order of states in an event, Kant notes that objective succession occurs according to a rule, and "according to such a rule the condition for a rule must lie in what precedes an event, according to which this event always and necessarily succeeds" (A 194/B 239). Here Kant distinguishes the general or second-order causal rule with its necessity from the particular or first-order causal rule that allows us to understand which event must succeed the other.

According to the *Critique of Judgment*, there is potentially an infinite number of different kinds of specific causal laws: "[A]nd each of these kinds must (according to the concept of a cause in general) have its rule that is law, and hence brings with it necessity: although we do not understand this necessity according to the character and limits of our faculty of knowledge" (Ak. v, p. 183). I take the remark that specific laws have a necessity in accordance with the general causal principle to be a statement deriving their necessity from that principle.

Buchdahl could respond that, even if the truth of singular causal statements entails the existence of some necessary causal law, it could be the case that they do not entail the existence of any particular causal law. However, this would be a different claim from the one advocated by Buchdahl and Allison that there can be events that are not subject to causal laws *per se* at all. Allison rightly emphasizes the fact that Kant allows for states that follow each other in an objective temporal order that are not related as cause and effect. But it does not follow from this that they are not covered by a causal law at all, as Allison suggests, motivated in part by his restriction of the causal principle to a relation between states of things. He cites an example of someone who is drunk and then falls. Although the person's drunkenness preceded his fall, another drug rather than the alcohol was the cause. Allison takes the example as evidence that the change from state A to state B is not always lawlike. By this he means that the first state, A, is not the cause of the second, B. This is obviously true, and thus Kant does not infer *post hoc ergo propter hoc*, as Schopenhauer charges. The sequence A B is contingent in the sense that any causal series could have had a different initial state, but it is not contingent in the sense that it might be causally undetermined as Allison takes it to be.[8] Kant nowhere indicates that the causes of a person's fall could not be distinct from and yet also simultaneous with a person's drunkenness, while also subject to strict causal determination. Indeed, he is at pains to point out that the causal order of events may not be immediately displayed by the relative position of those objects in time. Sometimes causes appear to be simultaneous with their effects. A ball's being on a pillow is the cause of the indentation of the pillow. There are states of the ball that are in the causal past of the indented state of the pillow. However, the continued presence of the ball on the pillow makes some of the states of the ball simultaneous with those of the pillow.

Allison has recently given a somewhat more plausible account of his thesis that the element involved in a succession may not be related according to empirical causal laws. Whereas he initially seemed to take the view that the general causal law involved no commitments concerning event-types, more recently, Allison has expressed his acceptance of Friedman's claim that the Kantian concept of causation involves the idea of event-types that are connected by a causal law.[9] While he now accepts the idea that there must be a causal covering law for any event if the general causal principle holds, he argues that this might have only a single application. He then denies that such a law would be a genuine law.

Allison appeals to Paton for support for the view that genuine laws must be characterized by regularity and repeatability.[10] It is possible for something to be repeatable, and hence form a very weak kind of regularity, without actually repeating itself. But, clearly, Paton and Allison have actual repetition in mind. When Kant maintains that the effect must follow its cause according to a rule, Paton takes this to require "regularity and repetition."[11] But then the causal principle would appear to require recurrent instances. Paton notes that in a universe governed by causal laws there might be no repetitions on the basis of which we could find out what those causal laws are. Thus, what seems initially to be an epistemic point about our ability to recognize laws, becomes a metaphysical point about the nature of laws.

Friedman makes repeated references to repeatability and regularity.[12] But it is not clear to me whether he would require the notion of regularity to involve actual repetition, as Paton and Allison seem to do, or whether Friedman would take the repeatability to be sufficient. For Friedman, the notion of a regularity is closely associated with that of law and uniformity. The notion of a uniformity suggests repetition, but does not actually entail it, while the notion of law does not seem to require any actual repetition. To be sure, Friedman overstates his case when he maintains that when individual events occur in objective succession as a result of the schema of the concept of causality they are also subsumed under a uniformity or general causal law.[13] While we presuppose that there is some causal law that covers the succession in question, we may not actually know what that law is. In that case we are not in a position to subsume the succession under that causal law.

Without the existence of some causal laws involving repeated instances, we would have no way of knowing individual causal laws. It seems doubtful that one could identify laws between event-types without any recurrence of event-types. This does not mean that, in every instance, knowledge of laws governing event-types would demand recurrence. Even Hume was prepared to argue in the *Enquiry* that we sometimes know causal laws governing events on the basis of a single token of a certain event-type. In general, a Humean will claim that one must know that an event-type A regularly follows on an event-type B in order to know in a particular case that A follows B. But even though generalizations about causal connections are in general based on repeated experiences, they are not necessarily based on repetition. It is perfectly possible to form inductive generalizations based on indirect evidence that apply only to one event-token.

Kant takes causal relations to hold between event-tokens as tokens of types rather than primarily between event-tokens. He does not so obviously take regularity in the sense of repetition to be a necessary condition for causal relations. The general causal principle entails lawlike connections between event-types of the kind that support counterfactuals, but it does not entail laws that cover recurrent event-types of the kind involved in a strict regularity theory of causation. Thus, although the general causal principle requires the existence of causal laws in nature that make changes recognizable, it does not obviously entail that we are actually capable of determining what those laws are.

There is nothing in the argument of the Second Analogy, according to Allison, which shows that particular causal laws, even if they must exist, must be knowable.[14] This claim deserves to be contested. For if particular causal laws were unknowable, then we would not be able to know whether a change in a particular substance had occurred. Since the principle that changes must be empirically significant provides the basis for the objective necessity that Kant assigns to causal relations, he cannot allow for the possibility of causal laws that have no empirical significance.

The Second Analogy does not itself provide any criteria for identifying the specific causal laws in terms of which events are actually to be ordered in time. However, the argument of the A-Deduction directly links a defense of the general causal principle to the existence of recognizable uniformities in nature. Kant states quite explicitly that an empirical rule of *association* must always be presupposed when one says that there is always some earlier event that a later event succeeds (A 112–113). Not only does association generally presuppose the recurrence of events, but it is difficult indeed to make sense of an empirical *rule* of association that is not based on the recurrence of events in experience. Kant makes this point in a context in which he stresses the independence of causal necessity from mere inductive generalizations.

The possibility that we might be able to provide a justification of the general causal principle without being able to justify the legitimacy of particular causal laws has suggested to a number of interpreters that the necessity of particular causal laws might be purely a function of their position in a systematic unification of nature.[15] Particular causal judgments have their tentative standing as statements of causal laws because they occur within the best systematic unification of experience available to us. But they have their status as statements of causal laws because they are instances of the general causal principle. All specific causal laws are metaphysical, because they cannot be derived from the transcendental conditions governing experience, but presuppose some metaphysical assumption about the world in which we exist (Ak. v, p. 181). They derive their status as causal laws from the presumption that they provide our best understanding of the necessary relations between events in virtue of which we are able to identify and reidentify events in time.

A PRIORI KNOWLEDGE OF PARTICULAR CAUSAL LAWS?

Kant's attitude towards how we know specific causal laws is somewhat ambiguous. On the one hand, he certainly wants to give an important place to empirical investigation. On the other hand, laws are only genuine laws for Kant to the extent to which they can be known to apply to all individuals in their domain with necessity and strict generality, otherwise they amount to mere empirical generalizations. Such empirical generalizations as "all swans are white" may have the provisional status of laws. But as soon as an appropriate counterexample is discovered, such as a black swan, their claims to be laws must be given up.

Given Kant's evident interest in the importance of empirical knowledge in science, some commentators have argued that Kant thought that specific natural laws cannot be known a priori. Thus Guyer claims that "Kant specifically denies that individual causal laws are known *a priori* (see A 196–197/B 241–242, or more generally B 142)."[16] The passages cited by Guyer do not support his assertion. B 142 does not make reference to causation or causal laws at all. Kant does note at B 142 that the judgment "bodies are heavy" is empirical and contingent even though the verb to be in this judgment expresses a necessity that is based on the transcendental unity of apperception. This suggests that even empirical generalizations can purport to be laws only insofar as they are supported by a priori principles. B 241–242 first notes that Kant's idea that we must presuppose a necessary and strictly general causal principle seems to contradict our practice of making generalizations concerning temporal sequence from different experiences of sequence, but he then goes on to claim that such a strategy in isolation would give us only a kind of imagined universality and necessity (i.e. Humean generality and necessity). As opposed to this view, Kant claims that causation is, like other concepts, a priori in that we can only derive it from experience because we have already constituted experience in accordance with it. Thus, if anything, the passage in question would seem to support the view Guyer rejects. For it suggests that we can only derive a necessity and universality claim from nature by antecedently investing nature with that very necessity and universality.

There is nothing in the *Critique* that suggests that causal laws could be knowable purely a priori, although the *Critique* does seem to require some a priori element to support an empirical generalization's claim to be a bona fide law, which Kant takes to be characterized by necessity and universality. At в 165n in the Deduction, Kant does say that particular laws cannot be completely derived from the categories because they concern empirically determined appearances. But then he asserts that experience is necessary in order to be acquainted (*kennen*) with these appearances. The fact that we need experience to become acquainted with certain regularities does not preclude the laws that we postulate from being a priori. However, this fact does suggest that we would first have to become acquainted empirically with regularities of the kind involved in causal laws. Kant can consistently argue that, even though the necessity and strict generality of laws is something that one would know independently of experience, it is still not possible for us to demonstrate the necessity of such necessary and strictly universal laws. In other words, such rules governing objects of experience would be necessary, but not necessarily necessary.

Now there are passages in Kant's later work that encourage the view that he came to regard all causal laws as knowable a priori:

Even the rules of consistent appearances are only called natural laws (for instance the mechanical ones), if one knows them either really a priori or at least assumes (as in the case of the chemical ones), that they would be known a priori based on objective grounds, if our insight went deep enough. (*Critique of Practical Reason*, Ak. v, p. 26)

Despite some of Kant's claims about the knowability of causal laws, no one has argued to my knowledge that he was committed to the derivability of all causal laws from the category of causation. It has been suggested by Friedman that the basic principles of Newtonian mechanics are thought by Kant to be a priori. According to Friedman, Kant also thought that all more specific physical laws would, in principle, be derivable a priori.[17] Even if Kant was attracted to such a view, he realized that the project of articulating a set of fundamental physical laws would have to count as a regulative principle of inquiry, rather than a goal that was already completed. It thus seems that the necessity and universality of laws would ultimately depend on the necessity for us of projecting a certain systematic unity of nature under laws if we are to regard our judgments about occurrences in nature to be justifiable and, hence, empirical truth to be attainable at all:

One can also not say that it [reason] has previously taken this unity according to principles of reason from the contingent character of nature. For the law of reason to look for it [the unity] is necessary, since without it we would have no reason, without that no connected use of the understanding, and without that no sufficient mark of empirical truth, and therefore in respect to the latter we must presuppose the systematic unity of nature as objectively valid and necessary. (A 651/B 679)

Kant's attempt to ground particular laws of nature in regulative synthetic principles a priori is based on the interest understanding has in postulating an intelligible order of natural laws. In the *Critique of Judgment*, Kant acknowledges that there are an infinite multiplicity of causal laws that we cannot know a priori, although he also maintains that the necessity involved in specific causal laws is a necessity that we must think of as a priori. These two statements are consistent to the extent that one takes causal necessity to be a priori while allowing that we may be incapable of determining a priori what the particular form of that necessity may be in the case of many individual laws. Indeed in the case of the laws of biology, Kant thinks that, in principle, it is impossible for our insight to go deep enough to understand the connection between biological laws and the mechanical laws of physics:

It is quite certain that we can never get a sufficient knowledge of organized beings and their inner possibility, much less explain them, according to mere mechanical principles of nature. So certain is it, that we may confidently assert that it is absurd for human beings to make any such attempt, or to hope that maybe another Newton will some day arise to make intelligible to us even the production of a blade of grass according to natural laws that no design has ordered. Such insight we absolutely deny to humanity. (Ak. v, p. 400)

Elsewhere in the *Critique of Judgment*, Kant also makes the point that organisms resist a purely physicalistic explanation. In this passage, he connects the point directly to the status of different kinds of causal explanation:

It is utterly impossible for human reason (even for any finite reason that might resemble ours in quality, however much it may surpass it in degree), to hope to understand the production even of a blade of grass from merely mechanical causes. For the possibility of such an object, the teleological connection of causes and effects is quite indispensable for judgment, and even if only to study it under the guidance of experience. (Ak. v, pp. 409–410)

Causal laws involve more than generalizations based on accidental regularities. They involve nomic necessities. But we can only know such nomic necessities, according to Kant, when we understand the kind of thing that we are investigating. We must know the dispositions of things belonging to a certain natural kind. That is, we know lawlike necessities when we know what things of a certain kind do under various physically possible circumstances. And we have no way of understanding such dispositions independently of what a thing of a certain kind would do under different circumstances. To understand the behavior of a certain kind of thing under different circumstances we need to be able to formulate a counterfactual conditional of the kind supported by causal laws.

Kant argues that without the supposition that nature divides into natural kinds in a manner susceptible to explanation in terms of the concepts we have, such knowledge of dispositional properties will not be forthcoming. That nature has a systematic unity susceptible to the formulation of hypotheses leading to true theories is an ideal guiding the formulation of empirical concepts of dispositional properties and lawlike causal connection. This transcendental postulate of the systematic unity of nature allows the truth of theories to be tested by a combination of internal coherence and empirical adequacy.

The inductive inference from singular causal judgments to corresponding causal laws must be supported by regulative principles of reason. If the lawlikeness of causal judgments must be supported by regulative principles which are antinomial, if treated as objective laws of unrestricted scope, then this will allow a role in inquiry for probabilistic laws. Kant certainly believes that laws make an implicit claim to unrestricted generality. But he also believes that this claim cannot be made good by us. Although we must strive to unify different causal laws under common principles, Kant believes that there are certain inherent limitations to our capacity to carry out this enterprise. Such an interpretation is suggested by the introductions to the *Critique of Judgment*.

ARE ALL CAUSAL LAWS DETERMINISTIC?

Kant's argument from time-determination to the a priori validity of the causal principle is compatible with the existence of indeterministic causal laws, as well as indeterministic applications of causal laws. Both Melnick and Guyer argue that the existence of statistical laws of nature does not threaten the universality and necessity that Kant attributes to causal laws.[18] This is clearly correct, since he countenances the existence of indeterministic natural laws:

Whatever concept one may hold, from a metaphysical point of view, concerning the freedom of the will, certainly its appearances, which are human actions, like every other natural event are determined according to universal laws. Since the free will of human beings has obvious influence on marriage, births, and deaths, they seem to be subject to no rule by which the numbers of them could be calculated in advance. Yet the annual tables of them in the major countries prove that they occur according to natural laws as stable as the unstable weather, where we cannot predict individual events, but which, in the large, maintains the growth of plants, the flow of rivers, and other natural events in an unbroken, uniform course. ("Idea for a Universal History from a Cosmopolitan Point of View" [1784], Ak. VIII, p. 17)

Kant regards probability as something subjective, roughly the plausibility of a certain hypothesis relative to a certain set of evidence, rather than as an objective property of nature, i.e. chance: "Probability is to be understood as a holding true on the basis of insufficient reasons, which however, have a greater relation to the sufficient ones than the grounds of the opposite" (*Logic*, Ak. IX, p. 81). Given this view of probability there is no reason to think that natural laws cannot be probabilistic. Our judgments about temporal relations and their correlative causal relations are uncertain, because they are subject to error, and so we can expect most of the laws that we formulate concerning causal relations to be inherently probabilistic. It is true that Kant seems to have thought that the fundamental laws of nature would be inherently unprobabilistic, but this is only because he thought they could be known a priori, and he seems to have thought they could be known a priori because he was convinced that we could know a priori that objects have completely determinate trajectories through space and time. This is a plausible assumption. But it is in conflict with the best theory of physical objects that we now have available to us. In quantum mechanics, the classical notion of a trajectory with a completely determinate position and momentum for a particle breaks down at the microphysical level. While quantum mechanics may eventually be replaced by a more fundamental theory that does involve the sharp trajectories of the kind Kant postulates, it is at least equally likely that this indeterminacy will remain in place in future physical theory.

THE COMPATIBILITY OF NATURAL CAUSATION AND
CAUSATION FROM REASON

At the level relevant to the explanation of human action, even Kant seems to think that the causal laws that apply are, at best, probabilistic. At least this is suggested by the passage from the essay on history cited above. Allowing for probabilistic causal laws governing actions helps one to see how he could argue that our actions might all have causal covering laws, and yet be such that they allow for a kind of causation by reason that is independent of natural causal laws. Kant's formulations of the causal principle in both the first and second editions suggest that they are designed to provide leeway with respect to the problem of the compatibility of non-physical causes and physical causal determination. In the first edition of the *Critique* (A 182), he asserts as a "principle of generation" that everything which happens or comes to be presupposes something which it is the consequence of according to a rule. This does not entail the existence of a temporal cause for every occurrence, although that could be understood to be his meaning. It certainly does not entail that we can have knowledge of what the specific cause of an event is. Different causes may be independently sufficient for bringing about a certain event-type, and hence no cause need be a necessary condition for the occurrence of a given event. In the second edition at B 224, the principle is restated in somewhat tighter terms as a principle of temporal succession according to the law of causality. All changes are now said to occur according to the connection of cause and effect. Again, every change must be describable in terms which allow one to identify a cause and an effect. Yet the formulae are compatible with an action being uncaused under a more fundamental description of that action as long as there is a temporal description of that action under which it is caused.

In causation from freedom, or from reason, an intellectual state causes a physical state but is not in turn caused by any antecedent physical state: "if reason has causality in respect to appearances, then it is a faculty *through* which the sensible condition of an empirical series of effects first begins. For the condition that lies in reason is not sensible and does not itself begin" (A 552/B 580). The uncaused event (the event which is the effect of causation through reason) is uncaused under its purely reason-based description, and caused under its description as an event belonging to a determinate temporal order. This leads to the thesis that incompatibilism and compatibilism are compatible so long as we distinguish the two fundamentally different aspects of how things are, namely, things as they must appear to us, and things as they are grasped by reason independently of the way they must appear to us.[19]

Kant's peculiar form of compatibilism is clearly consistent with the idea that every instance of singular causation entails the existence of a causal law which is true of it. Things would be more difficult if Kant were committed to the stronger claim that each individual cause entails a particular causal law. Given that individual causes do not entail the existence of particular causal laws, singular causation can, in some cases at least, consist in the temporal appearance of causation based on reasons for choice that are independent of the agent's causal history. The thesis that every physical event has a sufficient physical cause is compatible with the existence of non-physical events that serve as overdetermining causes of physical events. That is, it allows for the possibility that the occurrence of a physical event could equally well be explained in terms of a non-physical cause.

Interpreters who have been strongly influenced by Donald Davidson's account of free agency have argued that the key to Kant's account of the compatibility of free will and causal determination is that reasons serving as causes, or what Kant calls intelligible causes, provide "rationalizations" for what we do, but are not subject to causal laws.[20] On the view in question, mental events are anomalous, but token–token identical with physical events that are subject to causal laws. Initially, it would seem that this view of mental causation threatens to make all mental events and intelligible causes into mere epiphenomena of physical events. However, this is not so, for the view in question treats causation as an extensional relation. While mental events are only subject to causal laws under a physical description, they are causally efficacious in virtue of their nature as events. This, however, raises the following obvious problem for such a view of mental causation. On the view in question, reasons will be causally efficacious insofar as they are part of a person's psychological make-up. Now, insofar as these reasons are causally efficacious they will also themselves be subject to causal determination by antecedent causes. It is true that we will not be able to come up with causal laws governing such determination under the mental-event description of the event that instantiates a reason. However, such a mental event will belong to the causal order as an event, and, moreover, be token–token identical with a physical event that is subject to causal laws and thus, in principle, subject to deterministic causal laws. So it is hard to see how any progress has been made in rescuing Kant's intuitions about the compatibility of deterministic physical explanation with indeterministic reason-based behavior.

Kant argues that, as long as we are determined by causes that provide the conditions under which we are able to determine the relations between events at different times, we have only "psychological and comparative freedom" which would be nothing better than the "freedom of a turnspit, which also, once it is cranked up, goes through its motion on its own" (*Critique of Practical Reason*, Ak. IV, p. 97). The anomalous monism interpretation of mental-event causation does nothing to help Kant out of the dilemma that psychological freedom seems to be nothing but the freedom of a turnspit or a spiritual automaton. Unlike the anomalous monist, Kant insists that reason has to be genuinely causal in its own right, and not merely in virtue of being realized in the form of the psychological states of some agent, if freedom is to be saved. Now, from the second- or third-person perspective, Kant argues that we must attribute to human beings an empirical character that provides the basis for their choices, where such choices are themselves to be understood as a causal power of reason. But, since the empirical character is itself something that allows of a causal explanation, there can be no freedom:

[I]f we could research all appearances of choice to their ultimate ground, then there would not be a single human action that we could not predict with certainty and could not know with necessity from its preceding conditions. In respect to this empirical character there is therefore no freedom, and we can alone consider human beings according to this character when we merely **observe**, and physiologically investigate the moving causes of this action, as we do in anthropology. (A 550/B 579)

The important point to note is the conditional character of Kant's claim that all human actions would turn out to be completely predictable. We would have to be able to seek out the ultimate grounds of choice in a complete understanding of the person's empirical character and the other relevant causal circumstances, if we were to be able to explain a person's behavior in causal terms. Such a causal explanation is a regulative ideal governed by a principle of reason in our observations of ourselves and others (A 554/B 582). But this does not mean that, even in principle, we could ever have sufficient knowledge to fully carry out the required causal explanation.

A comprehensive explanation of the world is something that we are forced to strive for as rational beings, but it is also something to distrust because we are inherently incapable of realizing it given our finitude. Our reason brings with it the transcendental illusion that, in principle, we could attain such a comprehensive explanation. This illusion that one can provide such a comprehensive explanation is at the basis of his critique of transcendental realism.

Although it looks merely like a chain of causes here that does not allow an *absolute totality* in the regress to its conditions, this concern does not stop us at all; for it is already dealt with in the general consideration of the antinomy of reason. If we give way to the deception of transcendental realism: then neither nature nor freedom remains. (A 543/B 571)

The transcendental realist thinks that, in principle, he or she can presume to have all objects as they must appear to us in experience available to him or her, and then goes on to make inferences about what the world is independently of the way it must appear to us in our experience on the basis of that presumed closure in our knowledge of objects of experience. Kant maintains that the transcendental realist view cannot account for our knowledge of the necessity that laws of nature are supposed to have, and thus cannot account for nature. This might seem to leave the transcendental realist in a better position to deal with the problem of freedom. However, randomness is no more compatible with free agency than is complete causal necessity.

In contrast to the transcendental realist story in question, Kant argues that because our efforts to identify the physical causes not only of what we do, but of anything at all, are always going to be relatively incomplete, there is still always space for an alternative account or description of our action under which the occurrence of an action is explained by the rational principles that we adhere to, rather than by appeal to past facts about our causal history or about the causal history of the world. Causal overdetermination is sufficient to provide an alternative explanation for what the cause of a given event is.

Given the inherent incompleteness of our knowledge of causes, there will always be room both for an account of what we did that is determined by antecedent causal conditions, and an account that treats our adoption of the reasons for action that we adopt as genuinely independent of our past causal history and thus as inherently indeterministic. Kant insists that it is only in the latter case that we can legitimately regard the reasons for our action as ones that initiate a completely new causal series, rather than as mere parts of an ongoing series of causes. This way of resolving the competing claims made by the idea that all events are to be explained on the basis of natural causality and the claim that some are to be explained on the basis of causality from freedom does justice to the antinomial relation that Kant posits between these two ideals of explanation in the Third Antinomy (A 444/B 472 ff.).

SPONTANEITY

In discussing human freedom, and the idea that reason has causality, Kant ascribes to reason the capacity "to make its own order [of events] according to ideas with complete spontaneity, in which it fits in empirical conditions" (A 548/B 576). This complete spontaneity of reason derives from the link of reason with the spontaneity of self-consciousness:

Only a human being who otherwise knows the whole of nature only through the senses, knows [*erkennt*] itself also through mere apperception, and, that is, in actions and inner determinations that it cannot attribute to impressions of the senses, and is admittedly on the one hand a phenomenon, but on the other hand, it is, namely in respect to certain faculties, an intelligible object, since its action cannot be attributed to the receptivity of sensibility. We call these faculties understanding and reason, especially if the latter is properly and emphatically distinguished from all empirically conditioned forces, since it considers its objects merely according to ideas and determines understanding accordingly, which then makes empirical use of its (also pure) concepts. (A 547/B 575)

In claiming that we know ourselves to be intelligible objects through mere apperception, Kant is using knowledge or cognition (*Erkenntnis*) in the general sense that any representation of an object whatsoever may be called a cognition. He is not saying that we judge this to be the case. Instead, we have an immediate consciousness of ourselves in apperception that is independent of any empirical knowledge we may have about who we are. This capacity is the basis upon which our reason can then consider alternative possible causal orders of events with its ideas, which are concepts of totalities of objects. It is also the spontaneity of self-consciousness that allows us to regard our reason as a capacity that is distinct from empirically determined forces, and hence capable of causing events without itself being caused. Thus, the spontaneity of self-consciousness seems to involve a power of acting that is independent of any prior causes.

Kant undeniably distinguishes thought from self-consciousness by its spontaneity, that is, by its activity in contrast to the passivity of sensible experience. The spontaneity of thought that we have as finite rational beings is more restricted than the spontaneity of God with His ability to create things out of nothing. We can only have thoughts and perform actions in relation to information that is somehow given to us. However, it is controversial to what extent the spontaneity of thought is relative to or dependent on experience. Those who see freedom in judgment as relative, note its dependency on information that is simply given to us through our "receptivity." They emphasize the difference between freedom in thought and the full-blown freedom of the will in the Kantian sense that is supposed to be able to allow us to act regardless of the desires and beliefs we may otherwise have.[21] On the other hand, a number of commentators wish to ascribe an absolute spontaneity to us in thought.[22] They point to the close connection between the causality that Kant ascribes to reason, and the spontaneity of self-consciousness.

Significantly, Kant seems to draw the distinction between relative and absolute spontaneity within thought. If one assumes that there is an actual rather than a possible individual that is thinking, then this assumption will depend on experience and places a restriction on the spontaneity of the thought "I think." On the other hand, if one merely explores the analytic entailments of the proposition "I think," then there is no need to appeal to facts of experience at all. Thus, Kant ascribes to thought in its general form a kind of pure spontaneity that is completely independent of the passivity of sense. This purity of spontaneity is based on the fact that thought is exhausted in such cases by its functional role in logical inferences:

Thought, taken on its own, is merely the logical function, hence pure spontaneity of connection of the manifold of a merely possible intuition, and represents the subject of consciousness not at all as appearance, merely for this reason, since it pays no attention to the mode of intuition, whether it is sensible or intellectual. In this way, I do not represent myself either as I am, nor as I appear to myself, but rather I think myself as an object in general from whose intuition I abstract. (B 428–429).

From this passage, it seems safe to conclude that Kant allows for a kind of pure or absolute spontaneity when I think of myself as a thinker in general, a merely possible thinker, and analyze the analytic entailments of this notion of myself as a thinker without appealing to any facts that depend on experience. But Kant also goes on to note that already the proposition "I think," when it makes an existential claim in its assertoric use, "cannot take place without inner sense" and is "no longer mere spontaneity, but also receptivity of intuition" (B 429–430). Whenever the content of what I am judging depends in some way on the way the world actually is, I find myself forced to go outside of the analytic entailments of my concepts. Under those circumstances, I must appeal to my experience of the world. This experience of the world is passive in the sense that it is not completely up to me. I must receive information from the world.

Kant then contrasts the spontaneity of I thoughts that depend on the receptivity of intuition with the spontaneity to be found in morality, noting that in the kind of self-legislation involved in morality "one would discover a spontaneity through which our reality was determinable without needing the conditions of empirical intuition" (B 430). Thus, overall, the passage suggests that the spontaneity of thought is only a relative spontaneity when it depends on empirical facts about the world. It is only absolute spontaneity when it is not concerned with empirical considerations at all. Kant thinks that such complete independence from empirical considerations is characteristic of the moral will and our knowledge of logic.

The best argument for attributing some form of absolute spontaneity to thought even when it is concerned with empirical facts is based on Kant's conviction that the "I think" can accompany any of my representations, apparently regardless of my causal situation. This is a central idea of the Transcendental Deduction. But it is important to note that the "I think" also presupposes that there be something given to me in experience to interpret. This would include all facts about myself as a particular individual. However, if one ascribes absolute spontaneity to the subject, a problem seems to arise concerning the existence of other minds. If each person is absolutely spontaneous in their thoughts, then, in principle, those thoughts are completely independent of any antecedent empirical causal conditions that might govern the thoughts of other persons as well. The implication is that, even if another person's behavior seemed to warrant the ascription of thoughts to that person, I could never be certain that the other person was, in fact, thinking or for that matter a thinking being at all, since there would be no necessary causal connection between behavior of the kind which is usually taken to provide evidence for rationality and the actual existence of rationality. The argument is not decisive against the ascription of absolute spontaneity to thought, but it does seem to require that the manner in which persons appear to us be characterized only by a relative spontaneity that is compatible with causal explanation.

While self-consciousness may be thought of as absolutely spontaneous under a description that is purely first personal, when we turn to the second- and third-person point of view, we can only ascribe relative spontaneity to persons. Now, if one takes the claim of the Third Paralogism in A seriously, a claim I will discuss in the next chapter, the second- or third-person perspective is presupposed in any consciousness of oneself as a distinct individual in time with states of consciousness that have a distinct temporal position. From this, it would seem to follow that I cannot attribute absolute spontaneity to myself as a particular identifiable individual thinker in time. This claim derives further support from Kant's remark in the Antinomy that the observed behavior of an individual must, in principle, be regarded by us as completely predictable.

Kant thinks that there are principles governing the ascription of thoughts to others as well as to myself. But he does not think that we can show that either one's own thoughts or those of others must be as we must all represent them in order to make sense of them. Thus, it is perhaps most plausible to distinguish the relative spontaneity that thinkers have for the purposes of attributing experiences to them from the possible absolute spontaneity they have in themselves. Rational deliberation would be uncaused under the description of persons as things in themselves, but caused under a description of those same persons as objects of our experience.

In this chapter, I have attempted to place specific laws governing substances, causation, and interaction in Kant's scheme for determining the temporal (and spatial) relations between events and our experiences of them. I then attempted to fit Kant's notion of the possibility of causation from freedom into his overall account of action based on causal covering laws. This allows us to make sense of even a relatively strong interpretation of the idea that we are able as thinking beings to respond spontaneously to what we experience.

In the next chapter, I look at the kind of substantive metaphysical claims about the self that the first-person point of view provided by self-consciousness seems to support. I develop Kant's reasons for rejecting the idea that self-consciousness is a substance to which we can ascribe a metaphysical unity and personal identity that is independent of a body.

CHAPTER 8

Self-consciousness and the pseudo-discipline of transcendental psychology

In the last chapter, I noted that Kant takes reason to be concerned with the articulation of a totality of objects that can never be given to us in experience. The problem with the totality of objects in question is that it is nevertheless required by us in order to make sense of experience. This gives rise to what Kant calls a transcendental illusion:

The cause of this [illusion] is that in our reason (regarded subjectively as a human faculty of knowledge) lie basic rules and maxims of their use that have completely the aspect of objective principles and through which it happens that the subjective necessity of a certain connection of our concepts for the sake of our understanding is taken to be an objective necessity concerning the determination of things as they exist in themselves. This illusion is one that is unavoidable. (A 297/B 353)

In this chapter, I propose to look at the manner in which the "I think," "the proposition that expresses self-consciousness" (A 308-309), gives rise to a transcendental illusion that we can develop a "transcendental doctrine of the soul, which is falsely thought to be a science of pure reason concerning the nature of our thinking being" (A 345/B 346). As Descartes, and before him Augustine, noted, in using the expression "cogito," "I think," one cannot fail to refer to oneself as an individual who is thinking. The indubitability of I thoughts in contrast to the dubitability of thoughts about bodies suggested to Descartes the idea of a purely rational discipline based on the *cogito*. In this discipline, developed by Leibniz and Wolff, we seem to be able to articulate and even successfully defend metaphysical claims about the nature of the self based on evidence provided by the *cogito*. Thus, I initially seem to be able correctly to infer from the proposition that I am thinking that I am a thinking substance that has an intrinsic unity to it that must persist across time and be distinguishable from the identity of any body. Kant refers to the discipline in question as "rational psychology" or the pseudo-discipline of transcendental psychology (A 397).

In the Paralogisms of Rational Psychology, Kant is concerned with the kind of false inferences (paralogisms) to substantive facts about our nature as selves from the conditions governing our ability to ascribe thoughts to ourselves and to other rational beings that he takes to be constitutive of rational psychology. He wants to expose the transcendental illusion to which we are necessarily prone in thinking about ourselves as subjects of experience. With respect to the proposition "I think," Kant wants to show that *de dicto* notions of necessity, actuality, and possibility, that is, modal notions that are properties of propositions, or of statements, or sentences that express those propositions, cannot be appealed to in order to support *de re* modalities, that is, necessities, actualities, and possibilities that hold of a thing independently of the way in which we describe the thing. Kant takes the illusions that are generated by our ability to have I thoughts so seriously, because his own work prior to the *Critique* was infected by them.[1] Indeed, many commentators have ascribed views in the rest of the *Critique* to Kant that would seem to be based on paralogistic inferences from the proposition "I think." In particular, a number of commentators have argued that Kant himself illicitly moves from *de dicto* necessity claims about what we can become conscious of through I thoughts to claims of *de re* necessity concerning the objects of our I thoughts, while other commentators have argued that Kant's views are not as different from those of rationalists such as Descartes, Leibniz and Wolff as they initially seem to be.[2]

At first, a critique of rational psychology really seems to be inconsistent with Kant's own project of articulating a priori constraints on experience based on the possibility of becoming conscious of the different individual experiences that make up our experience as a whole. There is, however, an important difference between providing an a priori theory of the self and providing an a priori theory of the constraints imposed on our experience by the possibility of self-consciousness. If our self-consciousness imposes a priori constraints on the way we experience objects, then we will experience objects in accordance with those constraints. This does not imply that we have any knowledge of the way the self must be independently of such constraints on how we must represent the self. Kant's target in the Paralogisms is the view that we know the way the self is in itself. This would be to know the self in a manner that is independent of the way in which we must represent the self in order to ascribe thoughts to individuals.

THINKING OF ONESELF AND OTHERS AS THINKERS

Kant takes the Cartesian *cogito* as the starting-point for his reflections on the nature of self-consciousness and the self as it presents itself to self-consciousness. With Descartes, Kant notes that the self-consciousness expressed in the thought "I am thinking" has existential import and is self-verifying at the time the proposition expressed by the thought "I am thinking" is asserted by me. The referential force of the proposition "I think" is based on the empirical fact that I am thinking provided by inner perception. And "this inner perception is nothing more than the mere apperception: *I think*" (A 343/B 401). Taken in this sense, which Kant refers to as the assertoric use of the expression "I think," "the I think, is, as was already said, an empirical proposition, and contains the proposition, I exist, in itself" (B 422). There is, however, another sense in which the thought that I am thinking may be understood. Kant refers to the usage in question as taking the proposition "I think" "problematically":

Now I cannot have any representation whatsoever of a thinking being, through any outer experience, but only through self-consciousness. Objects of this kind are therefore nothing more than the transference of this consciousness of mine to other things, which in this way alone can be represented as thinking beings. The proposition: I think, is taken merely problematically here; not insofar as it contains a perception of existence (the Cartesian *cogito ergo sum*) but rather according to its mere possibility in order to see which properties might flow from this so simple proposition to its subject (whether it exists or not). (A 347/B 405)

When I use the proposition "I think" "problematically," the proposition "I think" is merely entertained as a possible thought, it is not actually asserted. Initially, it is unclear how such a problematic use of the statement "I think" is possible. The self-validating character of I thoughts to which Descartes appeals gives rise to difficulties here. There seems to be a (pragmatically) necessary connection between the conditions under which one can entertain the proposition "I think" and the conditions under which the assertion is true that I am thinking. It thus seems to be impossible for the proposition "I think" to be entertained without the proposition actually being true in virtue of being entertained. It then seems possible to infer that the constraints governing the ascription of thoughts to oneself and to others have the same self-validating character that is characteristic of the assertion "I think":

It must seem odd right away that the condition under which I can think at all, and that is therefore merely a property of my subject should be valid for everything that thinks, and that we can abrogate the right to base an apodictic and universal judgment on a seemingly empirical proposition, namely that everything that thinks is such as the expression of self-consciousness says it to be in me. The cause of this seems to lie in the following: that we must ascribe to things a priori all those properties that make up the conditions under which we can alone think them. (A 346/B 404)

Kant assumes with rationalist philosophers that our only grip on the notion of a thinker is based on our ability to ascribe to such a thinker a point of view that is like our own in the sense that we could conceive of ourselves as being able to take up the point of view of such a creature. However, this very process of transference that is the key to representing other minds allows us to understand what it might mean for me to represent myself as a thinker from whose actual existence I abstract. From the fact that I can think of someone else thinking, it does not follow that such a person actually exists. In thinking of another being as one of us, we think of that being as having a point of view that, in principle, is intelligible to us, and that could even have been our own had our history been sufficiently different.

In the feat of transference involved in thinking of what it would be like for *me* to understand or perceive the world from a different vantage-point I am no longer using the "I" that is represented by me in such transference to refer to an actual particular individual. I am using the expression "I think" *counterfactually*, or as Kant puts it "problematically," since I am thinking of what it would be like to represent the world from the point of view of that rational being.

In order for me to represent a point of view that might have been my own, but is not in fact my own, I must be thinking of myself in a quite attenuated way. In counterfactual self-reference, I am not referring to myself as the particular individual who I am. I cannot as a particular individual be identical with another individual, since each thing is that thing and not some other thing. Although I am still thinking of a permutation of myself, it is important to note that I am not thinking that Pierre Keller might be identical with Charles de Gaulle or the Red King, which would violate the principle of identity. The temptation is to think that I am then a thinking being that is no particular thinking being. This leads me to conclude that I have grasped what is essential to the very existence and nature of a thinking being, whereas in fact I have merely come to see what is required in order for me to think of another being as a thinker.

When I think of different alternative counterparts to myself in different possible experiences, I think of myself as a subject of experience that functions in a way analogous to a variable = x for which I can then substitute different individual constants. This is what Kant calls the representation of "a transcendental subject 'of thought = x" by means of the "simple and for itself completely empty of content representation: **I**" (A 346/B 404). I can think that I might have been Charles de Gaulle or the Red King rather than Pierre Keller. I am neither asserting that I as this particular individual exist nor that the other individual actually exists. Since I can interpret myself as a potential point of view among other possible points of view, I can even think of what it *would* be like to be conscious of myself as I am. Counterfactual self-reference applies not only to the thought of my being somebody else, but also to the thought of my having a particular possible point of view. While we can say that such counterfactual reference to ourselves underlies our understanding of others as rational beings, and even of ourselves, we cannot therefore conclude that we have the kind of natures as rational beings that such counterfactual reference to ourselves seems to suggest that we have.

In ascribing thoughts to others on the basis of the first-person perspective expressed by the statement "I think," I have effectively severed the thought "I think" from the pragmatic conditions of use that guarantee that the proposition it expresses is true. This means that I cannot take a logical analysis of the conceptual entailments of the proposition "I think" to tell me substantive metaphysical truths about the nature of thinking beings. It is not that my concept of a thinker is clearly an illegitimate one. It is just that it is my or our concept of a thinker. A certain concept may well be the only one we have available to us. But we are not therefore entitled to say that the only way the thing could be is the way that we must capture with our concept of the thing in question. So I cannot assume that the conditions governing my ascription of thoughts to rational beings must mirror the intrinsic nature of rational beings.

There is a strong temptation to think that one can establish substantive claims about the way all rational beings must be from the conditions under which we are compelled to ascribe rationality to ourselves and others. Succumbing to the temptation leads to what Kant calls a "transcendental use of the understanding" (A 348/B 406). By abstracting from the empirical conditions under which we use concepts, the putative use of concepts in question runs together our concept of a certain object with the inherent nature of that object (A 247/B 304). The temptation arises because of the link that holds for us between self-consciousness and our understanding of what it is to be rational. The temptation becomes compelling if one fails to distinguish the actual from the counterfactual form of self-reference. For then we seem to be able to infer how rational beings in general must be from the manner in which we are conscious of ourselves.

The connection between self-consciousness and rationality suggests that in articulating the structure of self-consciousness we are also articulating the nature of a rational being. But Kant insists that the "I think" is something that we must regard as a "*merely subjective condition*" of knowledge which we are prone to regard as a way of understanding the nature of rational beings:

> [T]he formal proposition of apperception: I think which proposition is admittedly no experience, but rather the form of apperception belonging to and preceding every experience, is to be regarded always only in respect to possible cognition in general as a *merely subjective condition* of it, that we wrongly make into a condition of the possibility of objects, namely into the *concept* of a thinking being in general, since we can only represent such beings by placing the formula of our consciousness in the place of every other rational being. (A 355)

There is a natural and, indeed, to some extent unavoidable tendency to confuse the conditions under which we make sense of rational beings with the conditions under which such beings can exist at all. The bearer of representations when represented as a self (as a representer conscious of being a representer) must be represented from the first-person point of view. This strongly suggests that the way the self is represented from the first-person point of view displays necessary facts about the bearer of that point of view. But these putatively necessary facts turn out to be nothing but artefacts of the way we must think of those to whom we ascribe rationality.

WHAT ARE THE PARALOGISMS?

Kant works through four different ways in which each of us as subjects of self-consciousness must represent ourselves. These four different ways of representing ourselves seem to verify themselves in any self-consciousness: (1) We are conscious of ourselves as basic subjects or substances. In self-consciousness we are conscious of whatever or whoever it is that has such self-consciousness. We cannot fail to refer to the bearer of self-consciousness in self-consciousness. (2) We are conscious of ourselves as absolutely unitary (as simple), that is, as individual egos. For we are conscious of ourselves as subjects of self-consciousness, as egos, that cannot be a mere collection of different subjects. (3) We are conscious of ourselves as being numerically identical selves in all our experiences of which we are conscious. For this is what it means to say of all these experiences that we are conscious of them as our own. Finally, (4) we are conscious of ourselves as being in a cognitive relation to possible objects that are external to us. For it is only in relation to these external objects that we think of ourselves as distinct individuals.

Kant argues that there are four aspects of self-consciousness that give rise to four natural fallacies concerning the nature of the self. It is these fallacies that underlie traditional metaphysics of the soul (self). It seems possible to infer the substantiality, simplicity, identity over all time, and independence of the self, from an analysis of the proposition "I think," since this proposition is a condition under which we ascribe thoughts to ourselves and others, and thus think of each other as thinking beings endowed with a self.

Kant diagnoses the four basic paralogisms of rational psychology as fallacies of ambiguity (*sophismata figurae dictionis*: A 402; B 411) that are based on a confusion of the problematic use of the proposition "I think" with the assertoric use of that proposition. The major premise of the syllogism lays out a definition of what it is to be a substance, a simple thing, a person, and a thing the existence of which is doubtful. Now, in a certain sense "the proposition that expresses self-consciousness: I think" (A 399) refers to something that satisfies the definition of what a substance, etc. is. For Kant insists that "the mere apperception (I) [is] substance in concept, simple in concept, etc." (A 400). In other words, apperception is the expression of the proposition "I think." And this proposition "I think" analytically entails that I am the absolute subject of my thoughts, that I am a single subject that has an intrinsic unity to it that I can call simplicity, that I am numerically identical over my different thoughts, and that I can distinguish myself as thinker from other things outside of my thought (see especially B 407ff.). Thus, the minor premise of the syllogistic inferences that Kant ascribes to rational psychology seems to be able to draw on the self-verifying and empirical claim that I am thinking in its claim that I have an existence that corresponds to the definition of substance, etc. The conclusion is then the claim that I am a substance, etc. However, the minor premise draws its support for the claim that I am a substance, etc. from the way I must think of myself and think of others in order to be able to think of us as thinkers at all. In other words, the minor premise depends on the problematic use of the expression "I think," which does not support bona fide existential claims, while presenting itself as based on the self-verifying status of the assertoric use of the expression "I think." The subtle mistake that underlies transcendental psychology is to conclude from the fact that the formal definition of substance, etc. is satisfied by the way in which each of us is compelled to think of him- or herself and others that each of us therefore knows that he or she and other thinkers are substances, etc.

The second edition of the Paralogisms clarifies the nature of the fallacy of ambiguity involved in the paralogistic inferences of transcendental psychology:

Thought is taken in both premises in a totally different meaning: in the major proposition as it applies to objects in general (hence as it may be given in intuition); but in the minor proposition as it subsists in relation to self-consciousness, whereby no object is thought, but only the relation to oneself < *Sich* [*sic*] >, as subject (as the form of thought) is represented. (B 411)

The major premise applies to all thinking beings regardless of how they are thought to be. It is explicitly said to include thinking beings that are given to us as objects of knowledge through intuition. It is a premise that is analytically true, since it merely analyzes the meaning of "substance," "simple things," "personal identity," or "external things." In the minor premise, thinking beings are taken only as they are available to us subjectively through our thoughts of ourselves. Due to the ineliminability of the first-person point of view, it is then tempting to infer that this description applies to oneself and others not just *as we must think of ourselves*, but without restriction.

In effect, the Paralogisms are based on running together two different senses in which thoughts about thinkers may be abstract. In the first case, thoughts are abstract in the sense that they apply to objects in general, absolutely all objects. This is the sense required in order to make substantive claims about thinking beings. This is a "transcendental use" of the notion of thought, that is, a use of something that serves as a condition for our experience as if the object that conformed to that condition could be given independently of our experience. It is an illegitimate extension from a definitional or purely logical use of thought. But, in ascribing thoughts, we are abstracting from facts about particular thinkers in a different way. We are thinking of them in terms of the conditions under which we ascribe thoughts to them. This does not license us to make claims about the way thinkers are in general, and in abstraction from the way we must think of them. Thus, it does not underwrite claims about how thinkers are in themselves.

The subject as represented in self-consciousness is not an object in the proper sense at all. It makes no sense to say that one might fail to be conscious of *oneself*, since this self is an internal accusative of self-consciousness. It does, however, make sense to say that one might fail to know who one is, as one can see from cases of amnesia. When I am conscious of myself merely as subject of self-consciousness, there is no room for reference failure. It is as some particular individual (as an object) that "I" can fail to refer to myself. Since such an object must be identifiable, the identification of who the subject is, as a certain particular (object), may fail. The "I" serves as its own formal object, but when I think of myself as this formal object I am actually abstracting from all objects in the normal sense of the word. Although "I" or rather "me" (its accusative form) serves as the grammatical object of consciousness, it need not correspond to any publicly identifiable or reidentifiable object.[3] Non-identificatory self-consciousness does not provide access to the self under any particular description. If one is self-conscious, one must refer to oneself. One also has a belief about a particular object. But the object of one's belief may not be the actual bearer of self-consciousness and thus it may not be the self to which one is referring in self-consciousness.

THE FIRST PARALOGISM

The second edition of the *Critique* provides only one explicit example of a paralogism, which apparently serves as a paradigm for how the others are to be reconstructed. It involves the notion of substance: (1) "That which cannot be thought other than as subject, exists in no other way than as subject and is therefore substance." (2) "Now a thinking being merely regarded as such cannot be thought of other than as subject." (3) "Therefore it exists also only as such, i.e. as substance" (B 410–411). The example displays the shift in scope that Kant takes to be characteristic of a paralogism in the second edition. We begin with an analytic principle that is little more than a nominal definition of substance. In the minor premise, we move to a principle expressing what is involved in our conception of a thinking being as such. However, in the conclusion, the restriction in the minor premise to the thought of a thinker as a thinker is ignored. Ignoring the restriction leads to the assertion of a synthetic proposition a priori on the basis of a definitional claim about the nature of substance and a claim about what the conditions are under which we think of ourselves and others as thinkers.

The basic problem with the argument is that it involves a fallacy of ambiguity. We begin with the idea that something that can be made sense of only as a subject, that is as a bearer of properties, is a substance. Then the Cartesian premise is introduced that a thinking being thought of *as a thinking being* can only be thought of as a bearer of thoughts. The restriction in the minor premise to thinking beings thought of *as* thinking beings is then dropped. Dropping the restriction leads to the fallacious conclusion that a thinking being can only be regarded as a subject of thought or bearer of thoughts. The problem is that a being might be a thinker without being essentially a thinker. Thinking might be only a derivative and non-essential property of the actual individual who thinks. The basicness of I representations to thought encourages one to assume that I am also ontologically basic as a thinker. The inference to my being ontologically basic is based on confounding the way I must represent myself as subject of judgment and of thought with the actual bearer of I thoughts.

Kant notes that "I" is a singular term that cannot be used as a predicative term. The fact that "I" can only be used as a singular term suggests that "I" refers to a substance, since a substance is precisely what one refers to by means of a singular term that is not predicated of other things, as general predicative terms may be. The "I" as subject of thought is a basic singular representation which cannot serve as a general representation that could be predicated of some more basic particular. Since the logical subject of the judgment is, in this case, a thinker, "I as thinking being," it seems to be licit to move from the logical basicness of the I representation to an assertion of the ontological basicness of me as a thinker. For here it is not just a linguistic expression which is the subject of the judgment, but a thinker, the subject of self-consciousness.

The inference in question is based on a use-mention fallacy. For it is still not acceptable to move from what is true of a representation of self in self-consciousness and thought to a claim about the bearer of that self-consciousness. I thoughts are logically basic as representations of whatever it is that is doing the thinking, but one cannot legitimately infer from this logical basicness of I thoughts that thinkers *qua* thinkers are basic particulars. Thus, while it is true that I must represent myself as a substance or basic particular when I think of myself as someone that thinks, it does not follow from the fact that I must represent myself as a subject that I know any substantive facts about the nature of the individual to which I refer in thought.

There is a trivial sense in which the self or thinker *qua* thinker may be said to be a substance. The self is an absolute subject of thought in the sense that it is whatever is represented *as* the bearer of thought. But this sense in which the self or thinker fits the definition of a substance, is an artefact of the first-person point of view:

Now in all our thought the *I* is the subject, in which thoughts only inhere as determinations, and this *I* cannot be used as the determination of another thing. Therefore everyone must necessarily regard himself < *Sich* [*sic*] *selbst* > as substance, and thought only as accidents of his existence, and determinations of his state. (A 349)

Since I represent the ultimate bearer of thought by means of the expression "I think," it is tempting to think that I as thinker must be the ultimate bearer of my thoughts. From this it would seem to follow that I as substance must be a thinking being. According to this non-trivial or substantive sense of substance, the real bearer, represented by "I," is essentially characterized as an ego or thinking substance. The important thing to note is that "*I*" who I think must be valid as *subject* and be regarded as something that cannot belong to thought merely as predicate is an apodeictic and even *identical proposition*; but it does not mean that I as *object* am a *being* subsisting for myself alone, or *substance*" (B 406).

In his Second Meditation, Descartes notoriously infers that the soul is a substance in the metaphysically interesting sense from the fact that it is a "substance" in the trivial one of being a self-conscious representer that is certain of its existence. Descartes argues from the certainty of *cogito* statements that thought is an essential property of me as a thinking being. He also argues independently that thought is not an essential property of body. From this he deduces that I as a thinking being have a property that my body lacks. This is the property of being essentially a thinker. And from this he concludes that there is a real distinction between me and my soul on the one hand, and my body, on the other. In the *Search for Truth*, Descartes develops the argument as follows:

Indeed, I do not even know whether I have a body; you have shown me that it is possible to doubt it. I might add that I cannot deny absolutely that I have a body. Yet even if we keep all these suppositions intact, this will not prevent me from being certain that I exist. On the contrary, these suppositions simply strengthen the certainty of my conviction that I exist and am not a body. Otherwise, if I had doubts about my body, I would also have doubts about myself, and I cannot have doubts about that. I am absolutely convinced that I exist, so convinced that it is totally impossible for me to doubt it.[4]

Kant's objection to the Cartesian claim about the nature of the soul is that it moves from the way one "must necessarily regard" oneself to the way one must be independently of being so regarded, that is, it shifts between a subjective necessity concerning the way things must be described by us to a *de re* necessity about the way things themselves must be. The self must be regarded as a substance, but in the sense that the ego to which one ultimately refers must be regarded as the real bearer of one's thoughts. Self-consciousness *per se* tells us nothing about the nature of the metaphysical relation between the ultimate bearer of thought and the representation "I" which we use to refer to that bearer of thought. For, in self-consciousness, I abstract from any knowledge of who the real bearer of my thoughts is, and regard myself purely as the point of view to which I ascribe different representations. The temptation, however, is to think that because one can think of a subject of thought in abstraction from its particular representations that one therefore has a grip on some real bearer that exists independently of all the representations that we may ascribe to it:

I think of myself for the sake of a possible experience by abstracting from all real experience and infer that I can be conscious of my existence also outside of experience and its empirical conditions. Therefore I conflate the possible *abstraction* of my empirically determined existence with the alleged consciousness of a *separate* existence of my thinking self, and believe that I *know* the substantial in me as the transcendental subject, while I merely have the unity of consciousness in thought that underlies all determination as mere form of cognition. (B 427)

THE THIRD PARALOGISM

In the Third Paralogism, Kant makes use of the relation of the mental to the physical as it presents itself to our experience from the first- and the third-person points of view to call into question traditional arguments for the persistence of the soul.[5] The first-person point of view of self-consciousness presents one to oneself as a thinker endowed with numerical identity over the times of which one is conscious. This seems to satisfy the definition of a person endowed with numerical identity. It is an analytic truth that, if one ascribes a sequence of beliefs or other representational states to oneself, one also believes that one is ascribing those representations to one and the same self. This is a feature of first-person self-reference, but it is dependent on taking a first-person point of view. Certainly, one must take a first-person point of view, but there may well be competing first-person points of view. The fact that these points of view compete with one another is disclosed by differences in the content of what they represent. Each of us represents the world from a different sequence of spatio-temporal positions. The different ways in which things appear to those positions give rise to competing conceptions of the unity of experience.

To think of oneself as *a* self, one must take oneself to be the same self through whatever set of experiences one ascribes to oneself. There has to be a single subject that represents a series of experiences to itself if those experiences are to be represented as part of a single experience: "On this basis the personality of the soul would have to be [*müßte*] regarded not even as inferred, but as a completely identical proposition of self-consciousness in time" (A 362). The basis in question is the way I relate all my inner states to my self.

With rationalist philosophers, Kant defines the soul as that which is conscious of the numerical identity of its self through different times. This provides the major premise for a syllogism. The minor premise of the syllogism then takes the soul to be a person as defined in the first premise, but the soul must be a person in this sense only from the first-person point of view. The fallacy of ambiguity involved in the Third Paralogism is again to take what is true from the first-person point of view and treat it as if it were true from any point of view, that is, as if it were true absolutely. This leads to the conclusion that the soul is a person in the sense of a particular that persists through different times and is conscious of that persistence.

The analytic truth that I must be conscious of my identity through all the states of which I am conscious is not clearly distinguished by Kant from another idea. This is the idea that one must be able to conceive of a standpoint that is not itself being successively replaced by some other standpoint in order to have a conception of succession itself. It is one thing to say that I am conscious of my identity through all the times in which I am conscious of myself. It is quite another for me to assume that there is a numerically identical self in all time: "I relate any and all of my successive determinations to the numerically identical self in all time, that is in the form of the inner intuition of myself" (A 362). Kant offers no argument for this strong claim.

There is an argument available to Kant for the strong claim that suggests itself from the First Analogy and its connection with the Transcendental Deduction. Succession requires one item to succeed or replace another item relative to something else that is not itself undergoing replacement. Thus, if one is to be conscious of succession, one needs to be conscious of a point of view that is not replaced in that succession. If I am to be conscious of successive states as successive, I must be able to order these states in time. But, in order to be able to set up a temporal ordering, I must be able to represent the temporal relations that constitute the form of inner representation in a way that purports to be independent of the way things merely appear to me now. I must be able to represent temporal relations in tenseless terms. To do this, I must be able to think of myself as being able to shift from one possible temporal position to the other.

To perform the kind of transference of the first perspective required to ascribe rationality, my consciousness of myself must, in a certain sense, be immune to reference failure by virtue of misidentification, that is, in being conscious of myself it cannot happen that I fail to refer to myself, and instead refer to someone else.[6] This immunity to reference failure allows me to contemplate alternative possibilities of how *my* life might have gone or even of who else *I* might have become. But this immunity to reference failure extends only to the use of "I" to refer to my representation of myself as a thinker, it does not guarantee my personal identity in a sense that satisfies third-person criteria.

I may be constrained to think of myself as identical through the experiences that I ascribe to myself, but my individual personal identity as it exists through a series of representational states is clearly something that can only be *known* from experience, indeed, through knowledge of my inner states underwritten by the identity of my human body over time: "the persistence of the soul, as a mere object of inner sense is unproved, and even unprovable, although its persistence in life is for itself clear, since the thinking being (as human being) is also an object of outer sense" (B 415). Personal identity is not something that can be inferred from the kind of self-consciousness expressed in the statement "I think" alone, even though I can legitimately claim that I am conscious of my identity as a subject through all those experiences of which I am conscious of myself (B 408):

The proposition of the identity of myself in respect to all manifolds of which I am conscious is also a proposition that lies in the concepts themselves, that is, an analytic proposition; but this identity of the subject of which I can become conscious in all its representations does not pertain to the intuition of that subject as it is given as an object, it can therefore not also mean the identity of the person for which to prove it the mere analysis of the proposition I think is not enough, but different synthetic judgments that are based on given intuition would be required. (B 408–409)

The necessity of the possibility of the kind of self-transferral involved in my being able to think of myself from different temporal positions can easily seem like an argument for the necessity of my actually existing at all of these different times. As an experiencer, my numerical identity would have to be taken as a basic given of experience. This leads to the temptation to argue from the first-person phenomenology of personal identity and survival to claims about the survival of my soul. From the first-person point of view of my time-consciousness, it makes no differ- ence whether I think of the time of my experience as belonging to the unity of my experience or whether I think of the unity of my experience as belonging to the unitary time in question:

For it really says nothing more than that in the whole time in which I am conscious of myself, I am conscious of this time as belonging to the unity of my self and it is the same thing whether I say: this whole time is in Me as an individual unity or I am to be found in all this time with numerical identity. Personal identity is therefore unfailingly to be found in my own conscious- ness. (A 361–362)

As long as we restrict ourselves to the first-person point of view, there is no distinction to be drawn between the way the different states of my life present themselves to me and the way that they really are. There is therefore no distinction to be drawn between the temporal order in which my different experiences present themselves to me and the actual temporal order of those different experiences. I am conscious of my numerical identity through the time in question because that time is the time of my time-consciousness. No distinction has yet been drawn between subjective and objective time, or between my subjective time and the subjective time constituted by another point of view.

Kant argues plausibly that the possibility of a second- or third-person perspective must become apparent to me before I can have a grip on the distinction between the temporal order in which things present them- selves to my self-consciousness and the temporal order in which they actually occur. It is only if one can conceive of a perspective different from the one which one actually has that one can understand the relativity of one's own perspective. One's very understanding of one's own personal identity thus depends on one's ability to perform the kind of feat of transference in terms of which one understands other persons.

From the purely first-person perspective, there does not seem to be any way of drawing a distinction between one's representation of one's identity over time and one's actual identity over time. In order to get a feel for this distinction, one must be able to shift from the first- to the second- or to the third-person perspective. Inner experience is, for Kant, essentially temporal. Mental states are constantly being replaced by other mental states. In immediate experience, no distinction is needed or drawn between a successive consciousness of inner states and a consciousness of inner states in succession. Although I relate all my successive states to a numerically identical self, it is not clear what is numerically identical here, nor can it be until I have been able to draw the distinction between the perspective of a representer and what is represented by the representer. I do not have full-blown consciousness of myself as an object of temporal experience until I am able to draw that distinction.

This is why I need to be able to take the perspective of an external observer in order to place myself in time. The vantage-point of the external observer is thus one which I myself must occupy in order to be aware of myself *as* an object of inner sense: "If I regard myself from the perspective of another (as the object of his external intuition), then this external observer considers *me* for the first time *in time*, for in apperception *time* is only actually represented *in me*" (A 363).[7] Kant makes the point somewhat less explicitly in the second edition: "Neither can the subject in which the representation of time has its original ground, determine its own existence through that [pure self-consciousness]" (B 422).

By taking up the perspective of a second person I am forced to represent myself in a different way. I have first-person access to my own representations, but another person's access to my inner states depends on inference. Such inferences are based on my outer states. This is why the states in question are considered to be inner and outer respectively. We represent outer states spatially, just as we represent inner states temporally. The other person must think of me as an embodied self, i.e. an object of external intuition (spatial representation). The only clear notion we have of being outside of something else involves something being in a spatial relation to something else. But as long as we have no distinction between inner and outer states we also have no way of representing the difference between a subjective and an objective time-series.

The point of view of the outside observer is not necessarily that of an objective time-series. The point of view of the outside observer may be just another subjective time-series, that is, another sequence of points of view:

For in that case the time in which the observer places me is not the one to be encountered in my sensibility but the one to be encountered in his sensibility, therefore the identity that is necessarily connected with my consciousness is not therefore [necessarily] connected with his, that is, with the external intuition of my subject. (A 363)

There is no way for me to think of my persistence as an individual as something distinguishable from the way I view my own history, as long as the only take on my experience that I have is first personal. In fact, I do not even have the full notion of what it is for something to belong to my own point of view, since I have no notion yet of another possible history with a point of view which is distinct from my own. By looking at myself from an outside spatial perspective, I come to see that my consciousness of my numerical identity does not entail that I am a numerically identical individual. As I think of myself from this third-person point of view, I come to see that the temporal series making up my inner experience may be unique, but it is unique precisely because it can be distinguished from that of other possible persons.

In a discussion, for instance, my knowledge of what I am now thinking precedes my knowledge of what someone else is now thinking, but the other person's knowledge of what s/he is now thinking precedes his or her knowledge of what I am now thinking. Different subjects may and often do represent the states of the same particular as temporally ordered in a way which is inconsistent one with the other. Reflection on this standpoint dependence of one's beliefs can lead one even to question one's own belief in one's persistence over time. Taking the perspective of another allows me to grasp the distinction between the self-identity built into my first-person perspective and my persistent existence as a particular individual.

The potential or actual existence of different sets of experiential episodes in different observers outside of me leads me to the idea of different competing temporal series. This suggests to me that my consciousness of my numerical identity through the temporal series of my experiences need not entail "the objective permanence of my self" (A 363). It is now apparent why Kant does not attempt to introduce an objective concept of time. The time to which we are referring, even when we look at things from the vantage-point of an outside observer, is just a further subjective time. The possibility of an alternative subjective time-series is already enough to make room for the distinction between the unity of time-consciousness that is necessary to the having of a point of view at all and the particular standpoint-dependent unity that characterizes different empirical knowers. This is because it already provides one with the possibility of contrasting the way things look from one's own perspective with the way they look from some other possible perspective. This other possible perspective leads to questions about how I could determine my personal identity over time.

The second- and third-person perspectives open up the possibility that my first-person perspective might be delusive and thus reveal to me that "the identity of the consciousness of myself in different times is only a formal condition of my thoughts and their connection" (A 363). I cannot therefore infer "the numerical identity of my subject" from the fact that I can use the same expression "I" to refer to my different states. Kant presses the point home about the defeasibility of first-person ascriptions by noting that my first-person take on my personal identity is based on my consciousness, and my consciousness of the past is based on my memories. While these memories cannot seem to me to be delusive, they might, in fact, turn out to be delusive. There might be a deviant chain of representations linking some of my memories to past occurrences. My memories of the past might have been taken over from other individuals, so that I was really only the last of a series of individual persons or person-stages: "The last substance would be conscious of all of the states of the substances changed before it as its own, since they would have been transferred to it with the consciousness of them, and yet it would not have been the same person in all these states" (A 364n). In such circumstances, one would have only a delusive quasi-memory rather than a bona fide memory of something that one believes to have happened to one.[8] The androids in the movie *Blade Runner* have such delusive quasi-memories. They have quasi-memories of a past that was not theirs, of a childhood which they never lived through. But we need not go so far afield. There is strong evidence that one can induce false memories in others which lead them to believe that they have had a different past than their actual one.[9]

Now, if the first-person point of view needs correction from a possible second- or third-person perspective, we cannot infer that we as individuals are identical over time from the data provided to us by consciousness and memory. So we certainly cannot infer that we are persons that exist forever from our inability to experience our own beginning in birth or ending in death. Thus, Kant's argument raises questions about any effort to take the consciousness of my identity over time as an indication that I am a person in the sense of a sempiternal substance that is conscious of its existence throughout time.

While the phenomenon of temporal succession leads Descartes and Leibniz to ascribe maximal certainty to self-ascriptions of actual occurrent cognitive states, philosophers such as Descartes and Leibniz were also attracted to the idea that the self is a sempiternal substance to which we have access through self-consciousness. The temporal implications of self-consciousness are most obvious with respect to Leibniz. Leibniz believed that in self-consciousness I have a somewhat unclear and indistinct grasp of the concept of my personal identity (of my individual essence). It is unclear because I may not be able to distinguish myself from others and it is indistinct because I am not able to give a complete analysis of my experience. But this concept of my personal identity includes everything that has ever, does, or will ever happen to me. From Kant's point of view, Leibniz assimilates the necessity that all represented be think*able* by the "I" to the thesis that there must be a soul which persists through all changes in experiences. Kant thinks that this is just what is going on in Leibniz's notion of the "I" as a simple substance which contains within itself the ontological basis for a complete time-series.

Kant wants to argue that, from Leibniz's standpoint, self-consciousness itself provides all that we need in order to know that we are each principles of change from which all the events in a particular time-series may be understood. While knowledge of the concept of a person would have to be provided for us by the reason that we have in virtue of being self-conscious individuals, once we were able to make our concept of ourselves clear and distinct, it would be enough to analyze the concept in order to know everything there was to know about me or you. It is far from obvious that "rationalist" thinkers, such as Leibniz, thought of the kind of reasoning required to see such consequences as the derivation of analytic entailments in Kant's sense of the word.[10] However, it is also unclear how Leibniz actually proposes to make sense of the concept of an individual, as he understands it. For all true propositions regarding the whole history of that individual are supposed to be entailed by the concept of that individual. One problem is that we do not actually have knowledge of such a complete concept for any individual. The problem also goes deeper. For it is not clear that we even understand what such a concept could be. This problem is reflected in the very idea of the identity of an individual as Leibniz understands that identity. For Leibniz, the content that distinguishes individual simple substances from each other consists ultimately in the differential way in which they represent other creatures representing them. With some justice, Kant can argue that Leibniz has no real way of giving any clear non-metaphorical sense to the different (non spatio-temporal) points of view of those representers that Leibniz must invoke to make sense of the differences in representational content that are supposed to individuate different simple substances. If we cannot make sense of those differences between simple substances and the different states of simple substances in their own right, we will also not be able to make sense of the idea of a spatio-temporal history corresponding to the different representations. Kant thinks that Leibniz falls into this difficulty because he attempts to draw metaphysical conclusions from the way objects must be represented from the first-person point of view belonging to self-consciousness.

Kant is not only interested in blocking any assumptions about the immortality of the soul that may seem to follow from my consciousness of my identity through time, he also argues for a restriction on our ability to have even phenomenal knowledge of the persistence of the self. Where the numerical identity of matter is concerned, direct observation from a third-person perspective seems to be possible. So we seem to have knowledge of the persistence of bits of matter. Even here there are difficulties. The medium size material objects that are our immediate objects of observation are persistent, but they are not themselves permanent even by the lights of Kant's theory. In the case of the self, there is a further complication. One must already put oneself in the position of another in order to ascribe consciousness to some other person. The actual ascription of conscious states to the other presupposes a shift to a third-person perspective that is itself inherently infected with the first-person point of view. This precludes one from having any immediate access to the other person's existence as a persistent entity.

The only thing that one can observe to be persistent is the other person's body. The precise relation of that body to the other person is quite a problematic matter. No empirical evidence seems to force us to identify the identity of the person with the identity of that persisting body, however plausible it is to do so. The persistence of a body is only contingently related to the possession of a numerically identical point of view which forms the basis for our ascription of personal identity to the other person. Given the fallibility of memory, this means that the persistence of a body may be the best criterion of personal identity that we have, but one the satisfaction of which provides no logically compelling guarantee of personal identity.

Once it becomes apparent that Kant does not intend to recognize any public knowledge of the persistence of the self, then his failure to introduce public time into his discussion of the role of the outside observer begins to make sense. Nor is this failure to recognize a public notion of inner time-consciousness an accident. Kant's general tact is to deny that inner experience can on its own provide any objective knowledge. In order to know objective facts, we must appeal to the behavior of physical objects in space. Our knowledge of public facts depends on our knowledge of external objects.

CHAPTER 9

How independent is the self from its body?

In the last chapter I developed Kant's general argument against the kind of inferences that lie at the basis of rational psychology. After looking at his general objections to efforts to infer substantive facts about our nature as thinkers from the way we must think of ourselves, on the basis of the way in which we must think of ourselves in order to ascribe thoughts to ourselves I then turned to his arguments against treating us as thinking things, in the sense of bona fide thinking substances or persons that have identity over time. In this chapter, I explore Kant's arguments in the Paralogisms against Cartesian metaphysical and epistemological dualism. I concentrate on the Second and Fourth Paralogisms.

THE SECOND PARALOGISM

The Second Paralogism attacks what Kant regards as the most illustrious champion to be found among the arguments of rational psychology. The "Achilles" of all rationalist proofs is the argument from the nature of thought to the metaphysical simplicity of the thinker who thinks. Kant's sympathy with the argument from simplicity has to do with his deep commitment to the logical simplicity of the "I." By this he means that our representation of self does not contain anything *per se* that would serve to distinguish one self from another self. For instance in the B-Deduction, Kant motivates the need for synthesis in order for one to be able to represent the identity of the self in different representations by noting that "through the I as simple representation no manifold is given" (B 135).[1] In that context, Kant contrasts the kind of simplicity of I representation that is supposed to characterize our discursive minds with the kind of intuitive intellect that could be ascribed to God.

Neither Descartes nor Leibniz would disagree with Kant's theory that rational psychology would have to be based on "the simple and for itself completely empty of content representation: **I**" (A 346/B 404). The simple representation "I" is the subject of consciousness represented as subject of self-consciousness. It is simple because it lacks any content beyond its self-referential form. Thought seems only to be possible if the thinker is characterized as a thinker by simplicity or absolute unity of consciousness. One cannot divide distinctive thoughts among different subjects without depriving those thoughts of their very existence. A verse or a sentence cannot be broken up into its constituent words and its constituent words represented by different individuals and still be that particular thought. From the inherent unity of particular thoughts it seems to follow that thought requires a metaphysically simple, or absolutely unitary subject. But Kant points out that the inference to the existence of an absolutely unitary bearer of thought is based on a presupposition that deprives it of most of its force.

We must presuppose a single logical subject, or subjective "I" (A 354) in order to ascribe to ourselves any thought. The logical subject lacks any content aside from that provided by that of which one is conscious. In this sense, the statement "I am simple" is an immediate expression of self-consciousness (A 355). But the fact that we can only represent ourselves as thinking by attributing unity to each of our points of view as thinkers does not establish that we are beings that have an absolutely unitary or simple nature.

Whenever we represent ourselves as the subject of different experiences, regardless of whether we are the same individual bearer that had all of those experiences, we represent ourselves as what Kant calls "the logical subject of a thought." The logical subject of a thought is just the subject that is represented by us as the thinker of that thought. The unity of the point of view does not guarantee the unity of the bearer of that point of view. Thus, an individual who had undergone fission, fusion, or had his or her experiences transplanted from those of another individual could still regard him- or herself as the same logical subject of all those experiences even though there was no individual bearer that had all of those experiences.

Thus, even many simple substances might again flow into one, without anything more being lost than the greater amount of subsistence, the one containing the degree of reality of all the previous ones together in it, and perhaps the simple substances that provide the appearance of matter could bring forth children souls through dynamic division of parent souls as *intensive magnitudes* (admittedly not through mutual mechanical or chemical influence, but rather through an influence that is unknown to us of which they are the mere appearance), while they might in turn replenish their loss through coalition with new stuffs of the same kind. (B 417n)

While the self presents itself to itself in self-consciousness as a unity that seems to be the unity of a real particular, this unity turns out to be, at least in some cases, a mere logical unity belonging to all the thoughts which that subject thinks of as belonging to him- or herself. Whether that subject is a thing with real unity, as well, is a matter for further investigation.

Self-consciousness involves a reference to self in abstraction from any description which distinguishes one from other individuals. Self-consciousness thus encourages us to think that the real subject of thought is simply identical with the logical subject of self-conscious thought. The logical subject of thought is just the point of view to which we ascribe a certain unity. From the intrinsic unity of a point of view, which Kant refers to as logical simplicity, one cannot establish the intrinsic unity or simplicity of the real bearer of that point of view. For one would have to establish the identity of the real with the logical subject of thought in order to infer that the bearer of thought is simple because the representation of that bearer is simple. The logically simple subject to which we ascribe individual thoughts might turn out itself to have an intrinsic unity of point of view that supervenes on a complex of many diverse real bearers. The proposition that a thought can only be the expression of the absolute unity of a thinking being is thus not analytic (A 353). It involves a substantive claim about the nature of thinking beings. Nor can experience alone provide the kind of evidence required to support a claim to necessity or absolute unity.

Kant thinks of the transcendental subject as the bearer of thought when it is conceived in abstraction from any of the features which distinguish one thinking being from another: "It means a something in general (transcendental subject) the representation of which must indeed be simple, precisely because one certainly cannot think of anything more simple than by means of the concept of a mere something" (A 355). But Kant insists that the simplicity of our representation of ourselves is not the simplicity of a real bearer of thought. Transcendental self-consciousness is the "I" attached to thought that "merely transcendentally designates" the real bearer of thought (A 355). It refers to the bearer of thought only insofar as that bearer is thought of as the condition for the possibility of thought, but not to any further features of that bearer. In self-consciousness, one refers to oneself where "oneself" is merely serving as the purely formal second term of a reflexive relation which picks up the reference involved in the use of the other term of that reflexive relation.

The plausibility of thinking of the self as simple rests on one's need to take the first-person perspective in order to ascribe thoughts.[2] The first-person perspective carries over to the ascription of thought to other persons. In the case of other rational beings, one must put oneself in the position of those thinking beings in order to be able to ascribe thoughts to them as well. Kant again insists that we can only represent another thinking being by transference from our own self-conscious reflection. He then explicitly rejects the inference as invalid that the self must therefore be simple. We are wrong in moving from the fact that self-consciousness is a necessary subjective condition under which we can make the notion of a rational being intelligible to ourselves, to the conclusion that the unity that we ascribe to ourselves as subjects of thought is a constitutive feature of the concept of a thinking being in general:

Thus here, as in the previous Paralogism, the formal proposition of apperception: I think, is the whole ground on which rational psychology dares its extension of its knowledge, which proposition is indeed no experience, but the form of apperception, which belongs to every experience, and precedes it, yet must only always be regarded in respect to possible knowledge as *merely subjective condition* of it [knowledge], which we unjustly make into the condition of the possibility of knowledge of objects, namely into a *concept* of a thinking being in general, since we cannot represent it [a thinking being] except by putting ourselves with the formula of our consciousness in the place of every other intelligent being. (A 354)

The form of apperception, the ability to represent experiences in terms of an "I think" through which we are conscious of ourselves being conscious of those experiences, is the basis for all experience (at least of intelligent beings, as we can understand them). Apperception is the basis for our representation not only of ourselves, but of other rational beings. Yet it is a subjective condition that we cannot construe as the objective basis for knowledge of *de re* necessities concerning the nature of rational beings. The only grip we have on what it is to be a thinking being is based on our ability to understand what it would be like for us to perceive or understand the world in a different way than we do. But it does not follow from this that the very nature of a rational being involves a connection to self-consciousness. The point of view that we attribute to thinking beings on the basis of our self-consciousness must be inherently unitary and indivisible, but we cannot legitimately conclude from this subjective necessity governing our ascription of thought that rational beings must have an inherently unitary nature.

In the second edition of the Paralogisms (B 420) Kant seems at first to endorse a more metaphysically loaded notion of the self's simplicity which suggests a much greater sympathy with rationalist critics of materialism. He notes that apperception is something real whose simplicity lies in its very possibility. The first-person point of view of self-consciousness demands that the subject of self-consciousness be a single unitary subject. Kant assumes as an independent premise that there is nothing in space that is both real and simple. He concludes from these assumptions that my character as a mere thinking subject cannot be explained by appeal to materialism. The assumption that what is spatially real cannot be simple expresses his thesis that points are abstractions from the real extended constituents of space together with the additional assumption that points are the only simple things that have spatial location. Both of these assumptions are problematic, since they involve a rejection of the existence of point-events.

The argument has some force against the very crude reductive forms of materialism with which Kant was familiar (Helvetius for instance), although it depends on an assumption about the nature of space that is now quite controversial. But even if we waive the worry that the argument has no force against someone who maintains that matter could be composed out of non-extended point-objects, it does not offer a very powerful objection to non-reductive materialism, which is prepared to argue that mental events are not reducible to physical events. Nor does the argument pose a problem even for a sophisticated form of eliminative materialism that treats the subjective point of view as something that has instrumental significance in understanding experience, but no ultimate real existence. A non-reductive materialist or even an eliminative materialist can allow for the existence of an emergent property of absolute unity or simplicity that cannot be adequately understood in terms of any of the individual bits of matter that collectively have this emergent property.[3]

Despite his rejection of materialism, Kant admits that the appeal to the simplicity of self-consciousness cannot establish the thesis of spiritualism or mentalism, that is, the independent existence of mental events, since the manner in which I exist is not determined by self-consciousness *per se*. Indeed, this is what is to be expected given the overall critical attitude to Cartesianism that underlies the argument of the Paralogisms. In the Cartesian tradition, the simplicity of the self as thinker has been used to support arguments for the immateriality of the soul. At first blush, Leibniz seems to be an obvious target for Kant's critique. Thus Leibniz argues in *Monadology*, section 17, that mental states cannot be explained in terms of mechanical composition, but have a unity that can only be understood by recourse to simple substances. Kant agrees with Leibniz that mechanism fails to explain representation, but he does not accept Leibniz's inference to the existence of simple substances. On the other hand, Leibniz argues for spiritualism from the simplicity of self-consciousness, not for immaterialism. In fact, he does not think that the soul or self can ever exist in a completely disembodied state (*Monadology*, section 72).

Although Kant directs his argument primarily against the Leibniz–Wolffian school of thought, Descartes is a better target. For Descartes does think that the soul is not only simple, but, in principle, can exist in a disembodied state. The status of embodiment in Descartes is, however, more complicated than it at first appears to be. In the Sixth Meditation, he rejects the idea that the soul is related to the body as a pilot to a ship. He argues that the human being *qua* embodied soul has the complex unity of an individual even though body and soul are different substances.[4]

Now, Kant argues that the statement "I exist as thinking" involves an element of experience. But, in order to show that I am a substance in any but a purely formal sense, I would have to show that it is in my nature to be an object that persists over time. Unfortunately, a persistent object cannot be found in inner experience alone, and hence I have no reason to assume that the formal identity of the self as subject of the experiences that I ascribe to myself or to others provides adequate grounds for making substantive claims about my relation as thinker to my body or other bodies. Kant concludes that no valid inference can be drawn concerning either the dependence or independence of the soul from the body. That Kant thinks that no inference can be drawn concerning the relation of consciousness to the body is only confirmed by a look at a parallel passage from "On the Progress of Metaphysics," Ak. xx, p. 308:

That he [the human being] is not wholly and purely corporeal may be strictly proven, if this appearance is considered as a thing in itself, from the fact that the unity of consciousness, which must be met with in all cognition (including that of oneself) makes it impossible that representations divided amongst various subjects could constitute a unified thought: therefore materialism can never be used as a principle for explaining the nature of the soul.

Kant first argues that the claim that human beings are not wholly and purely corporeal can be proved from the fact that the unity of consciousness cannot be distributed among different subjects, *if the human being as appearance is considered as a thing in itself.* But the whole point of the Paralogisms is that the antecedent of the conditional is something that we cannot take for granted. It is precisely the mistake of the rationalist and materialist philosophers that Kant wishes to criticize that they take what appears to us to be what that thing is in itself. But Kant argues that we cannot infer from the subjective conditions under which we can alone recognize other minds that all rational beings in general must be such as those constraints dictate to us (A 354).

In the "Progress" draft he then suggests that we can distinguish the body from the soul as phenomenon and still maintain that the external thing (the basis for the phenomenon of body) could itself be a simple being when taken as a thing in itself. In short, if we are not entitled to take the unity of consciousness in appearances as a unity of consciousness in things as they exist in themselves, the argument does nothing to contradict materialism. Given the conditional nature of Kant's argument and his own skepticism about the truth of the antecedent, I think one must reject Henry Allison's view that Kant takes this to be a compelling argument against materialism.[5] The argument provides the basis for rejecting the possibility of materialism only if we take the standpoint of the transcendental realist who maintains that inferences from the mental unity of appearances to the mental unity of things in themselves are legitimate. Thus, the argument has at best *ad hominem* force against a materialist who accepts transcendental realism.

How does Kant reconcile his rejection of both spiritualism and materialism as accounts of the ultimate nature of human beings? In our experience, the mental and the physical are distinct, since the mental is that which is essentially inner, and the physical is that which is essentially outer relative to the point of view of the representations which make up the mental. This leads Kant to favor property dualism, the view that mental and physical properties are distinct kinds of properties, at the phenomenal level of our experience. In the Paralogisms, Kant does not actually defend phenomenal substance dualism, the view that there are distinct mental things and physical things. However, he does distinguish objects of inner sense from objects of outer sense. And, in the *Metaphysical Foundations*, he maintains that life involves action that can only be understood in terms of desires that do not belong to outer sense. He concludes that "when we look for the cause of any change of matter in life, then we must immediately look for it in another substance that is however connected to matter" (Ak. IV, p. 544). Kant's claim that we must look to another substance as cause of change in life as opposed to the substances that cause change in matter strongly suggests that he was committed, at least at that time, to phenomenal substance dualism.

While Kant seems to be attracted to some form of substance dualism at the level of phenomena, he does not find such a dualism defensible at the level of things as they are in themselves. Such substance dualism would be forced on us if we were to treat the distinction between matter and mind as ultimate, as a feature of things as they are in themselves. But we cannot do this due to the limitations of what we can infer from the conditions under which we ascribe thoughts to individuals. Kant thus allows for the possibility of a form of naturalism at the level of things as they are in themselves which gives up substance dualism, and perhaps even property dualism, at the most fundamental level of reality:

If matter were a thing in itself, then it would be totally different as a composite being from the soul as a simple one. Now it is only external appearance whose substratum cannot be known through any predicates that can be given; hence I can well assume that it [the substratum] is in itself simple, although in the way that it affects our senses, it generates the intuition of the extended and hence of the composite. And I can assume that thoughts which can be represented with consciousness through its own inner sense belong to the substance in itself which in respect to our external senses has extension. In this way, precisely the same thing which in one respect is called corporeal would be in another a thinking being whose thoughts we cannot intuit, but whose signs in appearance we can intuit. Thus the expression would lapse that only souls (as particular kinds of substances) think; it would be said, as is customary, that human beings think, i.e. that precisely the same thing which is extended as external appearance is internally (in itself), a subject that is not a composite but rather simple and thinks. (A 359)

Kant argues that instead of talking about thinking substances, or souls that think, it might turn out to be more appropriate to treat of human beings as the bearers of thoughts as ordinary language does. In effect, he seeks a common ground of the mental and the physical or rather a concept of substance which is sufficiently rich to be able to explain both mental and physical properties in experience. This is a rather attractive position. Characteristically, Kant does not think that a substance that would have mental as well as physical properties is knowable by us (A 360). We have knowledge of matter and of our inner states. But matter, such as we know it, is a mere appearance, as are our inner states. There is something transcending appearance which is responsible for our *representations* of inner states as well as of material states. We do not know that there is an intrinsic difference between what would explain the properties of matter and what would explain mental events. At the deepest level, Kant is therefore suspicious of spiritualism and its claim that the mind is ultimately either more basic or independent of the physical, without being any more sympathetic to physicalism. Given his strictures on our capacity to know how things are in themselves independently of the conditions under which we can know them, Kant is also unwilling to endorse the hypothesis that there is a kind of common substance that underlies both mental and physical appearances.

THE FOURTH PARALOGISM

So far we have looked at three different determinations of self-consciousness that suggest rich metaphysical commitments. Self-consciousness presents itself to us, and hence also a thinker to us, as a logically basic subject that has identity over the different thoughts that it ascribes to itself. The subject of thought, and hence thinkers as they present themselves to us, has an intrinsic unity or simplicity to it that seems to distinguish them from material objects. In self-consciousness, I also distinguish my existence as a thinker from other things outside of my consciousness, including my own body. This suggests that I might have an existence as a thinker that is somehow independent of my body. But Kant rightly insists that the truth of the claim that I distinguish myself from other things in self-consciousness is analytic (B 409). It does not establish anything about the ultimate nature of my relationship to other things.

In the Fourth Paralogism in the first edition, Kant argues against the idea that the existence of things that are external to the self is doubtful. Descartes, for instance, famously argues in the Second Meditation that the existence of things outside of the self is doubtful in a way that the existence of thinking things is not. Descartes bases his real distinction between minds and bodies on the certainty of our knowledge of our mind and the uncertainty of our knowledge of (even our own) body. In the First Paralogism, Kant already rejects Descartess inference from the privileged epistemic status that thinkers have to the claim that they are thinking substances. In the Second Paralogism, he then rejects the claim that thinking things are, or even must somehow be, really distinct substances from material or extended things. In the present context,

Kant's concern is with rejecting attempts to infer that things outside of us have a different epistemic status than things as they are presented to us in thought.

Kant's general argument is directed against what he calls idealism. It is rather surprising to find a philosopher refuting idealism as something scandalous and vaguely pernicious, when he characterizes his own philosophy as a "transcendental idealism." Although Kant does refer to his own philosophical position as a form of idealism, he identifies idealism *tout court* (without predicative modifiers) with the denial of the existence of mind-independent objects. This is apparent in the *Prolegomena*:

> Idealism consists in the assertion, that there are none but thinking beings, all other things, which we think are perceived in intuition, being nothing but representations in the thinking beings, to which no object external to them really corresponds. Whereas I say, that things as objects of our senses existing outside of us are given, but we know nothing of what they may be in themselves, knowing only their phenomena, that is, the representations which they cause in us by affecting our senses. Consequently, I grant by all means that there are bodies without us, that is things which though quite unknown to us as to what they are in themselves, we yet know by the representations which their influence on our sensibility provides us with, and which we call bodies, a term signifying merely the appearance of the thing which is unknown to us, but not therefore less real. Can one really call this idealism? It is the very opposite of it. (section 13, Ak. IV, pp. 288–289)

Kant maintains that skepticism about the existence of external objects is generated by a commitment to transcendental realism. This transcendental realism is the thesis that objects as they (veridically) appear to us are things as they exist in themselves. Transcendental idealism, by contrast, maintains that we cannot know what things are in themselves. We can know facts only about appearances. Somewhat puzzlingly, Kant identifies transcendental realism with what is usually referred to as representational realism. For he maintains that the transcendental realist must assume that we have direct perceptions only of what is represented by us as represented by us. The direct or naive realist is inclined to reject any need to assume the existence of such epistemic intermediaries. The need to assume epistemic intermediaries is usually motivated by the need to provide an account of sensory illusion and other delusive experiences such as dreams. The representational realist insists that delusive and veridical perceptions should be treated symmetrically. If we do not assume any epistemic intermediaries, it is hard to understand how delusive experiences could occur. And, once we assume the existence of such intermediaries in the case of delusive perceptions, it is hard to see why such intermediaries simply drop out in the case of veridical perception.

Although the argument of the representational realist has some plausibility, it is hard to find it compelling. For it is open to the direct realist to argue that things as they are in themselves are just the way things appear to standard observers under standard circumstances, while delusive appearances are just the way things appear to standard or non-standard observers under non-standard circumstances. Once one makes this move, one must then spell out what standard observers and standard circumstances are supposed to be. The most plausible way to do this is in terms of the operation of certain causal mechanisms. The skeptic can then argue that, in principle, we are unable to know whether the causal mechanisms which cause standard observers under standard circumstances to perceive things as thus and such are in fact ever set up in the manner which we believe them to be. In this case, we will be systematically deluded about the world. We find ourselves forced to admit the possibility that empirical idealism could be true, in other words, that all of our beliefs about the external world might turn out to be false.

The key to an argument against empirical idealism within the framework of Kant's transcendental idealism is the combination of immediate consciousness of outer objects with a denial that the immediate relation to objects outside of one's subjectivity communicates (intuitive) knowledge of the things with which one is in an immediate relation. Kant identifies idealism with skepticism about our ability to justify claims concerning the external world. This is somewhat puzzling at first, since we are used to thinking of such a position as a consequence of metaphysical realism. But it turns out that idealism is to be understood as empirical idealism, and Kant thinks of such empirical idealism as a consequence of what is now generally called metaphysical realism, but which he refers to as transcendental realism. Empirical idealism is to be distinguished from empirical realism. The distinction between the ideal or mind-dependent and the real or mind-independent is a distinction which falls here within the domain of experience and the objects belonging to experience.

According to empirical realism, we have immediate perceptual knowledge of objects which are external to us. Kant also refers to empirical realism as dualism. We have direct perceptual knowledge of things, objects in space, which are not minds, and knowledge of inner states which are inherently mental, as well. Hence the term "dualism." Kant's use of the term "dualism" does not at first seem to suggest a commitment to substance dualism, but rather to a form of property dualism according to which mental and physical states are essentially distinct, at least in what appears to us in experience. However, he does conclude from the different character of the objects which we directly perceive to be temporal and spatial that inner and outer states are to be ascribed to different substances. He thus explicitly commits himself to substance dualism with respect to phenomena, that is, objects as we must experience them (A 379).

Kant is convinced that empirical idealism is a consequence of a commitment to transcendental realism "which regards time and space as something given in themselves, independently of our sensibility" (A 369). If space and time and the objects given in space and time are radically independent of our minds, then there seems to be no way of establishing that those objects must be as we think them to be. The transcendental or metaphysical realist must always allow for the possibility that all of our beliefs could be false. The transcendental idealist, by contrast, and Kant subscribe to transcendental idealism, and maintain that space and time are nothing apart from the sensible conditions under which we represent objects. Thus there would be at least no spatial objects to which our beliefs fail to conform so long as they satisfy the best standards we can have for the determination of whether our beliefs about objects external to us in experience are true. This raises more questions than it answers. For, in order to get a significant contrast between transcendental realism and transcendental idealism, Kant takes transcendental idealism to deny not that things existing independently of our sensibility could exist at all, but only that they are knowable for us. This seems to push the problem posed by idealism with respect to external objects back to the problem of how objects that are external to us in space relate to objects that are external to us in a sense that is independent of the way in which we experience them.

Even if the transcendental realist's attempt to provide an objective account of subjectivity is doomed to failure, this does not by itself rescue Kant's position from the pressures which threaten it. In the more extensive first edition discussion of the Fourth Paralogism, Kant seems to refute the skeptic only by granting to him or her everything that s/he requires:

I do not need to draw an inference with respect to the reality of external objects any more than I do with respect to the reality of the object of my inner sense (of my thoughts), for they are both nothing but representations the immediate perception (consciousness) of which is also a sufficient proof of their reality. (A 371)

While Kant insists that we have a direct perception of objects in a space which is outside of us, it turns out that this space and the bodies in it are mere represented, "the objects of which are something only through these representations. Apart from them they are nothing" (A 370). This refutation of idealism has nothing to recommend itself over Leibniz's most phenomenalist claims:

I judge without proof, from a simple perception or experience, that those things exist of which I am conscious within me. There are, first myself, who am thinking a variety of things, and then, the varied phenomena or appearances which exist in my mind. Since both of these are perceived immediately by the mind without intervention of anything else, they can be accepted without question, and it is exactly as certain that there exists in my mind the appearance of a golden mountain or of a centaur when I dream of these, as it is that I who am dreaming exist, since both are included in the one fact that it is certain that a centaur appears to me.[6]

Neither Leibniz nor Kant leave the matter at such immediate conscious-ness of objects.[7] They both see the need to distinguish between real and imaginary objects by means of coherence considerations. Thus, Kant claims that we can distinguish illusory appearances from bona fide perceptions of external objects by appeal to the principle that *"what is connected with perception according to empirical laws, is real"* (A 376). This is also a claim Berkeley could endorse. Thus Kant's refutation of idealism seems to have nothing to commend it over Leibniz's or Berkeley's similar arguments against skepticism about the existence of bodies. Indeed, refutations of idealism were standard in the handbooks of Leibnizian–Wolffian philosophy which Kant used for his own lectures.[8]

   Kant's first critic, Garve, or rather Feder, can hardly be blamed for assimilating Kant's position to Berkeley's phenomenalism.[9] Like Kant, Berkeley thought that the best response to the skeptic about external bodies was to argue that the only intelligible notion of bodies we have is one essentially tied to our sense representations. In responding to the criticism that his view was indistinguishable from Berkeley's phenom-enalism, Kant came to reformulate his criticism of empirical or psycho-logical idealism in the second edition of the *Critique*. He retains the idea that we have a direct perception of bodies, but he gives up the idea that these bodies are mere internal accusatives of perception.

In the next chapter, I turn to Kant's argument against Cartesian skepticism about the existence of external objects in the second edition Refutation of Idealism. Discussion of the Refutation allows me to flesh out the implications of my overall argument concerning the conditions under which our consciousness of ourselves as temporal and spatial beings is possible. I focus on the manner in which our temporal consciousness of ourselves as distinct individuals with distinct experiences is parasitic on our experience of objects that exist outside of us.

The Refutation of Idealism draws on the full resources of the analysis of the role of causation, and especially substance, in determining the temporal relations between inner episodes. For, in the Refutation, Kant argues that the mental lacks the autonomy required to fund the notion of persistence required to make sense of the very ascription of determinate temporal episodes to oneself needed in order for one to make sense of inner experience. From there, Kant argues that we cannot have any determinate beliefs about our inner states at all without also having beliefs about objects that exist outside of us. These objects turn out in the end to be objects that are outside of us in the transcendental, as well as the empirical, sense. Here, Kant fully exploits the idea that the inner–outer distinction is constitutive of any determinate consciousness of self by showing how the inner–outer distinction constitutes the particular consciousness of self that we have as individuals who have distinct experiences that, in principle, must be subject to some temporal order if they are to be comprehensible to us at all.

CHAPTER 10

The argument against idealism

Officially, the Refutation of Idealism is the only novel addition to the *Critique* in its second edition (B xxxixn). Given the other changes that Kant makes in the second edition, this admission may justify the amount of attention that has been devoted to such a small amount of text. He piques the interest of other philosophers by intimating that he has solved a problem that has been a "scandal" to philosophy and all reasoning persons:

Idealism may be held to be ever so innocent with respect to the essential purposes of metaphysics (which it in fact is not) it still remains a scandal of philosophy and of the universal reason of humanity that the existence of things outside of us (from which we however derive the whole stuff of cognitions even for our inner sense) must be accepted on *faith,* and not to be able to offer a satisfactory proof to someone if it should occur to him to doubt it. (B xxxix)[1]

Since Kant advocates his own form of idealism, transcendental idealism, the Refutation is not directed at all forms of idealism. The Refutation is directed against a specifically modern, and post-Cartesian skeptical worry about whether beliefs about outer states have the same degree of warrant as beliefs about inner states. The Refutation responds to the provisional skeptical position outlined in the first and second of Descartes's *Meditations on First Philosophy,* but Kant's more immediate target is the Humean position of his contemporary, Friedrich Jacobi. In the passage above, Kant alludes to Jacobi's claim that we need to appeal to faith or belief (*Glaube*) in order to support claims about the existence of the external world.[2]

Where Descartes worries about the possibility that my beliefs about external objects might all turn out to be false, Kant wants to show that any knowledge of inner states entails the existence of objects existing outside of me. In this way, he also hopes to show that Jacobi's claim that we have only an unjustifiable belief in the existence of external objects is unfounded. Kant aims to show not only that we have no reason to doubt the existence of the external world, but that we must assume its existence in order to have any determinate inner experiences at all.

The Refutation has a particular interest for my own enterprise of articulating the conditions under which a distinctive consciousness of ourselves is possible. Kant argues here that we can only know what is internal to our own individual experiences insofar as we are directly conscious of something that is external to our own individual experience. The Refutation thus links knowledge of oneself as an empirical self with the inner–outer distinction, while arguing that our consciousness of what is internal to our own distinctive point of view in experience is parasitic on what is outside of it in experience. In the Refutation itself, Kant is concerned only with the relation in experience between what is internal to a point of view and what is external to a point of view, but, in later personal notes, he then seeks to ground the distinction between the inner–outer within experience on the distinction between what is internal to experience and what is external to it. In this way, he seeks to show that any consciousness of oneself as an experiencer involves the empirical, as well as the transcendental distinction between the inner and the outer.

In responding to Descartes's problematic "material" or "psychological" idealism, Kant argues that Descartes is wrong when he takes inner experience to be indubitable and the experience of outer objects to be dubitable (B 275). According to Descartes, one has indubitable knowledge of any mental state that one is in purely in virtue of being in that state, while one's beliefs about outer objects are dubitable. This is the basis for the real distinction that he attempts to draw in the Second Meditation between mental and physical states and their respective bearers. Kant argues, by contrast, that one cannot even have knowledge of inner episodes except on the basis of a belief in the existence of outer objects that cannot be false. Kant does not address or even mention Descartes's appeal in the Fifth Meditation to the beneficence of God to warrant the reliability of our assumption that there is an external world. Kant would, however, reject such an appeal as based on knowledge of God that we do not have, and that is at any rate less reliable than our knowledge of the existence of an external world.

Kant's aim in the Refutation is to prove that experience would be impossible if there were no bodies and nothing that exists outside of consciousness. He has no argument against a person who is skeptical about having any experience or self-knowledge at all. This leaves a kind of gap in Kant's argument. He cannot refute a Cartesian skeptic who limits him- or herself to the *cogito*.[3] Kant does first note that Descartes's "problematic idealism" declares "only one empirical assertion (assertio), namely: *I am* for indubitable" (B 274), and Kant does set out to refute "problematic idealism." However, he soon goes on to describe his aim in the Refutation as that of showing that "even our *inner* experience, not doubted by Descartes, is only possible under the condition of *external* experience" (B 275). And Kant later notes that the representation "I am" is not experience, since one needs more than mere existence for experience, one needs some more determinate representation of the individual in time (B 277).

However, even if the argument has no force against a skeptic who is willing to retrench and restrict him- or herself to the certainty of the *cogito*, the argument is still quite ambitious. Kant attempts to show that one can only have a consciousness of oneself as existing in time, and hence the capacity to justify one's beliefs about one's own inner states, if one has some true beliefs about the existence of objects existing outside of one. He starts from the assumption that I am conscious of my own existence as determined in time. He then appeals to a conclusion of the First Analogy as an independent premise: all time-determination presupposes something permanent in perception (relative persistence is actually enough for the present purpose). What he wants to establish is that what persists cannot be an intuition in me. Representations make up the only bases in me for determining my existence. And as representations they themselves also require something persistent that is distinct from them. For something is needed in relation to which representations may be said to change and in relation to which my existence in time may be determined.

Two conclusions are supposed to follow: (1) the perception of what is persistent or permanent is only possible through a thing existing outside of me and not through the mere representation of a thing outside of me; (2) the determination of my existence in time is only possible through the existence of actual things that I perceive outside of me. Since the Analytic as a whole has argued that consciousness in time is necessarily tied to the possibility of time-determination, Kant can then also avail himself of this claim as a premise from which he draws the final conclusion of his argument: (3) since the existence of things outside of me is a condition for time-determination, consciousness in time is necessarily tied to the existence of things outside of me. This is just another way of claiming that consciousness of my own existence is also an immediate consciousness of things that exist outside of me.

UNDERSTANDING THE ARGUMENT

The Refutation of Idealism links empirically determined self-consciousness to the existence of permanent objects existing outside of the self. Kant states the thesis of the Refutation clearly enough: "The mere, but empirically determined, consciousness of my own existence, proves the existence of the objects in space outside of me" (B 275). There is, however, a certain ambiguity to the notion of "the mere, but empirically determined, consciousness of my own existence." It is initially unclear whether consciousness of one's existence is empirically determined by the mere fact that it entails the existence of some indeterminate empirical representation, or whether empirical determination requires determination of the position (and hence the content) of that empirical representation in time.

In the literature, empirically determined consciousness of my own existence has been rightly understood in this latter, stronger sense.[4] Kant explicitly denies that the mere consciousness of our own existence requires an experience of outer objects (B 277). Thus, the kind of representation of self to be had by transcendental apperception alone is not sufficient to provide a premise for the argument. In fact, recent interpreters have rightly taken this consciousness to be the inner experience that Kant identifies with self-knowledge.[5] Kant uses the term "experience" in many places as a synonym for knowledge, in which we are even said to know the objective temporal relations of what we perceive (see B 219). And in his own subsidiary remarks to the Refutation, he identifies inner experience with knowledge (B 277).

Once we assume that we have self-knowledge the argument lends itself to a straightforward reconstruction. Self-knowledge requires knowledge of a certain temporal order among one's inner states. Knowledge that inner states have a certain temporal order requires that there actually be a certain temporal order governing those inner states. And, assuming that such a temporal order is only determinable with respect to something that is outside of us, then there must be something that exists outside of us.

In the argument, Kant first appeals to a premise from the First Analogy. All time-determination requires something permanent in perception. We may recall that consciousness of one's inner states is inherently successive. The replacement of one state of consciousness by another state of consciousness after it, is not enough to support a representation of succession. There must be something that is represented as constant through that transition. It is then through one's representation of this item that persists over one's representations, while other contents of representation undergo change, that one becomes conscious of the transition from one temporal state to another. Even to have a belief that something has occurred at some point in time, I need something that I represent as persistent or even permanent relative to which something can appear to me to be an event.

Initially, it seems that what I take as permanent might merely be something that is represented by me as permanent, without it, in fact, being permanent. How can it be successfully argued that my own existence in time presupposes something permanent that cannot itself be a mere represented? While Kant assumes in the First Analogy that all permanent objects are objects that are to be met with by us in space, he does not attempt to offer any proof that this is so in that context. The proof of this claim that he offers in the *Metaphysical Foundations* has severe difficulties, as we have already seen. But, in order to provide a proof of the dependence of beliefs about inner states on the existence of external objects, the Refutation must also argue for the claim that only objects to be met with outside of me can be permanent.[6]

The permanent object that I need to order my subjective states in time cannot be purely private, for I would then have no way to distinguish between a veridical and a non-veridical temporal ordering of my mental events. If all I had to go on were my own private experiences, then I would not even have the notion of a temporal perspective that is different from the one I am taking and then I would have no basis for thinking that any of my beliefs about the temporal order of my experiences could ever be false. However, even if I need some representation of the possibility of a different take on my inner experiences than the one I have now in order to be able to take myself to be making a judgment about my inner states, it is still not obvious that this cannot be just another inner take of mine with which I might compare my present experiences. This initially suggests that regularities in the occurrence of purely inner psychological states could be sufficient to allow for the determination of the relations of co-occurrence and successiveness of states.

Henry Allison argues that consciousness of a succession of representations is, at the same time, a succession in my consciousness.[7] But this view would be rejected by someone like Paul Guyer, who thinks that one can have a momentary consciousness of a succession of states. Now, regardless of whether one could represent a succession of states at a moment or not, and regardless of whether one could then represent something persistent at a moment or not, a representation of something persistent from the vantage-point of a purely subjective take on things would give me, at best, an apparently persistent object. The claim that the persistent or permanent might be a mere representation would reduce the permanent to an apparent permanent. Such a merely apparent permanent would then yield only an apparent temporal order requiring in its turn a spatio-temporal permanent which could not be in turn purely temporal on pain of infinite regress.[8] Thus, without some permanent that is outside of my inherently successive inner experiences, I would not even be able to make veridical claims about the order of those inner experiences, and so I would not have inner experience at all. This seems to be part of the claim that Kant is making in a note added to the preface to the second edition, in which he argues that representations themselves "require as such a permanent distinct from them in respect to which their replacement-change and hence my existence in time, in which they replace themselves, can be determined" (B xxxix).

We need not have an uninterrupted perception or representation of a particular in order for that particular to serve as a basis for providing a temporal order for our representations. The permanent is supposed to be something that we can assume to continue to exist during any interruptions of our conscious experience, such as when we sleep. Without the notion of something that continues even while our own train of representations is interrupted, we would have no basis for accounting for non-conscious periods of our existence within our experience:

[T]he representation of something *permanent* in existence is not identical with a *permanent representation*; for this [representation] can be very changeable and subject to replacement-change, as all of our representations and even those of matter [are], and relates itself to something permanent, which must therefore be a thing that is distinct from all my representations and external [to them], the existence of which is necessarily contained in the *determination* of my own existence and makes up only a single experience with it [the determination of my own existence] that would not even occur internally, if it were not (in part) also external. (B XLI)[9]

Kant admits that even our representations of physical objects are not themselves enduring representations. But his concession does not matter, since the persistent or permanent cannot be something that is merely represented as persistent. Everything in me exists only insofar as it can be represented by me. If it is true that the permanent cannot be something merely represented by me, then it follows that the permanent cannot be something in me, something internal to consciousness itself. Kant concludes that the permanent must be something outside of me.

The assumption that the permanent objects outside of us are to be understood as spatial objects is introduced in the second note to the Refutation. According to the note, the permanent objects in question must be material objects. Kant's observation has some force that we do, in fact, derive our consciousness of temporal relations from changes in such external objects as the sun. But solar motion relative to terrestrial objects is relative motion. Each of these objects undergoes changes, and none of them can be regarded as permanent from a cosmic perspective. None of the objects that we perceive are permanent objects in the strict sense. The fact that the objects that we perceive are not permanent, forces Kant to admit that we do not derive the permanence of external objects from external experience (B 278), but presuppose it a priori as a condition for determining temporal relations. This certainly seems to put objects in space on a par with objects existing only in time, in other words, with representational states.[10]

The problem of change and hence of permanence also arises for purely spatial objects. For, even though Kant thinks that physical properties are only to be regarded as temporal states in virtue of their relation to mental events, such physical properties do present themselves to us as temporal states of physical objects. However, in the case of physical objects and their states, it is possible for us to give a tenseless characterization of those objects, while we cannot provide any such account of mental states from the standpoint of inner experience. We can assign a determinate tenseless temporal order to our inner states, but we are able to do this only by appeal to the existence of physical objects that are not essentially tensed in the same way that mental states are.

Now it is important to note at this stage that external objects are privileged in the determination of the temporal order of events (including mental events) because they are public objects. Failure to appreciate the fact that external objects must be understood as public objects has seriously undermined some discussions of the Refutation. Thus, C. D. Broad argues that the external objects together with the spaces to which they belong which we perceive are something *private* and dependent on the mind of the individual percipient.[11] But it is only once one realizes that external objects cannot be private objects precisely because they are external objects that the significance of external objects in providing an independent standard for determining the temporal order of our beliefs becomes apparent. Whatever external objects may turn out to be, it is their very externality from the contingent order of succession of states in my or your consciousness that makes them an appropriate basis for assigning a temporal order to my or your states. For it is their very externality to my or your consciousness that makes them capable of providing independent confirmation or disconfirmation of the temporal order that each of us subjectively assigns to our individual states and thus gives sense to such a subjective order in the first place.

THE ROLE OF IMMEDIACY IN THE ARGUMENT

The Refutation of Idealism is, in many respects, a revision of the argument articulated against skepticism about the external world in the Fourth Paralogism in the first edition of the *Critique*. There, Kant also attempts to show that we have an immediate experience of the external world, as he does in the Refutation: "that is, the consciousness of my own existence is also an immediate consciousness of the existence of other things outside of me" (B 276). But, after this, the argument diverges substantially. For in the first edition Fourth Paralogism, Kant is content to argue for this immediacy on the basis of the fact that external objects are objects represented by me immediately in my outer sense, just as my inner states are immediately represented to me through my inner sense (A 371). In the new argument in the Refutation, by contrast, my consciousness of my inner states turns out to be mediated by a consciousness of objects outside of me. And these objects outside of me are precisely not mere represented, as the argument in the first edition had maintained.[12] The argument attempts to establish that one's consciousness of one's own existence is coupled to an immediate consciousness of things which are distinct from it.[13]

Although it is clear that Kant wants to claim that outer objects are supposed to be experienced directly, it is less clear if one has any direct consciousness of the objects of one's "inner time-consciousness." The evidence on this issue is somewhat ambiguous. In private notes devoted to rethinking his argument, Kant claims that "empirical consciousness of myself, which constitutes inner sense by no means occurs immediately" (Reflection 5653, Ak. XVIII, p. 306). But this does not really settle the question of whether one has immediate knowledge of the objects of inner experience. The process of introspection may in some sense be mediated by its relation to external objects while still providing one with non-inferential knowledge of one's inner states. This possibility seems to have been overlooked by Guyer, who cites the Reflection as evidence against the immediacy of inner experience.[14] In the Refutation, Kant states that "inner experience is itself only mediate and possible through external" experience (B 277). But there is no evidence that he wants to suggest that our knowledge of inner experience is therefore purely inferential, as Guyer suggests that he does.

It would appear that, for Kant, the non-immediacy characteristic of my empirical self-consciousness is a function of its mediation by consciousness of objects outside of me. The claim that all inner experience is parasitic on outer experience might be taken to mean that all inner experience is also at the same time an experience of something outer, or it might mean something weaker. It might, for instance, mean only that inner experience somehow presupposes outer experience.[15] Kant needs the stronger claim that any determinate consciousness or belief about something temporal must involve a consciousness of something spatial. This is the full import of his thesis that "the representations of *external senses* make up the actual content of inner sense with which we occupy the mind" (B 67). On the other hand, it is also true that any consciousness of something outside of me is also a consciousness of something that is present to my consciousness and hence a part of my inner experience.

Kant would hardly deny that our experience of objects in space is itself mediated by consciousness of inner states. For according to him, objects in space are only in time in virtue of their relation to our inner states. Without the mediation of our time-consciousness one could not even experience objects as persistent through changes in their states. There would not be any changes in state there to be experienced in the first place. At best, Kant can sustain the claim that while our consciousness of inner and outer objects are mutually dependent, such mutual dependence does not preclude immediacy of awareness.

The asymmetry with respect to the immediacy claim must be between the way judgments about inner states and about outer states is to be justified. As knowledge that is expressible in a judgment, our knowledge of the external world is propositional, but it is also the non-inferential articulation of what we immediately perceive and hence involves direct apprehension. Immediate knowledge of the external world thus has features of both immediate propositional knowledge and of direct apprehension. Now judgments about inner states can only be justified by appeal to knowledge of outer states. By contrast, judgments about outer states could be justified even if we did not have any self-knowledge at all, although it would be impossible to have any knowledge of outer states without some consciousness of our inner states. For outer states are only (successive) temporal states in virtue of their relation to inner states.

The claim that all knowledge of inner states is parasitic on knowledge of outer states has some strong support in Kant's position. Remember that the application of categories is supposed to make objective claims about spatio-temporal events possible. Now there is strong evidence that Kant restricts the direct application of the categories to the spatial objects of outer sense (B 291ff.).[16] This restriction requires that all mental events have corresponding physical states. While Kant does not seem to believe that mental events must have corresponding physical states, he does believe that we can have no experience of mental states that do not have corresponding physical states. The very conditions governing ascription of mental states collapse in the case of disembodied souls. We cannot really make sense of the representational states involved in the praxis of disembodied souls, since the conditions governing our ascriptions of content do not hold with respect to them. We do not have any self-knowledge at all which does not also include knowledge of objects in space.[17]

Despite the emphasis Kant puts on immediacy of representation in the Refutation, Guyer has argued that the proof for "the immediate consciousness of the existence of external things" and the proof "that external experience is immediate" (B 276–277n) cannot be taken seriously. This is supposedly because Kant does not appeal to any premise involving immediacy in his argument.[18] Kant does claim that the immediate consciousness of things outside us is not assumed, but proven (B 277n). Guyer suggests that there is no premise entailing immediacy available to Kant.[19] In part, Guyer's claim is based on Kant's alleged commitment to a premise that is undeniably to be found in the first edition, that one only has immediate consciousness of one's representations.[20] This thesis may be found in the Fourth Paralogism in the first edition (A 371). However, Guyer offers no argument to show that Kant retained commitment to this particular immediacy thesis in the second edition. The Refutation of Idealism seems, rather, to be based on rejecting the restriction of immediate awareness to representings that formed the cornerstone of the argument against idealism in the first edition of the Fourth Paralogism.

The natural reading of the immediacy claim in the Refutation is that our knowledge of external objects (rather than knowledge of our representings) must be immediate if it is to justify claims of self-knowledge. Guyer maintains that this cannot be the case because claims to knowledge of external objects will be justified in many cases by appeal to putative instances of self-knowledge.[21] Now it is true that putative instances of self-knowledge could provide inductive support for some knowledge claim about external objects. But this self-knowledge will itself always presuppose some knowledge of external objects. Apart from such potential dependence of certain knowledge claims about external objects on claims to self-knowledge, there does not seem to be any reason to attribute to Kant the view that self-knowledge *per se* ever provides a basis for confirming or disconfirming knowledge claims about external objects.

Guyer asserts that only if claims concerning self-knowledge and knowledge of outer objects are on a par can the argument of the Refutation be saved from circularity. Causal knowledge must be derived from induction on subjective successions while knowledge of subjective succession depends on knowledge of causal laws.[22] The worry of circularity that Guyer raises against Kant disappears once one recognizes the possibility of direct awareness of subjective succession. And so it does not seem necessary to go to the expedient of appealing to our knowledge of external causes to account for our being able to justify our beliefs about our inner states. But, given Guyer's interpretation of time-consciousness, it is not surprising that the argument which Guyer views as an appropriate substitute for an argument from an immediate consciousness of things outside of me is based on inferential causal knowledge of objects outside of us.[23] This is, however, a singularly unpromising line of attack. In giving up the immediacy premise, Guyer winds up attributing to Kant and defending a version of precisely the kind of idealism Kant officially sets out to refute! In diagnosing the position of "problematic idealism," that he wishes to reject, Kant notes that the "problematic idealist" assumed that:

the only immediate experience is an inner one, and that one merely *infers* the existence of external things from it, and that, as in general, when one infers *determinate* [specific] causes from given effects, [this is] undependable, because the cause of the representations, which we perhaps falsely attribute to external things, may lie in us ourselves. (B 276)

Any judgment to the effect that a certain causal relationship holds between the objects of our beliefs and those beliefs themselves seems to be open to skeptical attack. If all we know are the effects of a certain causal connection, our belief that those effects are the result of a certain kind of cause is itself always open to skeptical doubt. A different set of causes than the ones which we hold to be the source of our beliefs might in fact turn out to be their true source. Something we believe to have a cause outside of us may turn out to have a cause inside of us. The criticism of causal explanation as a basis for belief in the external world is also echoed in later Reflections, as well as in the Fourth Paralogism of the first edition (Reflection 5654, Ak. XVIII, p. 312; A 368). So this is one of the few points that remain unchanged in Kant's arguments against idealism.

The Refutation does not rule out the possibility that one has a direct experience of objects outside of one based on one's causal relations to those objects. Kant's worry about skeptical doubt concerns the postulation of particular causes as explananda for our representations. On the other hand, he is committed to the Humean idea that causal connection is imperceptible (A 138/B 177). The imperceptible character of causal connection makes it difficult to see how we could have immediate (non-inferential) knowledge of causal relations in any sense. And Guyer does interpret the fact that 'we can only know our existence in time in commercio' (Reflection 6311, Ak. XVIII, p. 612) to mean "that we must perceive *our bodies* in causal interaction with the other bodies we use for time-determination."[24] It is rather odd to base the argument of the Refutation on a premise that Kant not only never states but also explicitly denies in the Schematism which is supposed to lay the groundwork for his theory of time-determination: "no one will say that this [category], for instance causality, can be intuited through the senses and is contained in appearance" (A 177/B 138). Another, I think more plausible, reading of Kant's claim, is that our inner experiences must be causally connected to our bodies. And our bodies are in turn, of course, causally connected to other bodies. Causal interaction immediately links our representations and objects outside of us, but the causal link in question is not something that we perceive. We have an immediate perception of objects outside of us because we interact causally with them. But our knowledge of the causal relation is inferential and part of a global systematization of nature, whereas our knowledge of the perceptual object is immediate.

THE REFUTATION AND THINGS OUTSIDE OF US IN THE
TRANSCENDENTAL SENSE

Eckart Förster maintains that, by arguing that the determination of my existence in time is possible only through a *thing* outside me and not through the mere *representation* of a thing outside me, Kant refutes not only Cartesian idealism, but also his own transcendental idealism, since the latter requires "that what we call outer objects are nothing but *mere representations* of our sensibility" (A 30/B 45, my italics). Förster concludes that either the Refutation of Idealism refutes Kant's own transcendental idealism, or it fails to *refute idealism* at all.[25] The objection fails to take account of the two different senses of the expression "external" that Kant works with. In the Fourth Paralogism, Kant notes that "the expression *outside of us* carries with it an unavoidable ambiguity, in that it sometimes means something that exists distinguished [by us] from us *as a thing in itself* and sometimes means that which belongs to external *appearance*" (A 373). The ambiguity in the notion of externality carries over to the notion of internality. The distinction between appearances and things in themselves itself turns out to be ambiguous in a manner that is analogous to the ambiguity in the inner–outer distinction. For we can draw a distinction between appearances and things in themselves within experience. In this case the distinction between appearances and things in themselves corresponds to the distinction between what is inner to experience, in the sense of what is part of an individual point of view, and what is outer, in the sense of what is external to an individual point of view. But we can also draw a distinction between appearances and things in themselves in which anything belonging to our experience (including what is external to individual points of view) is an appearance, and anything which is completely external to experience is a thing as it exists in itself.

Thus, both the inner–outer distinction and the distinction between appearances and things in themselves are ambiguous. There is a distinction to be drawn *within* experience between the private and the public, and a distinction between what is public, but nevertheless dependent on the way we must together experience the world, and the way the world is independently of being experienced by us. The distinction between appearances and things in themselves within experience is an empirical distinction, while the transcendental distinction concerns the relation of experience to what is outside of experience itself.

Kant's response to Cartesian idealism in the Refutation is based on an empirical understanding of "external." Transcendental idealism is committed to denying that external objects as represented in the empirical sense are external to us in the transcendental sense. The context of A 30/B 45 in which he stresses his thesis that what is external to us in the spatial sense is not as such a thing in itself indicates that he is concerned with what is "outer" in the empirical sense.

In fairness to Förster, an argument against idealism in the empirical sense does not address the question of whether the external world might not turn out to be the representation of an individual mind after all, once we move to the level of transcendental reflection.[26] But, on the other hand, the thesis that consciousness of oneself in time presupposes the existence of things in themselves existing outside of that self-consciousness in a transcendental sense, is not only compatible with Kant's transcendental idealism, it can even make a distinctive contribution to the ultimate success of his argument against skeptical idealism. For, without a defense of the existence of radically mind-independent things in themselves, the problem posed by skepticism seems to be merely pushed back a stage.

Some commentators have inferred that objects outside of us must be things in themselves because they are not objects existing purely in my private space. This is clearly the wrong reason for inferring that they must be things in themselves.[27] Kant's thesis that objects in space are transcendentally ideal, and not transcendentally real as things in themselves would have to be, means that, at the very least, the same object cannot be transcendentally ideal and transcendentally real under the same description. But it need not mean that the object cannot exist both independently of us in the spatial sense and in a much more radical sense. Under a spatial description, it may turn out to be dependent on our subjectivity, while it may turn out to be completely independent of our subjectivity under some other description.

The Refutation of Idealism makes no explicit reference to things as they exist in themselves, and the passage at B XLI that I have already quoted makes it quite clear that Kant thinks of the objects outside of us that are required for inner experience as themselves belonging to experience. They cannot be things in themselves in the transcendental sense of the term. However, in later reflections concerning the problematic of the Refutation, Kant does try to argue that inner experience is tied to the existence of things in themselves in the transcendental sense. These are thoughts he put to paper in response to queries by Kiesewetter. In meditations dating from the 1790s, he argues that the transcendental ideality of objects provides the basis for a refutation of skepticism concerning the existence of things in themselves. To the extent that he can make this claim stick, he has a compelling response to those who claim that he has simply given the game of responding to skepticism away by restricting his knowledge claims to appearances.

The idea that our knowledge of the independent existence of appearances should somehow be linked to some consciousness of things as they exist in themselves independently of the conditions governing our knowledge should not be a surprising one when viewed from the perspective of a dual-aspect interpretation of transcendental idealism. According to the dual-aspect interpretation, appearances and things in themselves are two different descriptions of the same things. To describe something as it is in itself is, of course, to describe it in more fundamental terms than the way it must appear to us spatio-temporally, but these are nevertheless two distinct ways of describing something. In order to provide an adequate response to skepticism, a refutation of idealism must at least prove that I have knowledge that things exist in themselves outside of my mind. Now the Refutation is successful at making good on this demand at the empirical level. Objects outside of me in space are genuinely outside of my mind, as my mind must appear to me. However, it might still be argued that there could be no objects that are independent of my individual mind, as it is in itself.

In the 1790s, Kant tries to address this worry, by showing that we do have a kind of knowledge that there are radically mind-independent objects, although we cannot know how we should describe such objects. This does not violate critical strictures on knowledge of things as they are in themselves. Indeed, Kant regards knowledge that things in themselves exist as transcendental knowledge. It is not knowledge of the nature of those things as they exist in themselves. Such knowledge would be transcendent knowledge for him. The notion of a thing in itself must be intelligible, and hence representable by us in some very minimal and negative sense if we are to make sense of the distinction between appearances and things in themselves. Otherwise this is a distinction without a difference, and transcendental idealism collapses into transcendental realism.

In general, Kant does not commit himself to the non-representable character of things in themselves, but rather to their being unknowable according to the canons of theoretical knowledge. This leaves room for an immediate relation to things in themselves so long as this awareness is not interpreted as full-blown theoretical knowledge.[28] Such knowledge that there are things in themselves cannot entail substantive knowledge of the nature of those things in themselves. It does, however, commit one to a form of negative theology; one knows, for instance, that things in themselves cannot be spatio-temporal objects when conceived in themselves. To affirm the impossibility of treating objects in space as available under some non-spatio-temporal description is just to deny the legitimacy of the double-aspect approach to transcendental idealism in favor of some form of double-object theory. Even some interpreters who have advocated a double-object approach have also argued that the Refutation requires reference to things in themselves.[29]

Kant maintains that representations of objects in space are only possible to the extent that there is some thing in itself to which we are in a "real" relation:

> But if it is shown that the determination of our own existence in time presup-
> poses the representation of space in order even to represent to oneself the
> relation of the determinations of inner intuition to a constant object <*zum
> bleibenden Objekt*> ... then external objects can be secured a reality (as things in
> themselves) precisely through one's not taking their intuition as that of a thing
> in itself; for if it [the intuition of space] were of such [a thing in itself] and the
> form of intuition were the form of a thing, (which) were to belong to it [that
> thing] in itself even without the particular character of our subject, then it
> would be possible that we would have the representation of such a thing
> without that thing existing. However there is a particular kind of intuition in us
> which cannot represent what is in us, hence what exists in the change of time
> <*Zeitwechsel*>, since it would then be thinkable in the mere representation of
> temporal relations, therefore such a representation must subsist in the real
> relation <*wirklicher Beziehung*> to an object outside of us and space really
> means something which in being represented in this form of intuition is only
> possible through the relation to a real thing outside of us. – Therefore Refuta-
> tion of skepticism. Idealism. Spinozism. also of materialism, predetermin-
> ism. (Reflection 6317, Ak. XVIII, pp. 627–628)

We cannot have a representation of a spatial object without that object somehow existing outside of our spatial intuition. The thing in itself is represented by us as a real object in space, although, in fact, it is also in a real relation to the subject that cannot be spatio-temporal in character. The suggestion is that metaphysical or transcendental realism is false. Metaphysical realism insists that our beliefs about the world may be completely false, since the objects of our beliefs are completely independent of our beliefs. The complete independence of the world from our beliefs opens up the prospect of skepticism. There is no way for us

decisively to determine·from the nature of our beliefs whether they are radically misguided or not.

The reflection offers some indications as to how skepticism about the external world may be refuted. We must reject the assumption that we could have spatial representations of objects divorced from real relations to objects existing outside of our subjectivity. Kant does not leave it at this *petitio principii*. He also attempts to offer a vestige of an argument for the rejection of this assumption. The argument turns on the distinction between the representation of a spatial and the representation of a temporal relation. The key premise of the argument is that a spatial representation cannot be a representation of what is in us or of the passage of time, "Zeitwechsel." This appears to be another *petitio*. We want precisely to establish that we have a representation of something that is truly outside of us. We need to demonstrate that space is not merely a representation of inner experience. If space turns out to be a representation of inner experience and inner experience is essentially temporal, then our representation of objects in space would also involve a representation of a passage of time.

Fortunately, Kant offers a sketch of how the distinction between the faculty of representing things temporally and the faculty of representing things spatially might be justified. The argument would have to rest on a proof of the conditional with which he begins the reflection. One would have to show that temporal relations can only be established by appeal to some persistent object in space that is not essentially temporal. Objects given to us a priori through our temporal representation are by definition essentially temporal. One must show that consciousness of temporal relations is parasitic on consciousness of objects in space that are not essentially temporal. Then one may argue with some conviction that it is only in virtue of a mode of givenness of objects that is independent of the essential temporality of inner experience that we can experience temporal relations at all. Our consciousness of objects of inner sense, and indeed of inner sense itself, will turn out to be parasitic on the existence of the spatial objects of outer sense. Kant insists that both an intellectual consciousness of things outside of me and a determination of those things in space must co-occur with the determination of my existence in time. In making this claim, he links empirical self-consciousness to an immediate consciousness of things outside of one in both the transcendental and empirical senses.

Emphasis on the immediate givenness of one's existence through a purely intellectual self-consciousness leads Kant to fall back on his old term for intellectual self-consciousness. In Reflection 5652, the consciousness of things outside of me is referred to as an "intellectual intuition," where this intellectual intuition provides one with "no knowledge of things." The immediacy of existence provided by the act of self-consciousness had suggested the notion of an "intellectual intuition" to him in the seventies. Kant now endeavors to link this immediacy of existence not only to an event in time, but also to the immediate consciousness of something in space outside of me. He insists however that from this immediate consciousness "I [know] my own empirically determined existence no more than that of things outside of me (which, what they are in themselves I do not know)" (Reflection 5653, Ak. XVIII, p. 306).

Kant maintains that the immediacy in our consciousness of external things is the basis upon which such an interpretation must build. But, according to Guyer, the *mere occurrence* of intuitions with either temporal properties or even the phenomenological form of spatiality is not itself sufficient to provide even a representation of the temporal relations of these representations, so that questions of immediacy or mediation arise only once we have interpreted spatial and temporal experience.[30] It is, of course, true that the discussion of the status of consciousness as immediate or inferential is a topic of more abstract reflection, but this is not because representations only represent when they are interpreted or judged. For Kant clearly does not think that representations need to involve inference in order to be represented at all.[31] In fact, he pushes a point that is quite different from the point that Guyer derives from the passage.

Kant argues that we have an immediate and, hence, non-inferential consciousness of ourselves as passive beings, as beings to whom data is merely given. This is his justification for the claim that space cannot be within me. The assumption is that anything in me is a function of my spontaneity. Without an immediate consciousness of oneself as a passive being, one could not even represent things as being outside of oneself. Although the concepts of passivity/receptivity and activity/spontaneity are highly charged technical terms of philosophy, he suggests that they serve to articulate an immediate experience of the world and, indeed, the content of one's own experience as not completely of one's own making. If one is a passive being, then there must be things which exist outside of one, because otherwise one could not even have an inner experience.

The intuition of a thing as outside of me presupposes a determinability of my subject in which I am not myself the determinator, which therefore does not belong to spontaneity, because the determinator is not in me. And in fact I cannot think any space as in me. Therefore the possibility of representing things in space in intuition is grounded on the consciousness of a determination through other things, which [consciousness] means nothing other than my Original passivity in which I am not active. That dreams bring about deception concerning existences outside of me does not demonstrate anything against this; for external perceptions would have had to precede them at any rate. It is impossible to get a representation from something outside of me without being in fact passive. (Reflection 5653, Ak. xviii, p. 307)

The refutation of idealism ultimately depends on the idea that consciousness of a mere subject of thought is not enough for representing anything as genuinely in space and time and, hence, for representing anything as distinct from space and time themselves. One must be able to represent some particular as distinct from one's own subjectivity, if one is even to represent oneself as a numerically identical particular in time. Without some other individual that is external to one, one does not yet have a grip on the numerical distinctness of one's own identity as a particular individual.

The link between intelligibility for us and the content of beliefs also provides some support for a rejection of global skepticism. It undercuts the obvious objection that we may have concepts and quasi-perceptual experiences (imaginings) of many things that do not actually exist. It cannot be that everything that appears to me in perception is actually there, since there are delusive perceptions. The best that can be hoped for is an argument against global error together with a framework for tracking down local error. Our capacity to identify and reidentify particulars across different spaces and times, together with our ability to classify them into sorts, goes a long way to dealing with the problem of local error. Global error would undermine the conditions under which we can give representations whatever content they have.

Without the premise that global error is impossible, Kant has no serious prospects for blocking the claims of subjective idealism. He argues for the impossibility of global error by appeal to a version of the principle of charity. In order to take some claim as a judgment one must be able to make sense of that claim. However, one can only make sense of a claim against the background of certain other beliefs that one can also take to be true.

The appeal to some form of the principle of charity gives rise to another form of idealism however. But the idealism in question is a conceptual idealism. The governing idea of this conceptual idealism is that we cannot make sense of the notion of a world that does not conform to the conditions under which we can apply concepts at all. Even insistence on the existence of things in themselves does not violate this principle. Kant thinks that we can conceive of things in themselves only as objects of an understanding stripped of the conditions governing sensibility. This is why he often identifies things in themselves with noumena (intelligible objects). Since Kant acknowledges the possibility of merely imagining the existence of particular external objects – this possibility is the topic of the third and final note to the Refutation – he must have some premise that blocks the move from local skepticism about external objects to global skepticism about their existence. The intelligibility premise also undercuts skepticism about other minds, since it calls the skeptic's assumption that we could be completely wrong in our ascription of minds to other beings into question.

If self-affection, that is the determination of the content of one's experience, were possible completely independently of one's environment, then the empirical idealist's position would be unassailable. Since inner sense involves self-affection, saying that self-affection is possible without affection by external objects is another way of saying that an inner sense is possible without an outer sense. Kant tries to rule out such a possibility by arguing that it is incompatible with the existence of consciousness of oneself as a spontaneous being:

If we were only affected by ourselves but without noticing this spontaneity, then only the form of time would be found in our intuition: and we would not be able to represent any space to ourselves (an existence outside of us). Empirical consciousness as a determination of my existence in time would therefore go around in a circle and presuppose itself – above all it would be impossible, since the representation of something persistent would be missing, in which there is no continuous synthesis as in time. (Reflection 5653, Ak. XVIII, p. 308)

For those who find the idea that we are spontaneous beings implausible to begin with, this does not have much bite. In somewhat more general terms, Kant argues that we cannot make sense of ourselves as interpreters of experience without the idea that there is something in experience that is not up to us. We can only have the representation of our activity of interpreting, if there is something of which we are also immediately conscious that we must represent as distinct from this activity. This is why Kant infers the existence of an immediate consciousness of passivity or receptivity from the existence of an immediate consciousness of our spontaneity: "the concept of the mere passivity in a state of representation . . . is not inferred, since we do not perceive in us the cause of the existence of a perception, yet it is an immediate perception" (Ak. xviii, pp. 307–308). The immediate consciousness of our spontaneity is something we can only be aware of if we have an equally basic consciousness of our receptivity. Once we have a consciousness of our spontaneity we are then in a position to know that experience of objects in time as a form of inner sense must be connected to an immediate experience of objects in space. Now it is not altogether implausible to argue that we have an immediate experience of things not being up to us, but also of things needing interpretation by us. This could indeed be argued to be constitutive of our self-consciousness as finite rational beings.

While Kant could have argued for the existence of a fundamental distinction between what is internal to an individual point of view and what is external to all of our points of view had he not insisted on a sharp distinction between the conditions under which objects are intelligible to us and the conditions under which they are intelligible *tout court*, it is significant that in the end he wants to argue that our very consciousness of ourselves as experiencers depends on the existence of objects that are not only publicly and spatially accessible to us, but which are also radically independent of us.

CHAPTER 11

Empirical realism and transcendental idealism

In the last chapter, I explored Kant's argument that we can only make sense of claims to self-knowledge if we commit ourselves to the existence of objects that exist outside of us. Kant identifies this realism with respect to objects that are experienced as outside of us in experience with empirical realism. More controversially, he argues that the kind of knowledge of external objects that empirical realism requires, can only be established by appeal to his doctrine of transcendental idealism. It is to this doctrine of transcendental idealism that I now turn in closing my general argument.

EMPIRICAL REALISM AND TRANSCENDENTAL IDEALISM

In the Transcendental Aesthetic, Kant maintains that space and time are unavoidable representations. He makes the point clearest with respect to space: "we cannot represent to ourselves the non-existence of space." He maintains that the existence of space and time, while not logically necessary, is necessary to any experience that is intelligible to us, and necessary to any of our efforts to distinguish particular objects. Kant was inclined to draw far-reaching conclusions from his thesis that there is a distinctive non-logical and non-conceptual necessity involved in our capacity to distinguish inner from outer within experience. He saw the intuitive necessity in question as the basis for distinguishing what belongs to our experience from the way things are independently of our experience. This gives rise to what he calls a transcendental distinction between the inner and the outer, where everything that we experience is to be regarded as inner relative to what is completely independent of the sensible pre-conditions governing our experience.

Kant's conception of transcendental philosophy as an analysis of the pre-conditions of experience is closely associated with the thesis that we can know theoretically only what appears to us in accordance with the

sensible pre-conditions of experience (B XXIX). He refers to this thesis as
transcendental idealism, which he also glosses as the claim that objects
of experience are inherently subjective. Here subjective does not mean
private, but rather dependent on absolutely general conditions governing at least all human experience. Transcendental idealism is the thesis
that "such properties which belong to things in themselves can never be
given to us through the senses" (A 36/B 52), where we are to understand
things in themselves as things in themselves in the transcendental, and
not the empirical sense. Here the senses refers not only to the five senses,
but also to the a priori forms of our sensibility. This is thus not the
traditional claim of representational realism that we do not perceive the
primary qualities of things, such as mass, force, wavelength, and extension, while we do perceive secondary qualities such as heaviness,
warmth, color, smell, taste, and sound. The traditional distinction
between secondary and primary qualities corresponds roughly to the
distinction between appearances and things in themselves within experience, that is to the empirical distinction between appearances and things
in themselves. The transcendental claim is rather that our notion of
mass, wavelength, and force are themselves restricted to the way things
must appear to us. They presuppose the notions of extension, space, and
time, and these notions in turn depend on our a priori forms of
sensibility.

   Human beings can have sensory disabilities that make them unable to
experience certain kinds of sensations and hence certain secondary
qualities. The properties that objects have in virtue of being represented
by us in terms of the specific make up of our sensory apparatus are
contingent. They are not representable by all human beings (A 28–29).
The way things appear to us from a certain position in space and time is
also contingent. Thus an appearance in the empirical sense is the way
something looks, tastes, sounds, feels, or is experienced, from a particular spatio-temporal standpoint. By contrast, the properties that empirical objects have in themselves are those which "in universal experience
among all different positions relative to the senses, are determined thus
and in no other way in intuition" (A 45/B 63). These standpoint-
independent properties that objects of experience must have for all
observers regardless of their standpoint in space and time are not ones
that can be directly perceived through the senses, since sense perception
is inherently perspectival. Empirical objects regarded in themselves
have a spatial and temporal position that is the same for all observers.
They also have standpoint-independent properties that allow us to

locate them in a space and time that is the same for all observers, even though they appear differently to different observers depending on the spatio-temporal standpoint and psycho-physiological make up of those observers.

The transcendental distinction between appearances and things in themselves is a distinction we draw between the ways in which we know objects a priori (A 12/B 25). The only properties of objects that are available to us are ones that are essentially spatial or temporal. We would not know what the objects or their properties would be like in abstraction from space and time. The key thesis of transcendental idealism is that even the standpoint-independent spatial and temporal properties and relations that characterize objects of experience are themselves dependent on the way absolutely all human beings must experience objects, and have no existence that is independent of the forms according to which we and creatures relevantly like us must experience the world. Thus, from a transcendental point of view, even the seemingly standpoint-independent properties of objects turn out to be dependent on the standpoint that we must occupy as human experiencers. Things taken in themselves in the transcendental sense would by contrast be things that are radically independent of the way we as human beings must experience the world.

The claim that space and time are ideal when things are regarded from the transcendental point of view is a function of the fact that we represent space and time by means of the forms of our sensibility. Space and time cannot be represented as features that belong to things when they are reflected on by reason alone in abstraction from the sensible conditions that govern our experience, for our concepts of space and time are supposed to be parasitic on our capacity to represent objects in terms of the forms of our sensibility:

Our expositions teach therefore the *reality* (i.e. the objective validity) of space in respect to everything that can occur to us as an external object, but also the **ideality** of space in respect to things, insofar as they are regarded by reason in themselves, i.e. without regard to the character of our sensibility. (B 44)[1]

The affirmation of the reality of space and time with respect to all objects of our experience, the assertion of what Kant calls their objective reality, is connected with the denial of their absolute reality. For it is precisely because space and time are necessary structures of the mind that spatial and temporal objects must have observer-independent properties that, in principle, are cognitively accessible to us. To the extent that objects in space and time are themselves parts of space and time, they must also be conceived of as objects that cannot be represented by reason alone. Kant wants to argue that they cannot have absolute reality to the extent that they cannot be represented by reason alone. If we identify absolute reality with being an object of reason alone, then we can understand the thesis that spatio-temporal objects are mere appearances for us, but are not represented by us as things as they exist in themselves. But still we are inclined to wonder why we should think that things with absolute reality can only be objects accessible to reason alone.

THE DIRECT ARGUMENT FOR TRANSCENDENTAL IDEALISM

Kant presents the argument for the transcendental ideality of space and time as a conclusion from the arguments developed in the Metaphysical Expositions of Space and Time (A 23–25/B 38–40; A 30–32/B 46–48), as well as the Transcendental Expositions of Space and Time (B 40–41; 48–49). He thus assumes that once one has accepted these arguments one will also accept transcendental idealism (A 28/B 44; A 35/B 52). It is in the Conclusions from these Concepts (referring to the concepts of space and time developed in the Metaphysical Exposition) and the Transcendental Exposition that Kant explicitly commits himself to the *mere* subjectivity of space and time (A 26/B 42; A 32/B 42).

The Metaphysical Exposition defends Kant's thesis that space and time are a priori intuitions, because space and time are immediate and non-conceptual representations of a form according to which we must order objects. The Transcendental Exposition is an addition of the second edition which shifts the discussion of geometry out of the Metaphysical Exposition, develops it in more detail, and articulates the dependence of change and hence the laws of motion on the structure of time.

Kant articulates his worries about the legitimacy of the idea that space and time might exist completely independently of the mind by attacking the absolute and relational theories of space and time as incoherent. Following Clarke's exposition of the absolute theory in his famous exchange with Leibniz on the nature of space and time, Kant takes the adherent of an absolute theory of space and time to regard space and time as properties of things in themselves (in Clarke's theory, properties of God), whereas, for the relationalist, space and time are relations between things in themselves. From the premise derived from the Metaphysical Exposition that space is an a priori intuition, together with the premise that one cannot intuit determinations a priori and hence prior to the existence of things in themselves, Kant then infers that space is not an absolute or relative determination applying to things as they are in themselves and thus, by implication, that neither the absolute nor the relational theory of space could be true.

Space does not represent any property of things in themselves, nor does it represent them in their relation to one another. That is, space does not represent any determination that attaches to the objects themselves, and which remains even when abstraction has been made from all the subjective conditions of intuition. For no determinations, whether absolute or relative, can be intuited prior to the existence of things to which they belong, and none can be intuited *a priori*. (A 39/B 56)

The expression "for" in the final sentence indicates that the claim that one cannot intuit a priori determinations prior to the existence of things is being appealed to as a premise in the argument. The non-spatiality of things in themselves is supposed to follow from the nature of space as an a priori intuition.[2] Kant seems to place weight on the idea that neither space nor time could be properties or relations that depend for their existence on things in themselves. He talks of them as being determinations that cannot be "fastened" ("anhaften" A 26/B 42) or "attached" ("anhängen" A 33/B 49) to things in themselves. The implication is that space and time cannot be a priori conditions while also being properties or relations that owe their existence to the things in themselves that have them. For Kant's notion of the a priori requires that these properties or relations be necessary to all of the objects that have them. Clarke would not have wanted to say that space or time are necessary properties of God, and Leibniz would not have wanted to say that space or time are necessary relations of the things which induce them. This argument thus has some historical force. Kant also anticipates the possibility of thinking of time as something that exists for itself, but rejects this possibility because he thinks that time cannot be an object in its own right and so would have to be real without any real object (A 33/B 49). This seems to be based on the then universally held, but now widely rejected, assumption that time could not be a kind of thing or object with dynamic properties of its own.

Even if one accepts the arguments of the Metaphysical Exposition, one is entitled to be skeptical of the premise that one cannot represent absolute or relative determinations of things in themselves prior to the existence of those things. Kant's claim that one cannot intuit determinations prior to the existence of things seems to rule out an a priori intuition of the structure that any objects have. It thus seems to preclude us from having an a priori intuition of objects that we experience (appearances) as well. Since logical priority is part of the meaning of being a priori, *a priori* intuition must involve an immediate representation of objects that is logically prior to the existence of those objects.[3] Kant must mean that a thing that has properties or relations that we can intuit a priori would not be a thing in the absolute sense. It would not be fully independent of the mind.

Kant's line of thought seems to go as follows: things as they exist in themselves, in principle, could have spatio-temporal features that are necessary to either their possible or their actual existence. But they would not have such features in virtue of being represented by us according to a certain intuitive form. An intuitive form is distinguishable from a logical form precisely because its non-existence entails no contradiction. This is why we cannot prove that there cannot be other forms of intuition than the ones which human beings must have (B 72). Since there is no contradiction in the non-existence of a form of intuition, its existence is metaphysically contingent. This metaphysical contingency of our form of intuition is connected with its capacity to present us with objects that actually exist, as opposed to mere conceptual connections.

Something whose very existence depends on the contingent fact that there are representers like us who must represent the world in a certain way cannot be a thing which exists in itself because it cannot be a fully independent thing. It is, rather, an essentially relational thing which cannot exist independently of being representable by us. Spatio-temporal properties are essentially relational in the sense that we cannot form a concept of them independently of the way objects *must intuitively appear to us*. One might object that, while some objects may be necessarily spatio-temporal in the sense of being objects of a priori intuition, this need not preclude other objects from being spatio-temporal in the sense that they fall under concepts of space and time. But to affirm this possibility would be just to deny Kant's claim that our concepts of space and time necessarily depend on a priori intuition. The only concepts of space and time which we have are ones that are (putatively) based on a priori intuition. There are then no concepts of spaces and times in terms of which we could make sense of spaces and times that are completely independent of us. Thus we cannot make sense of spaces and times which conform to the way things appear to us only contingently.

The argument for transcendental idealism in the Transcendental Exposition provides support for this reading. From the assumption that we have a priori knowledge of geometry, it is inferred the objects of geometry are necessarily mind-dependent (B 42). For it is said that an external intuition that precedes its object can only belong to the mind and determine the concept of an object a priori, if it exists only in the subject. Kant demands that this intuition be the formal condition for being affected by objects and thus an *immediate representation* of them. The same argument is developed more explicitly at the end of the Transcendental Aesthetic in section 8 (A 46ff./B 64ff.). First Kant argues that geometry is synthetic. He notes that no purely conceptual analysis can show the impossibility of a closed geometric figure which consists of two straight lines. He insists, more tendentiously, that for this one has to go to intuition. Such intuition must be a priori if it is to justify propositions that are necessary and strictly general. He then argues that geometry can only be regarded as objective, as applying to the objects of geometry in themselves, if these objects cannot also exist independently of being intuited by us. The only way we have (according to Kant) of representing the objects of geometry is by means of the particular form of externality which forces itself upon us. This form of externality is assumed by him to be Euclidean and three-dimensional in structure, although this assumption depends on his views about the possibility of constructing mathematical objects in space. The key assumption, however, is that the only representation one could have of objects with spatial (or temporal) properties is the one which is provided by a priori intuition. Kant was convinced that, if the objects which we know as thus and such with necessity and strict generality could exist in abstraction from the conditions imposed on them by our experience, then all our claims to make objective assertions about these objects are in doubt.

Now if a faculty of intuiting a priori did not lie in you; if this subjective condition were not also as regards its form the general condition a priori under which alone an object of this (external) intuition is possible; if the object (the triangle) were something in itself without relation to your subject: how could you say that what lies necessarily in the subjective conditions for constructing a triangle, must also apply to the triangle itself? (A 48/ B 65)

Only by taking space and time to be inherently subjective can we be certain that the claims that we make on the basis of how possible objects must appear to us spatio-temporally are in fact objectively true of spatio-temporal objects. It might be thought that Kant's claims depend on the general nature of necessity claims. This is the way Kant's argument is understood by Paul Guyer with whose reconstruction I am otherwise in considerable sympathy.[4] But then the implication would seem to be that the notion of a mind-independent object would be either completely vacuous or incoherent. For any conceivable object must conform to the demands of logic. This possibility can be avoided if we take the argument to depend on the kind of non-logical necessity provided by intuition.

TRENDELENBURG LOOPHOLE

There appears to be a gap in Kant's argument, generally known as the Trendelenburg loophole after the nineteenth-century German philosopher who first brought it to the general consciousness of the philosophical public. It is not obvious why objects as they are intuited by us spatially and temporally cannot correspond to things in themselves that are themselves spatio-temporal. Henry Allison has done the most to rehabilitate Kant's transcendental idealism and is responsible for revived interest in the Trendelenburg loophole. Allison appeals to his principle of formal idealism as the key to Kant's argument against the possibility that the absolute or relational theories of space and time can account for the function of space and time as forms or conditions of human experience.[5] The purported principle of formal idealism forms the basis for what Allison takes to be Kant's strategy for dealing with Newton's and Clarke's theories of absolute space and time as well as Leibniz's relational theory of absolute space and time: "regarding space as an ontological condition (is) incompatible with also regarding it as an epistemic condition."[6]

However, in fairness to Allison, his specific argument for the transcendental ideality of space and time is supposed to depend on a priori conditions of the mind which are distinctively sensible. In transcendental reflection, we may think of something in terms of the forms according to which objects are given to us (the forms of our sensibility), or in terms of the forms according to which we must interpret objects (the forms of our thought). Something which merely appears to us is something which we represent according to the forms of our sensibility, whereas something which exists in itself is something which can be understood without reference to the forms of our sensibility. Unfortunately, when Allison tries to close Trendelenburg's loophole, he uses the general notion of a form of representation. The specifically sensible or intuitive character of our representation of space and time plays no obvious role in his argument.

There may be things that are logically possible, which we cannot make sense of in terms of the specific ways in which objects are given to us by our forms of sensibility. This raises the question whether something which we represent according to our forms of sensibility cannot also be understood without reference to those forms of sensibility. Allison considers two possibilities. There might be objects that are independent of our forms of sensibility but numerically identical with the objects which must conform to the a priori forms of our sensibility. Alternatively, there might be objects that are qualitatively, but not numerically, identical with the objects which must conform to our forms of sensibility. Allison dismisses the possibility that space or time might be numerically identical with what is independent of the mind, although the double-aspect view of transcendental idealism, which he defends, requires that one and the same thing be available under radically different aspects or descriptions, indeed as a mere appearance and as something that may be represented as it is in itself. He then argues that it would be incoherent or at least utterly vacuous to maintain that mind-dependent features could be qualitatively identical with mind-independent features of things. Since the notion of space and time as forms of intuition entails that what exists in these forms is something represented or mind-dependent, the notion of things in themselves having intuition-independent and hence mind-independent features is meaningless.[7] Unfortunately, this line of thought would seem to lead one to a form of solipsistic phenomenalism that is inconsistent with Kant's empirical realism. For we could raise the same objection with respect to any purportedly mind-independent features. Allison could appeal for support to a remark from Kant in which he distances himself from Berkeley's idealism:

I should be glad to know what my assertions must be in order to avoid all idealism. Undoubtedly, I should say that the representation of space is not only conformable to the relation which our sensibility has to objects – that I have said – but that it is completely like the object – an assertion in which I can find no meaning anymore than if I had said that the sensation of red has a similarity to the property of cinnabar which excites this sensation in me. (*Prolegomena*, Ak. IV, section 13, pp. 289–290)

Kant is assuming the thesis of representational realism that empirical objects (objects as they are to be regarded in themselves from the empirical standpoint) are not colored. Colors are mind-dependent secondary qualities, to which there are corresponding dispositional primary qualities in physical objects. The analogy to the relation between primary and secondary qualities to which Kant himself appeals in rejecting any relation of similarity between space and its objects suggests a plausible alternative account of the relation between space and time as features of things in themselves and space and time as forms of what is represented. The sensation of red and cinnabar are not similar with respect to the predicate red according to Kant. While the distinction between primary and secondary qualities does not strictly preserve qualitative identity, it does provide us with an analogical use of predicates which is neither vacuous nor incoherent. For we can speak of a red sensation, and a red sample of cinnabar, even though the sensation is not red in the same sense that the cinnabar is. It is difficult to understand how there could be a coherent use of analogical predicates across the empirical distinction between appearances and things in themselves while the use of analogy across the transcendental distinction would be illicit. Thus this passage gives some support to Allison's reading of Kant, but not to the substantive claim he wants to make.

There is a deeper difficulty with Allison's general line of argument, as well. For it rules out the possibility that things in themselves could be grasped in purely conceptual terms as well as in terms of our intuitions of spatio-temporal objects. If it never makes sense to say that an object can have the same features when represented as when it is understood in abstraction from being represented, then the whole notion of a thing as it is in itself threatens to become incoherent. Thus we could say, if space and time are forms of what is represented in intuition, things in themselves cannot coherently be represented spatio-temporally. But this would only be because things in themselves cannot be coherently represented at all. For this would be to represent something via a form of representing that is defined as independent of any form of representing. What is missing in Allison's account is a way of distinguishing the necessary mind-dependentness of objects subject to our forms of intuition from the mind-independence of objects that are subject only to forms of understanding. He tries to provide such an account by distinguishing logic from epistemic conditions, but the consequence of that view seems to be that we then have no representation of a thing in itself at all.

More recently, Allison has come to accept much of the force of this objection to his position.[8] While he earlier rejected Jill Buroker's argument for transcendental idealism from right- and left-handed objects (incongruent counterparts) as the basis of Kant's idealism, he now concedes that a generalized version of this idea is just what Kant needs.[9] For he now argues that something like Lorne Falkenstein's distinction between a presentational order for spatial and temporal properties of the kind provided by intuition and a comparative order for properties that can be grasped purely conceptually would be required in order to establish Kant's point that there is a sharp distinction between appearances and things in themselves.[10]

Falkenstein argues that if space and time were properties or relations of things as they exist in themselves, they would have to be based on a comparative order of internal properties such as that characteristic of the quality "space" of our sensations rather than the presentational order which Kant believes to be characteristic of the form of objects represented by us spatially (and temporally). The notion of a thing in itself is taken to be defined as allowing only relational properties that are reducible to non-relational properties. Objects that appear to us spatio-temporally would be the kind of objects that we must grasp in terms of an essentially relational, comparative order (right, left, earlier, later), while things in themselves would be the kind of things that can be grasped in a non-relational, purely conceptual manner.

Such a view seems clearly to have played a role in Kant's transcendental idealism, as his appeal to incongruent counterparts in support of his idealism indicates.[11] However, the idea that distinctions between right, left, earlier, later cannot be exhaustively expressed in terms of purely conceptual relations seems to be on rather shaky ground, since they can be given a rigorous mathematical formulation. And, even if we accept the distinction between a comparative and conceptual order, we must still demonstrate that only a comparative order of internal properties can exist independently of our sensibility. Otherwise, Kant, at best, will have established that we can only conceive of a presentational order by appeal to our sensibility, he will not have established the stronger claim that space and time cannot exist independently of our sensibility.

Kant assumes that because space and time are forms of our sensibility they cannot be forms which also exist independently of the way in which we order objects. But this claim, that because space and time are forms of our sensibility they can only be *mere* forms of our sensibility, raises precisely the neglected alternative suggestion made by Trendelenburg.

Perhaps the most direct approach to the loophole, that taken by Guyer, has a different, although related difficulty. Guyer argues that the loophole is closed by Kant's assumption that the necessity and universality involved in the a priori must be coextensive (B 4), so that, if something is known to be necessarily thus and such, it must belong to the same domain with respect to which we are able to make universal claims.[12] This provides an answer as to why Kant would rule out the idea that space and time might turn out independently of us contingently to have the features that we necessarily represent them as having; it does nothing, however, to show why they cannot necessarily have the properties that we represent them as having independently of us. And it raises the question as to whether the contrast between the way things must appear to us and things as they are in themselves is itself intelligible to us. For the very generality of the (necessary) a priori knowledge that we have, including, as it does, purely conceptual knowledge as well, seems then to preclude us from having any notion of an object that is not subject to necessary constraints.

THINGS IN THEMSELVES AND NOUMENA

There are a priori conditions for Kant governing even the concept of an object in general. These a priori conditions are provided by formal logic. If an object were necessarily mind-dependent in virtue of being subject to a priori conditions for thought in general, then the very notion of an object which exists independently of being represented by us would entail a logical contradiction. But then the distinction between an object which appears to us and an object as it is in itself would amount to just the distinction between an intelligible and an unintelligible object. In this case, the very claim that we can know only appearances but not things as they are in themselves would collapse into the trivial point that we cannot know what is unintelligible. Thinking of things as they are in themselves as unintelligible would conflict with Kant's tendency to identify things as they are in themselves with noumena or intelligible objects, objects of understanding alone. The problem with such objects is that they are vacuous for us, not that they are unintelligible. Kant's view, by contrast, is that the range of the logical a priori determines what is intelligible.

Since Kant does not think that there can be alternative logics to the term logic of his time, he does not think that there can be alternative logics with more or less equal claims to plausibility. It is thus reasonable for him to take the a priori of general or, rather, universal, logic ("allgemeine Logik") to determine what can intelligibly be said to be. It thus has a general criteriological character for ontology. This assignment of a general criteriological function to logic in ontology is reasonable even from a more contemporary point of view that is bound to be more skeptical about the neo-Aristotelian and Stoic term logic which Kant thought to be largely, but not wholly, immune to revision. Something resembling first-order quantification theory with identity seems to be very close to any adequate way of fleshing out basic assumptions governing thought. At the very least, logic is that part of our corpus of beliefs which we must hold to be most resistant to revision in the face of experience.

It seems reasonable to look to general logic for the concept of an object that can be thought independently of any sensible intuition. And, given the completely general character of logic, we might hope that logical notions would provide us with some representation of a thing that is independent of sensibility. But here we run up against the limits of what reason can provide us with. We do have the general idea of an object that could be grasped by reason without appeal to experience. Kant introduces the noumenon as a thing "that ought to be thought of not at all as an object of the senses, but rather as a thing in itself (merely through the pure understanding)" (A 255/B 310). The identification of what would be represented by a pure understanding in abstraction from sensibility with a thing in itself fits his view that it is because space and time and their objects are given to us by our forms of sensibility that they cannot be things as they exist in themselves. This notion of a noumenon is not itself self-contradictory, Kant maintains, since one cannot say of sensibility that it is the only possible form of intuition. But he does argue that our concepts are restricted in their meaning and application to the domain of sensibility. Even general logic can only be applied to objects if those objects are somehow given to us. This means for him that a noumenon, or a thing represented as it is in itself, cannot be an intelligible object for our understanding. We are to think of a thing in itself as something which could only be thought by a radically different kind of intuition than our own, a non-sensible intuition (A 256/B 312). For such an intuition, there is no distinction to be drawn anymore between the way objects are given and the conditions under which they can be thought. Indeed, the very notion of objects being given to such an intuition loses any meaning. Kant admits that the very possibility of such an intuition is problematic. This leads Kant to conclude that the notion of a noumenon involves the representation of a thing of which we can neither say that it is possible nor that it is impossible, since we do not have the kind of intuition required to make sense of it (A 287/B 343).

Kant denies in many places that we do or can know whether there could be objects which are not spatial or temporal. This is the dominant view in the sections on Phenomena and Noumena (A 255/B 310) and the Amphiboly of Concepts of Reflection (A 276–277/B 332–333). He thus leaves the question open whether there could be things which exist as they are in themselves independently of the way we represent things spatially and temporally. So interpreted, the thing in itself is a limiting concept for theoretical reason of which we have no theoretical knowledge. The question of whether things in themselves are spatio-temporal or not is meaningless, since it requires resources outstripping the enabling conditions of meaningful discourse. Space and time cannot be taken by us to exist independently of the mind because we have no concept of them that would make their mind-independent existence intelligible. If we cannot have a concept of space and time that is independent of the way objects must be given to us by the contingent fact that we must represent the inner–outer distinction as we do, then we cannot make sense of the idea that space and time themselves exist completely independently of us. Kant is clearly right that, even though space and time may be necessary to the way we experience the world, we cannot regard their existence as logically necessary. Still, even if this is true, it is too weak a claim to establish that space and time cannot be things as they exist in themselves or properties or relations of those things. The best that Kant can hope for is that he has established that space and time are not the kind of things that can be regarded by us as things in themselves or their properties or relations. This interpretation fits Kant's tendency to refer to the distinction between things in themselves and appearances as two ways that we have of regarding things, rather than as a distinction that applies to things completely independently of our reflection.

Most of our beliefs might turn out to be false, and the best standards of knowledge we have might turn out to be inadequate by the lights of the noumena presented to an intellectual intuition. But we do not even know that the perspective of intellectual intuition is possible. It is not really intelligible to us and might turn out to be unintelligible in a more general sense. Here we find the basis for a modest version of transcendental idealism, according to which there is a way in which together we must understand and experience the world, although we cannot be certain that this way of experiencing the world is compelling for absolutely all creatures. This anodyne notion of transcendental idealism leaves it an open question whether there can be things that are intelligible independently of the conditions of our spatial and temporal representations of them. This epistemically modest version of transcendental idealism is a view which should be very attractive for anyone who thinks that there can be transcendental arguments in the theory of knowledge which compel us to think of the world as structured in a certain way.

Those passages in which Kant pushes the idea that the notion of a noumenon is necessarily empty for us, make it difficult to understand how Kant can think that "it is indubitably certain and not just possible or probable" that space and time are forms only of appearances rather than things in themselves (A 49/B 66). The epistemically modest notion of transcendental idealism allows for the logical possibility of something that is distinct from the way objects must appear to us, and thus provides us with a purely negative notion of a thing in itself, but Kant often wants something much stronger:

In fact, when we regard objects of the senses as mere appearances, as is appropriate, then we admit that a thing in itself is their ground, although we know it not as it is in itself, but only its appearance, i.e. the way our senses are affected by an unknown something. The understanding therefore in assuming appearances also admits the existence < *das Dasein* > of things in themselves, and in this respect we can say that the representation of such beings that are the ground of appearances, that is, mere beings of the understanding, is not only admissible, but also unavoidable. (*Prolegomena*, Ak. IV, section 32, pp. 314–315)

If space and time are merely subjective in contrast to things in themselves, then we can conclude from the existence of space and time as mere subjective forms that there must be things in themselves. For without the existence of things in themselves there would be no justification in claiming that space and time are *merely* subjective. The notion of a "mere appearance" requires some form of real distinction between appearances and things in themselves, and some thing that exists in itself to which what appears merely appears to be thus and such. To establish a real distinction between appearances and things in themselves one would need some knowledge or at least some conception of how things are or might be in themselves apart from the pre-conditions of our knowledge. This would commit one to a substantive concept of a thing as it exists in itself.

The claim that things as they appear to us cannot be things as they exist in themselves is the basis for Kant's rejection of transcendental realism "which regards space and time as something given in them-selves, independently of our sensibility" (A 370). The contrast between transcendental realism and idealism thus depends on a distinction between things in themselves and appearances that seems only to be articulable by rejecting the very epistemological criterion of reality upon which that distinction might be founded. Kant maintains that we cannot have bona fide theoretical knowledge of things as they are in themselves, except in the manner in which they must appear to us. But then the worry is that we have no way of knowing that they must, indeed, be distinct from the way that things must appear to us. If we cannot know that things in themselves must be distinct from the way things must appear to us, we cannot know that transcendental idealism is true.

There is an inherent ambiguity in Kant's notion of a thing in itself even when one disregards what he calls the physical or empirical notion of a thing in itself. In one sense, a thing in itself is an object of an intellectual intuition, a kind of intuition which we cannot have as finite rational beings. In this sense, Kant consistently denies that we can have a concept or cognition of things in themselves. Even our understanding of an intellectual intuition is purely negative. It has powers of compre-hension that our intellect and our intuition do not have. On the other hand, Kant also thinks of moral properties and the individuals to which they belong as existing in and of themselves. The Aesthetic, for instance, contrasts the notion of space, belonging only to appearances, with the notion of right, that belongs to things in themselves; the contrast with space makes it clear that Kant does not have in mind the claim that right is a property of things in themselves in the empirical sense: "right cannot appear at all, its concept lies rather in the understanding and represents a property (the moral one) of actions which belongs to those actions in themselves" (A 43/B 61).

In the *Critique*, Kant no longer allows for any grasp of things in purely conceptual terms by theoretical reason, as he seems to in the *Dissertation* where he identifies purely conceptual knowledge of things with meta-physics (Ak. II, pp. 395–396). But he continues to think that, from a purely practical or moral point of view, we can say that there are real things that are not spatial and temporal. Thus the passage in the Aesthetic is very much in the spirit of a similar passage in the *Dissertation* where Kant also notes that our moral concepts may be confused, that is, not such that we could pick out their objects by means of necessary and sufficient conditions, but that their objects are known by the pure intellect itself (Ak. II, p. 395). Kant tends to regard the practical notion of a thing in itself as something that we merely postulate as ultimately real in order to express the primacy of moral agency. Things in themselves in this sense are not objects of an intellectual intuition, but rather a way of looking at the sensible world in abstraction from what is sensibly determined about it and, hence, as an object of pure practical reason (A 808/B 836). When we relate to the world in moral terms, we relate to it in a way which abstracts from the sensible conditions which govern what must merely appear to us. This purely intellectual conception of the world also grasps the world as it is in itself in abstraction from sensibility. But the notion of a thing in itself is not, in this case, independent of our practices, although it is something substantive.

The assumption that we understand the way the world really is from the moral point of view has some force. It is hard to find it completely compelling, since this primacy of the moral point of view is something that can only be understood once one has already accepted the moral point of view. Also, its bearing on most objects of theoretical reflection is indirect. Nature is connected to rights and the moral point of view only indirectly. For instance, when we take a natural object to be something we regard as property, we are conceiving of nature in the framework of rights. But some sense can be given to the initially implausible assumption that moral agency must be somehow independent of the spatial and temporal conditions otherwise governing agency. The categorical imperative articulated in Kant's moral theory spells out a procedure for universalizing the maxims that we derive from everyday deliberations. This promises a way of understanding what we are doing that applies regardless of our spatio-temporal context. To the extent that we adopt and act according to those universalized maxims solely because of their universality, we may be said to act from motives that abstract from spatio-temporal content. Even here there is the problem that moral law has content only through the way it generalizes from our experience. It is thus somewhat doubtful that we have succeeded in representing an action in a way that is genuinely independent of our sensibility. But we can take this to be a representation of the sensible in terms of purely intellectual concepts, as Kant does in the *Critique*.

Kant's transcendental idealism is most plausible when it presents itself in its modest form. Otherwise it requires a compelling reason to believe that the concept of an object which could be grasped in abstraction from a priori intuition is not altogether empty of real content. Kant has admittedly an initially plausible motivation for denying spatiality and temporality to things as they exist in themselves. Our ability to know necessary facts about space and time, and the objects that are to be found in space and time, is based on the way the mind is constrained to represent the world. If the features that those objects must have in virtue of the way we must represent the world were features that those objects might not have independently of being represented by us, then we would be left with what might seem to be a subjective necessity of the kind Hume attributed to our fundamental beliefs. We could not be certain that the structures in terms of which we make the world intelligible to ourselves are not mere projections on to the world of what we must believe about the world. But this challenge could also be met by rejecting the subjectivist interpretation of necessity in favor of the idea that we have no reason to doubt that the necessities in question hold independently of what we as humans must believe. Kant seems to have been prevented from endorsing such a move by worries that ascribe metaphysical necessity to things other than God, but this does not really seem to be a compelling worry, even for someone with religious beliefs.

Even if the legitimacy of what we must believe about the world is, in principle, subject to challenge, this challenge will have to come from inside what we must believe. The worry must be taken seriously that what we take to be facts might not be genuine facts about anything but what we must believe. But this worry is much less serious than the more pressing worry that we will fail altogether to identify anything that we all, even as human beings, must believe. This is the place where Kant needs to take a stand against Hume's notion of psychological necessity. Genuinely a priori knowledge is enough, if it can be had. We do not need to worry about the way things might appear to a point of view that we cannot even make intelligible to ourselves. Thus it seems that Kant's concern with how to draw the distinction between what is inner, in the sense of private, and what is outer, in the sense of public, is ultimately more fruitful than his attempt to work out how we are to understand the further distinction between what is inner, in the sense that it is internal to the experience that we all share in common, and what is outer, in the sense that it is completely independent of us. However, despite the reservations that are in order concerning the substantive negative claims that Kant makes about the nature of things as they are in themselves, he seems to be right that our conception of the world must provide for both of these inner–outer distinctions.

Conclusion

I have traced a path that began with the idea that a distinction between what is internal to one's point of view and what is external to one's point of view is constitutive of the kind of consciousness that we have of ourselves as finite rational beings. I have argued that the most fundamental way in which we distinguish what is internal to our point of view from what is external to our point of view is by appeal to the idea that we experience what is internal to our point of view successively, and hence temporally, while we experience what is external to our point of view in spatial relations that are only contingently successive. Spatial relations, and the objects that occupy them are ultimately the basis upon which we are able to ascribe a determinate position even to the successive representations that are constitutive of our individual point of view. At the same time, we cannot make sense of objects that we experience as outside of us without representing them temporally.

The idea that experiencing objects spatially and temporally is unavoidable for us, indeed the more general idea that the only grip that we have on existence is in terms of existence in space, or at least time, leads Kant to claim that space and time are necessary forms of our experience. The logical possibility that there might be objects that are not spatial or temporal leads him to argue that space and time constitute necessary forms of our experience only. In this way, we come to have the idea of objects that might be outer to us in a very radical way; they might be outside of the conditions governing our experience. This, in turn, leads to the conception of objects that we experience as objects that are inner in a new, transcendental sense; they are internal to our experience. Kant then, unfortunately, succumbs to the temptation to argue that these objects that are completely outside of the conditions governing our experience would have to be neither spatial nor temporal. This is an idea without much plausibility to it. And, fortunately, it is not a view that he consistently espouses. Sometimes he opts for the more

235

modest view that we cannot make sense of real objects that are not spatial or temporal. It is more fruitful to think of such non-spatial or temporal objects as mere logical possibilities, rather than as correct descriptions of objects as they would have to be completely independently of our experience.

We distinguish the inner from the outer within experience, and the outer as what is completely independent of the way we must experience the world, on the basis of the consciousness that we have of ourselves. The consciousness that we have of ourselves has two aspects to it. On the one hand, we are conscious of ourselves as individuals who have distinctive experiences that distinguish us from all other individuals, each of whom has his or her own distinctive point of view. These experiences are distinguished on the basis of their different spatial and temporal content. On the other hand, we are also conscious of ourselves as individuals who have a point of view that might have been a different point of view had our experience gone differently than the way it actually has gone. This gives us some understanding of what it is to have a point of view in a more general sense. In the end, our only grasp of our own distinctive point of view seems to be based on what is distinctive about it and our ability to grasp that depends on our capacity to grasp other possible points of view.

The capacity to grasp different points of view as possible ways in which one might experience the world is what Kant thinks of as the capacity for certain representation of one's numerical identity. One must be able to represent oneself as identical through different experiences and representations in a more general sense, for this is an a priori condition for the ascription of determinate and communicable content both to our representations and to the representations of any other sentient being. To regard another creature as sentient, at least in principle, is to recognize the representations of that creature as ones that could have belonged to one's own experience had that experience only been sufficiently different. It is to treat the states of that creature as potentially connectible together in a system of self-ascribable representations in which one's own representations would also have a determined position. This system of different self-ascribable representations is our best way of making sense of the notion of an object of experience that is independent of my, or even our, particular take on what we experience. The system in question takes its starting-point from what we experience, so it is not completely arbitrary, but the only way we have of getting on in understanding what we are experiencing.

Our grasp of concepts is based on the distinctive ability for self-conscious abstraction that we have. For concepts are just capacities that we have to represent things in ways that make sense not only to each of us individually, but also potentially to each and all of us, collectively. We develop and exercise our understanding of concepts in terms of our understanding of a whole battery of concepts that we systematically apply to our experience. And it is this systematic unity of conceptualized reality that provides us with the very distinction between a correct and an incorrect use or application of a given concept in a judgment. It is this systematic unity in what we experience that thus provides the only way we have of distinguishing what is true from what merely appears to us to be thus and such from our own distinctive point of view.

Our capacity to use concepts to interpret what we experience as inner or outer to us is based on our capacity for self-consciousness. But the self-consciousness that allows us to do this must be thought of as an impersonal one. For it is based on the capacity to stand back from or abstract from the way things are for each of us individually. Such a subject of thought is the condition for the possibility of the kind of neutrality with respect to differences in point of view that characterize our conception of objectivity. The impersonal point of view gives judgment its target of truth. We conceive of what is true as holding independently of what each of us may happen to believe or take to be true. But, in order for this idea of independence to be coherent, we must assume the possibility of a point of view from which what we happen to take to be true might turn out to be false. We can only do that to the extent that we are willing to allow for the possibility of alternative takes on reality, and for us to do that we must be able to consider the possibility that our own distinctive take on things might have been, or could be, a different one.

The very abstractness of our representation of self, expressed in tokenings of "I," makes it capable of representing both the impersonal point of view and a particular point of view as a point of view that shares something in common with other points of view, but also differs in some respect or other from those different points of view. The impersonal consciousness of self to which I have been referring is an enabling condition of personal identity, but it is not to be conflated with one's empirical personal identity. Acknowledgement of the possibility of being conscious of oneself in such a way that one thinks of oneself as a consciousness that is yet not identified with any spatio-temporal location is an important dimension to our ability to understand and use concepts.

For the very impersonal way in which one represents the self allows the impersonal representation of self to serve as a pre-condition of communicable experience and communicable representations. In particular, it underwrites our capacity for judgment and to come up with concepts that articulate what we experience and otherwise grasp in ways that we can communicate to others. Such a self-consciousness allows one to conceive of space and time and the objects of experience in space and time as a unitary system of permutations on potential standpoints that I might assume with respect to spatio-temporal experience.

It might seem that only our capacity to form concepts and make judgments with them that have objective import is based on our capacity for abstractive self-consciousness. But, in fact, not only our grasp of concepts, but our very grasp of the distinction between inner and outer and the distinctive temporal and spatial form that it takes for us, is based on the kind of capacity for abstraction that comes with the capacity for self-consciousness. For this is a structure that is abstract in the sense that each of us attributes it to him- or herself, and yet it is also a general condition under which each of us individually is capable of experiencing him- or herself, as well as the world. The self can represent itself spatially and temporally in abstraction from the empirical objects that present themselves to various particular spatial and temporal locations. This is to represent oneself as having a point of view, but in abstraction from the particular context in experience which makes one the distinctive person one is. Any arbitrary self-conscious individual may think of him- or herself as existing here and now, and in each case something different will present itself to him or to her in accordance with the change in context within spatial and temporal experience. Thus the abstract representation of self as the possessor of a spatio-temporal experience provides the most general notion of the self as an object of self-consciousness which relates to itself as a distinctive object and to other possible objects as distinguishable from it. The different objects that present themselves to different spatio-temporal subjects, together with those subjects, each of which may, in turn, be regarded as a spatio-temporal object, may be ordered in a standpoint-independent way by each self-conscious individual in a way that is consistent with each of their different spatio-temporal perspectives. In order for them to order episodes in this standpoint-independent way, subjects set up a common Cartesian co-ordinate system with four different axes corresponding to the three dimensions of space and a fourth dimension for time. They can then assign tenseless relations of earlier, later, simultaneous, and spatial co-ordinates to all objects. To do this, they, and indeed each one of us, must be able to apply the concepts of causation, interaction, and substance to experience, for only if we can legitimately apply these concepts to all of our experiences will we be able to determine the temporal relations and positions of all episodes within experience.

The unity of spatio-temporal experience manifests itself in the possibility of our having determinate beliefs and representations about spatio-temporal objects. Beliefs about objects experienced in space and time are determinate because there is a determinate procedure for confirming and disconfirming (verifying and falsifying) those beliefs. We can make out something permanent in spatio-temporal experience that provides the basis for a determinate procedure for confirming and disconfirming our beliefs. The very notion of an object as something permanent in experience, or as something that is numerically identical through space and time, turns out to be a function of our need to assume a self-conscious standpoint that allows us to regard our experience as an experience that can be captured and expressed in intersubjectively communicable concepts.

The communicability of beliefs presupposes the possibility of a consciousness from which we may distinguish ourselves. Our possession of determinate beliefs also requires the existence of objects existing outside of us. For only such objects can provide us with the permanence which we need as a reference-point for determining the content of our beliefs in some way which promises potential criteria for success and failure in our self-ascriptions of beliefs and cognitions. Without permanent objects whose existence is not at the mercy of our immediate representations, we would fail to have any basis for believing that we had correctly or incorrectly ascribed a belief or other representation to ourselves or to someone else.

Kant's transcendental idealism suggests that we can only give determinate content to our beliefs at the cost of subjecting them to substantive restrictive constraints, such as that every event must have a cause or that every event must be the state of a permanent substance. These are constraints on the self-ascription of spatio-temporal representations. Thus Kant finds himself defending the claim that all non-logical theoretical knowledge is restricted to spatio-temporal objects. These objects might, however, in principle be subject to some other more fundamental mode of description that would not be spatio-temporal at all. But, even where Kant seeks to find such a description in the dimension of action motivated by impersonal reasons, he does not give up the basicness of the idea of a numerical identity of the self that is a priori. For this notion is the very basis for his defense of the impersonal point of view. Nor does he give up the idea that the immediacy of experience is something that we must conceptualize in a manner that sustains the publicity of what we represent. The publicity of what we represent continues to express the numerical identity of an impersonal point of view. And this impersonal point of view, in principle, is available to us in any arbitrary context of experience.

While the constraints that self-consciousness imposes on experience may be necessary to any experience that we may conceive of as such, it is not obvious that we can dictate that the world must be such as to conform to conditions on the ascription of belief. This is the sense in which Kant is entitled to defend his thesis that objects of experience are transcendentally ideal, that is, inherently mind-dependent. We cannot know what they would be like independently of the conditions under which we must ascribe beliefs about them to us and to other thinkers. The thesis that our only access to the world is constrained by pre-conditions on experience governing that access, is a weaker construal than Kant often gives to his transcendental idealism. For he often insists that we can know that things as they exist are not spatial or temporal, and sometimes even claims that we can be certain of the non-spatio-temporality of things as they exist in themselves. The most that the purely epistemic dimension of Kant's transcendental idealism allows him is that we can only make sense of the world in terms of the spatio-temporal conditions governing our experience. It does not licence the further claim that space and time could not exist independently of the role that they play in allowing us to identify and reidentify objects of experience, and our cognitive states as well.

Kant is most successful in spelling out a framework in terms of which we can think of how to make sense of our position in the world. It is this framework that I have tried to develop. I have sought to restore the standpoint of an impersonal self to the status it deserves as the crucial starting-point for understanding our capacity to understand our individual identity and our place in the world relative to other selves and to material things. In the process, I have argued that Kant's transcendental self-consciousness is not just a logical capacity that we associate with the capacity for judgment, although it is crucial to our capacity for judgment. Nor does transcendental self-consciousness simply collapse into consciousness of personal identity. But transcendental self-consciousness is the key to drawing the distinction between inner and outer experiences and recognizing inner experiences as inner and outer experiences as outer. It is on the basis of this capacity to distinguish between inner and outer experiences that we are then able to apply concepts to our experience in judgment.

Notes

I INTRODUCTION

1 The objection that Kant must appeal to an unintelligible notion of subject in his conception of transcendental self-consciousness is well articulated by Rüdiger Bittner, "Transzendental," in H. Krings *et al.* (eds.), *Handbuch philosophischen Grundbegriffe* (Munich: Kössel Verlag, 1974), vol. 5, pp. 1524–1539.

2 Interpreters who have treated Kant's theory of the identity of apperception as a theory of personal identity include: Graham Bird, Robert Paul Wolff, Dieter Henrich, Paul Guyer, and Patricia Kitcher. I discuss their interpretation of the representation that we have of our numerical identity in chapter two.

3 I will argue in chapter four that the interpretation that Henry Allison provides of transcendental apperception collapses all self-consciousness for Kant into knowledge of objective states of affairs, or at least into judgments that purport to be objective; see H. Allison, *Kant's Transcendental Idealism* (New Haven: Yale University Press, 1983), see esp. p. 155: "In other words, a subjective unity of consciousness is not a unity *of* self-consciousness, although it can (as objectified) become a unity *for* self-conscious thought."

4 In his classic discussion of Kant, *The Bounds of Sense* (London: Methuen, 1966), P. F. Strawson is careful not to run together the identity of the subject of transcendental self-consciousness, which is concerned with the possibility of experience, with empirical personal identity. A priori identity of self-consciousness is supposed to be the basic condition for the possibility of empirical self-ascription without being actually identical with that possibility (p. 108). Strawson rightly notes that, for Kant, objectivity has something to do with transcendental self-consciousness and that personal self-consciousness has something to do with how each of us experiences the world in our own distinctive ways. Strawson is also clearer than many contemporary commentators about the dependence of empirical self-consciousness on transcendental self-consciousness that Kant emphasizes in the same context. But Strawson does not spell out how transcendental self-consciousness is supposed to help us to understand the connection and distinction between the subjective and objective (*Bounds of Sense*, p. 107). While he notes that transcendental

self-consciousness is supposed to be the core of empirical self-consciousness, he has nothing to say about how it might serve as the core of empirical self-consciousness. Indeed, he has almost nothing substantive to say about what transcendental self-consciousness might be.

5 Kant's general line of thought is articulated in an interesting way by Theodor Lipps, *Leitfaden der Psychologie* (Leipzig: Engelmann, 1903), pp. 34ff.: "I know .. . immediately only of my *own* consciousness or of 'me'. But this consciousness is *not* in itself something individual, but rather simple consciousness; and this I is not in itself 'my' I or 'this' I, but it is simply *I*... Not until I know of other I's does this I become 'this', 'mine', one among many, in short individual." A similar claim is developed in Theodor Lipps, *Inhalt und Gegenstand: Psychologie und Logik* in *Sitzungsberichte der philosophischen-philologischen und der historischen Klasse der Königlichen Bayerischen Akademie der Wissenschaften* 4 (1905), p. 564. Kant does not demand that I actually know that there are other egos in order to ascribe beliefs or desires to myself. But he does think that one must have the concept of other possible individuals endowed with self-consciousness in order to have a grasp of the individuality of one's own self-consciousness.

2 INTRODUCING APPERCEPTION

1 J. Tetens, *Philosophische Versuche über die menschliche Natur und ihre Entwicklung* of 1771 reprint: (Berlin: Reuther and Reichard, 1912), identifies inner sense with apperception. In his *Psychologia Empirica* of 1738 reprint (Hildesheim: Georg Olms, 1968), section 25, Christian Wolff argued that "apperception is attributed to the mind insofar as it is conscious for itself of its perception." Kant criticizes the identification of inner sense with pure apperception in *Anthro*, Ak. vii, p. 161, and with apperception in the B-Deduction at B 153.

2 Andrew Brook, *Kant and the Mind* (New York: Cambridge University Press, 1994), p. 145. Brook interprets Kant's distinction between actual self-consciousness and the possibility of self-consciousness and that between empirical and transcendental apperception as the difference between optional and non-optional acts of synthesis. The mind only sometimes engages in acts of attentive awareness, however the mind is supposed to represent itself to the self through the self's activity of synthesis all the time. Now Kant does distinguish between acts of attentive awareness and non-attentive awareness, but he also distinguishes between self-consciousness and consciousness, and there is little of no textual support for the claim that the distinction between attentive and non-attentive awareness corresponds to that between self-consciousness and consciousness. Conflating the two distinctions also seems to be intrinsically implausible. The view that apperception is not about self-awareness is also shared by Patricia Kitcher, *Kant's Transcendental Psychology* (New York: Oxford, 1990), esp. p. 138.

3 Graham Bird, *Kant's Theory of Knowledge* (London: Routledge and Kegan Paul, 1962), pp. 136ff., sees Kant as responding to Hume's worries about personal identity. R. P. Wolff, *Kant's Theory of Mental Activity* (Cambridge, Mass.: Harvard University Press, 1963), pp. 134ff. Wolff argues that Kant came to

know Hume's critique of self-identity through Beattie's *Essay on the Nature and Immutability of Truth* in *Beattie's Works* (Philadelphia: Hopkins and Earle, 1809), translated into German in 1772. The argument is presented in detail in R. P. Wolff, "Kant's Debt to Hume via Beattie," *Journal of the History of Ideas* 21 (1960), 117–123. More recently it has been articulated with vigor by Patricia Kitcher, *Kant's Transcendental Psychology*, pp. 97ff. Kant's conception of self-identity a priori is said by Patricia Kitcher to be a response to Hume's worries about self-identity. She argues for this in "Kant on Self-Identity," *The Philosophical Review* 91 (1982). 41–72, and in *Kant's Transcendental Psychology*, p. 97. Paul Guyer also maintains that Kant's conception of the numerical identity of the self a priori is intended as a reply to Hume in *Kant and the Claims of Knowledge* (Cambridge University Press, 1987), pp. 76, 137, 147. Other interpreters, such as Strawson, note similarities and differences between the two views of self-identity, but are more circumspect in their claims of influence, cf. *Bounds of Sense*, pp. 169–170. Wolfgang Carl, *Die Transzendentale Deduktion der Kategorien in der ersten Auflage der "Kritik der reinen Vernunft": Ein Kommentar* (Frankfurt: Klostermann, 1992), is an exception to this approach to the identity of self-consciousness; Carl sees the German philosopher and psychologist Tetens as the target of Kant's critique, pp. 60ff.

4 David Hume, *A Treatise on Human Nature*, L. E. Selby-Bigge (ed.) (Oxford: Clarendon Press, 1888), Book I, Part IV, Section VI, pp. 250–251.

5 Graham Bird, *Kant's Theory of Knowledge*, pp. 120ff., thinks that Kant runs together apperception as involving personal identity and apperception as providing a unity for objective judgment and conceptual rules.

6 Strawson, *The Bounds of Sense*, pp. 164–165. Dieter Henrich, "Identity and Objectivity," in *The Unity of Reason* (Cambridge, Mass.: Harvard University Press, 1994.

7 The inflated view of a priori consciousness of self-identity is defended by Dieter Henrich, "Identity and Objectivity," in his *The Unity of Reason*, pp. 187ff., and Peter Rohs, "Über Sinn und Sinnlosigkeit von Kants Theorie der Subjektivität," *Neue Hefte für Philosophie* 27/28 (1988), esp. 66ff. Henrich argues that we have Cartesian certainty of our numerical identity over a series of states. Rohs maintains that self-identification across time is criteria-less and certain. He has nothing to say about the possibility of delusive quasi-memories which threaten such a claim.

8 Paul Guyer's critique of Henrich is first presented in his review of *Identität und Objektivität* (the original German version of "Identity and Objectivity"), *The Journal of Philosophy* 76 (1979), 151–167. Henrich's response may be found in "The Identity of the Subject in the Transcendental Deduction," in E. Schaper and W. Vosenkuhl (eds.), *Reading Kant: New Perspectives on Transcendental Arguments and Critical Philosophy* (Oxford: Basil Blackwell, 1989), p. 279.

9 Guyer, *Kant and the Claims of Knowledge*, pp. 146–147.

10 *Ibid.*, p. 148.

11 *Ibid.*, p. 303.

12 A variant on Guyer's interpretation is defended by Lorne Falkenstein, he argues that, even though intuition is itself a manifold, when it is though it is then collapsed into an absolute momentary spatial unity, i.e. that of a particular shape. "The mind seems to distinguish automatically the moments of time over which the intuitions occur, and so, whereas it collapses the manifold in space at any instant as an 'absolute unity,' it continues to distinguish the different times over which the intuition occurs as so many successive and distinct representations." *Kant's Intuitionism* (University of Toronto Press, 1995), pp. 76–77. Apart from the fact that Kant never claims that thought transforms the manifold into an absolute unity, and that it is hard to see how a particular shape could be an absolute unity, this view has the difficulty that it also requires powers of temporal discrimination of the kind rightly criticized by Parsons. Falkenstein's interpretation also seems to be inconsistent with the position that Kant maps out in Reflection 5390: "All appearances stand as representations in time and are determined in time. As a part of a whole appearance it [*sic*] cannot be determined (genetically apprehended) in an instant, but only in a part of time."

13 *Ibid.*, pp. 148–149.

14 P. Guyer, "Placing Myself in Time: Kant's Third Paralogism," in G. Funke (ed.), *Akten des 5ten Internationalen Kant-Kongresses* (Bonn: Bouvier, 1985), pp. 532–533.

15 Guyer, *Kant and the Claims of Knowledge*, p. 140.

16 *Ibid.*

17 *Ibid.*, pp. 135–136.

18 Jonathan Bennett, *Kant's Analytic* (Cambridge University Press, 1966), pp. 105–106.

19 A certain capacity for recognitional awareness also characterizes the intelligence of higher animals. Kant maintains that, while subhuman animals, such as dogs and hares are not able to develop bona fide concepts, they do learn from the animals which they are pursuing or who are pursuing them (*Metaphysics Lecture K3* (1794/5), Ak. XXIX, p. 949). This is a longstanding view of Kant's. In a 1762 paper, Kant notes that animals can distinguish objects based on their sensations and desires, "the dog distinguishes the roast from the bread, because he is differently affected by the roast than by the bread" (Ak. II, p. 60). The distinctive feature of (subhuman) animal awareness is, for him, its lack of the capacity for universalization and full-blown concept use: "Animals are acquainted [*kennen*] with objects, but they do not know [*erkennen*] them." (*Logic*, ed. Jäsche, Ak. IX, p. 65). Knowledge or cognition ("erkennen," "cognoscere") involves consciousness while the acquaintance ("kennen," "gnoscere") requires only the associative capacity to represent something in comparison with other things. Norman Kemp-Smith's brief discussion of Kant's views on human and animal intelligence is quite helpful, *A Commentary on Kant's "Critique of Pure Reason"* (London: Macmillan, 1923), pp. XLVII–L. There is also a useful discussion on the contrast between animal and human intelligence in J. Michael Young, "Kant's View of the

Imagination," *Kant-Studien* 79 (1988), esp. 150, and S. Naragon, "Kant on Descartes and the Brutes," *Kant-Studien* 81 (1990), 1–23.

20 Thomas Nagel seems to me to be right when he argues in "What is it like to be a bat?," in *Mortal Questions* (Cambridge University Press, 1979), pp. 168ff., that it makes sense to talk of what it would be like to have the experience of non-self-conscious being, such as a bat. However, I would argue that we can make sense of this idea that there is something that it is like to be such a creature and hence of its having a point of view only by thinking of such a being *as if* it had self-consciousness. We understand representational content as such only from the vantage-point of the kind of creature that can ascribe representational content to itself and to others.

21 It is not entirely clear whether Kant thought he had a completeness proof for the forms of judgment and the categories available or not. In a famous Rostock dissertation, *The Completeness of Kant's Table of Judgments* (Palo Alto: Stanford University Press, 1992), Klaus Reich argued that Kant had thought through such an argument. Reich's argument moves from constitutive features of the unity of apperception (self-consciousness) to the individual logical functions and from there to the categories. A more recent book by R. Brandt, *Die Urteilstafel* (Hamburg: Meiner, 1989), attempts a new reconstruction based on the nature of judgment and the different manner in which the nature of judgment manifests itself in the structure of concept, judgment, and inference. The argument from the nature of judgment to a completeness proof has been further developed by Béatrice Longuenesse, *Kant et le pouvoir de juger* (Paris: Presses universitaires de France, 1993) and Michael Wolff, *Die Vollständigkeit von Kants Urteilstafel* (Frankfurt: Klostermann, 1995).

22 In the second edition of the *Critique*, Kant admits that we would not give a reason why the understanding requires the kind and number of categories it supposedly does, or even why we have these and no other functions of judgment, or, for that matter, why space and time are the only forms according to which we can perceive objects (B 146). Great weight is given to the passage from section 21 in the critical examination of Reich's argument for the completeness of the table of judgment forms and categories undertaken by Lorenz Krüger, "Wollte Kant die Vollständigkeit seiner Urteilstafel beweisen?," *Kant-Studien* 59 (1968), 333–355.

23 Wilfried Sellars, "this I or he or it (the thing) which thinks," *Proceedings and Addresses of the American Philosophical Association* 44 (1971), 11.

24 *Ibid.*, 7–8.

25 Sellars, "Metaphysics and the Concept of a Person," in K. Lambert (ed.), *The Logical Way of Doing Things* (New Haven: Yale University Press, 1969), pp. 248–249.

26 Sellars, "This I or he or it (the thing) which thinks," 19n.

27 *Ibid.*, 21.

28 Kitcher, *Kant's Transcendental Psychology*, esp. pp. 111–112. Ralf Meerbote generally endorses Kitcher's claim that Kant's account of representations is

functionalist because it makes representations depend on each other by virtue of their content, although he insists that sensations cannot be understood by Kant purely functionally, see R. Meerbote, "Kant's Functionalism," in J.-C. Smith (ed.), *Historical Foundations of Cognitive Science* (Dordrecht: Kluwer, 1990), esp. pp. 162, 170.

29 *Ibid.*, pp. 122–123.

30 Kitcher, *Kant's Transcendental Psychology*, pp. 111ff.

31 *Ibid.*, p. 143.

32 A somewhat different version of the functionalist interpretation is defended by Andrew Brook, *Kant and the Mind*, esp. pp. 12ff. Like Kitcher, Brook emphasizes the importance of synthesis, the process of connecting representations, in the constitution of representations for Kant. Brook meets the problem posed for Kitcher by the unity of the mind by identifying the mind with the unity of its representations (*Ibid.* p. 209). Where Kitcher insists on the synthetic character of the claim that we can become conscious of our representations, Brook takes it to follow trivially from the self-intimating character of representation.

33 Sellars, "This I or he or it (the thing) which thinks," 19.

34 Sellars's functionalist interpretation of the Kantian notion of the self has been developed and defended by Jay Rosenberg, *The Thinking Self* (Philadelphia: Temple University Press, 1986), and C. Thomas Powell, *Kant's Theory of Self-Consciousness* (New York: Oxford University Press, 1990). In particular, Powell has noted the tendency to misinterpret Kant's claims for consciousness of self-identity as claims to knowledge that we are identical particulars. But Powell pushes this insight too far. He interprets the self of which we are conscious in self-consciousness as an illusion. We must represent different states only as if they belonged to a single consciousness (*Ibid.*, p. 56). This prevents him from ascribing a constitutive role to self-consciousness which merely becomes a stand-in for objective constraints on experience that are themselves intelligible independently of self-consciousness.

3 CONCEPTS, LAWS, AND THE RECOGNITION OF OBJECTS

1 Richard Aquila, *Matter in Mind: A Study of Kant's Transcendental Deduction* (Bloomington, Indiana: University of Indiana Press, 1989), pp. 168ff.

2 Christian Wolff also claims in his *Psychologia Empirica* of 1738 (Hildesheim: Olms, 1968), section 173, that a reproduced idea is recognized when we are conscious of already having had it. This is said to be memory. I owe the references to Wolff to Wolfgang Carl, *Die Transzendentale Deduktion*, p. 162n. The same point is made by Baumgarten in section 579 of the *Metaphysics* (1757) handbook that Kant used as the basis for his lectures (Ak. xv).

3 Kant connects the notion of a concept as a universal representation with its function as a rule. Concepts are universal representations in two different senses. They can be shared by different individuals with different intuitive states, and they represent intuited particulars in repeatable terms. Kant does not simply identify concepts with rules. In his discussion of the

subjective deduction, R. P. Wolff maintains that rules are concepts. This leads him to detect "a conflict which runs through all the *Critique* and which Kant never successfully resolves. On the one hand, his rationalist orientation and concern with the conditions of knowledge incline him toward an emphasis on concepts, judgments, reasoning, and the other conscious processes of cognition. On the other hand, his discovery of the problem of consciousness, and his distinction between appearances and reality, force him to assign the generative processes of the mind to a pre-conscious limbo. Kant obscures this ambiguity to a certain extent by attributing the non-conscious functions to faculties of the mind whose operations are customarily considered conscious, by distinguishing synthesis itself from the bringing of synthesis to concepts (A 79). This won't do, however, for the concept is simply the rule according to which the synthesis is performed, and hence must precede, now follow it. " *Kant's Theory of Mental Activity*, p. 131. Wolff confuses the concept with its schema. It is no surprise that Wolff cannot make sense of Kant's notion of a schema, since it is the schema rather than the concept corresponding to it that precedes the synthesis to be performed.

4 A helpful discussion of the different uses of the term "object" to be found in Kant may be found in Charles Parsons, "Objects and Logic," *The Monist* 65 (1982), 491–516.

5 Henry Allison, "Transcendental Affinity – Kant's Answer to Hume," in L. Beck (ed.), *Kant's Theory of Knowledge* (Dordrecht: Reidel, 1974), esp. p. 123.

6 Further remarks about the relation of Goodman's problem to Kant's position may be found in Ralph Walker, *Kant* (Routledge and Kegan Paul, 1978), pp. 172ff. as well as Gordon Brittan, *Kant's Theory of Science* (Princeton University Press, 1978), pp. 188ff. Neither author relates the Goodman problem specifically to Kant's notion of the affinity of nature.

7 Further discussion of the notion of a projected systematic unity of nature may be found in Gerd Buchdahl, *Metaphysics and the Philosophy of Science* (Cambridge Mass.: MIT Press, 1969), chapter 8, as well as in the papers collected in his *Kant and the Dynamics of Reason* (Oxford: Blackwell, 1992). Philip Kitcher, "Projecting the Order of Nature," in R. Butts (ed.), *Kant's Philosophy of Physical Science* (Dordrecht: Reidel, 1986), pp. 210–235, and a discussion by Paul Guyer and Ralph Walker of "Kant's Conception of Empirical Law," *Proceedings of the Aristotelian Society, Supplementary Volume* 64 (1990), 221–242, and 243–258, are also extremely interesting. Systematic unity has been discussed more recently by Susan Neiman, *The Unity of Reason* (New York: Oxford University Press, 1994), pp. 7off. and especially Michael Friedman, *Kant and the Exact Sciences* (Cambridge, Mass.: Harvard University Press, 1992), esp. pp. 244ff.

4 SELF-CONSCIOUSNESS AND THE DEMANDS OF JUDGMENT IN THE B-DEDUCTION

1 Robert Howell, *Kant's Transcendental Deduction* (Dordrecht: Kluwer, 1992), pp. 18off.

2 Allison, *Kant's Transcendental Idealism*, p. 137.

3 D. Henrich, "The Proof Structure of Kant's Transcendental Deduction," in R. C. Walker (ed.), *Kant on Pure Reason* (Oxford University Press, 1982), pp. 76–77.

4 P. Guyer, "Kant on Apperception and *A Priori* Synthesis," *American Philosophical Quarterly* 17 (1980), 210, *Kant and the Claims of Knowledge*, p. 141.

5 Hector-Neri Castañeda, "The Role of Apperception in Kant's Transcendental Deduction of the Categories," *Nous* 24 (1990), 153ff.

6 Thomas Nagel, "Brain Bisection and the Unity of Consciousness," in *Mortal Questions* (Cambridge University Press, 1979), pp. 147–164.

7 Terence Wilkerson, "Kant on Self-Consciousness," *Philosophical Quarterly* 30 (1980), 56ff.

8 Manfred Baum, *Deduktion und Beweis in Kants Transzendentalphilosophie* (Meisenheim: Königstein, 1986).

9 Guyer, *Kant and the Claims of Knowledge*, p. 117.

10 P. Guyer, "The Transcendental Deduction of the Categories," *The Cambridge Companion to Kant* (New York: Cambridge University Press, 1992), p. 151, sees Kant's claim that the unity of consciousness is sufficient for cognition as a blatant error.

11 Allison, *Kant's Transcendental Idealism*, p. 145.

12 *Ibid.*, p. 144.

13 *Ibid.*, p. 154.

14 *Ibid.*, p. 155.

15 *Ibid.*, p. 155.

16 *Ibid.*, p. 260.

17 *Ibid.*, p. 261.

18 *Ibid.*, p. 262.

19 *Ibid.*, p. 263.

20 *Ibid.*, p. 79.

21 According to Allison, the only things of cognitive significance for Kant are objective states of affairs. This is because objective states of affairs are the only things of which we can be conscious in apperception. Allison's restriction of self-conscious experience to objective states of affairs also seems to encourage him to give an absolute reading to the spontaneity or independence from causal determination that Kant ascribes to self-consciousness in epistemic contexts. For Allison, self-consciousness is more completely independent of sensible information than it is for functionalists and other philosophers who interpret the theoretical subject as only relatively spontaneous. See H. Allison, "Autonomy and Spontaneity in the Self," in his *Idealism and Freedom*, pp. 132–133.

22 By treating objective validity as the target of judgment, I avoid the difficulties that beset the interpretation that is defended by G. Prauss in his *Erscheinung bei Kant* (Berlin: De Gruyter, 1971), pp. 86ff. and by H. Allison, *Kant's Transcendental Idealism*, pp. 72–73, according to which objective validity consists only in the possibility of a judgment having a truth value. This

would hardly be enough to provide the truth with which Kant repeatedly identifies objective validity.

5 SELF-CONSCIOUSNESS AND THE UNITY OF INTUITION: COMPLETING THE B-DEDUCTION

1 The point that intuition involves unity or rather singularity of what is represented by definition is emphasized by Hoke Robinson, "Intuition and the Manifold," *Southern Journal of Philosophy* 22 (1984), 405.

2 Henrich, "The Proof Structure of Kant's Transcendental Deduction," 70–71. J. Claude Evans has recently defended Henrich in "Two-Steps-in-One-Proof: The Structure of the Transcendental Deduction of the Categories," *Journal of the History of Philosophy* 28 (1990), 563ff.

3 Friedrich Tenbruck seems to be the first interpreter to have emphasized the two-step character of the proof in the B-Deduction in "Die transzendentale Deduktion der Kategorien nach der zweiten Auflage der 'Kritik der reinen Vernunft,'" Ph.D. Thesis, Marburg (1948). Tenbruck sees the first step as establishing that the categories apply to all representations of which we are conscious, since all such representations must be unitary. He also thinks that there is some question whether "all the manifold must be given in One empirical intuition" (p. 50). This is because he takes the first step in the proof to be analytic, expressing a merely hypothetical necessity. The second step must then provide a premise from which a categorical necessity may be derived. Tenbruck traces this second premise back to the a priori unity of intuition defended in the Aesthetic. According to Bernhard Thöle, "Die Beweisstruktur der transzendentalen Deduktion in der zweiten Auflage der 'Kritik der reinen Vernunft,'" in G. Funke (ed.), *Akten des 5ten Internationalen Kant-Kongresses* (Bonn: Bouvier, 1981), pp. 302–312, and *Kant und die Gesetzmäßigkeit der Natur* (Berlin: De Gruyter, 1991), the first step (sections 15–20) demonstrates only the possibility of thinking (not of knowing) objects through the categories. A second step is required (sections 22–25) in order to show that there is a synthesis of empirical intuition corresponding to the intellectual synthesis of thought. A third step then shows that the function of synthesis in judgment is identical with that performed by the imagination in the synthesis of perception and unity of time. Henry Allison divides the argument into a proof of the objective validity of the categories in which categories are only shown to apply to objects in a logical sense (step 1) and a proof of the objective reality of categories in which they apply to real empirical objects (step 2), *Kant's Transcendental Idealism*, p. 158; cf. also his "Apperception and Analyticity in the B-Deduction."

4 Raymond Brouillet, "Dieter Henrich et 'The Proof-Structure of Kant's Transcendental Deduction.' Réflexions critiques," *Dialogue* 14 (1975), 647–648; Hans Wagner, "Der Argumentationsgang in Kants Deduktion der Kategorien," *Kant-Studien* 70 (1980), 365–366; and Robert Howell, *Kant's Transcendental Deduction*, pp. 131ff., and 367n.

5 Manfred Baum, "The B-Deduction and the Refutation of Idealism," 104, and especially *Deduktion und Beweis*, p. 201.

6 Edwin McCann, "Skepticism and Kant's B-Deduction," *History of Philosophy Quarterly* 2 (1985), esp. 72, 74, 76, 78.

7 J. Claude Evans has recently defended Henrich in this way in "Two-Steps-in-One-Proof," esp. 563ff.

8 The objection that an analytic first step would give the first step no substantive role in the argument is forcefully made by Patricia Kitcher, *Kant's Transcendental Psychology*, p. 172.

9 McCann, "Skepticism and Kant's B-Deduction," 78.

10 A. Pistorius, "Review of Kant's *Prolegomena zu einer jeden künftigen Metaphysik,*" *Allgemeine Deutsche Bibliothek* 59 (1784), 385. It has seemed, even to some recent commentators, that self-consciousness for Kant must be a form of self-knowledge. Edwin McCann argues, for instance, that one cannot even think of oneself as a self without having the determinate self-knowledge that is the basis for the argument of the Refutation of Idealism; McCann, "Skepticism and Kant's B-Deduction," 84. But this reconstruction of the argument of the Deduction would leave it wide open to the objection made by Pistorius.

11 Kemp-Smith translates "das, worinnen sich die Empfindungen allein ordnen, und in gewisse Form gestellt werden können" (A 21/B 35) as "that in which alone the sensations can be posited and ordered in a certain form," *Kant's "Critique of Pure Reason"* (New York: St Martin's Press, 1968), p. 66, treating "sich ordnen" as if it were not a reflexive expression referring back to "sensations."

12 Karl Ameriks, *Kant's Theory of Mind* (Oxford: Clarendon Press, 1982), p. 241.

13 Henry Allison appeals to Reflection 5423, Ak. xviii, p. 186, in support of the ascription of Kant of the bar substratum view of the self when it comes to judgments concerning inner sense: "All inner experience is a judgment in which the predicate is empirical and the subject is I. Independently of experience, therefore, there remains merely the I for rational psychology; for the I is the substratum of all empirical judgments." Allison is clearly right when he says that Kant is referring here to the I *qua* subject of judgments as something non-empirical. It is also true for Kant that the I as such cannot be known empirically. Kant is left with the bare substratum view Allison ascribes to him if one denies the empirical existence of the self as anything but an object of reflection. Allison does claim that "a subjective unity of consciousness is not a unity *of* self-consciousness, although it can (as objectified) become a unity *for* self-conscious thought," *Kant's Transcendental Idealism*, p. 155. On this view all (empirical) consciousness of oneself as a particular individual is knowledge of oneself as an object. Put more bluntly all *self*-consciousness that is not self-*knowledge* seems to be pure apperception for Allison. This is difficult to reconcile with Kant's references to empirical apperception as self-consciousness. Kant's reference to that object of reflection as *self*-intuiting indicates that the non-empirical or logical I of (pure) apperception may refer to itself as the possessor of a certain individuating spatio-temporal history.

14 Paton, *Kant's Metaphysic of Experience*, pp. 238–242; cf. also Allison, *Kant's Transcendental Idealism*, p. 266.

15 Robert Howell, "Apperception and the 1786 Transcendental Deduction," *Synthese* 47 (1981), 385, 424ff., also *Kant's Transcendental Deduction*, pp. 194ff.

16 "Kant takes the *I* to be an a priori representation of thought, a representation that gives me no awareness *of* any particular object called the subject of thought, but instead gives me only the awareness that there is an entity – whose nature is not further revealed to me – that we can call the subject of thought. Hence by an appeal simply to his revisionary view of knowledge, Kant takes the *I* to yield me no (empirical) intuition or intellectual representation *of* any particular entity at all, let alone any representation that displays to me the nature of such an entity. And Kant takes the *I* to yield me no such intuition or representation despite the fact that, as he sees it, the relevant type of *I think*-related unity does obtain among my representations." R. Howell, "Apperception and the 1786 Transcendental Deduction," 433.

17 *Ibid.*, 424.

18 *Ibid.*

19 The attribution of the reflection theory of self-consciousness to Kant has enjoyed a certain vogue in the German philosophical literature. Henrich develops this view of Kant's theory of self-consciousness at greatest length in "Fichtes 'Ich'," in his *Selbstverhältnisse* (Stuttgart: Reclam, 1982), pp. 61–65. But he also makes some remarks about Kant's purported reflection theory in "Die Anfänge des Subjekts (1789)," in A. Honneth et al. (eds.), *Zwischenbetrachtungen im Prozeß der Aufklärung* (Frankfurt: Suhrkamp, 1989), pp. 106–170. The reflection theory is developed and discussed in more detail in his essay "Self-Consciousness: A Critical Introduction to a Theory," *Man and World* 4 (1971), 3–28. Henrich's interpretation of Kant has been followed in this regard by Ulrich Pothast, *Über einige Probleme der Selbstbeziehung* (Frankfurt: Suhrkamp, 1971), p. 18; Ernst Tugendhat, *Self-Consciousness and Self-Determination* (Cambridge, Mass.: MIT Press, 1986), p. 41; and Manfred Frank, "Intellektuelle Anschauung," in E. Behler and J. Hörisch (eds.), *Die Aktualität der Frühromantik* (Paderborn: Schöningh, 1987), pp. 96–126. Tugendhat devotes most of his attention, *nota bene*, to criticizing Henrich's and Pothast's theory of self-consciousness (pp. 39–76). Charles Larmore notes in his review of Tugendhat's book, *Philosophical Review* 98 (1989), 104–109, that Tugendhat does not escape the circularity difficulties in the analysis of self-consciousness which he diagnoses in the reflection theory. Dieter Henrich argues the same point in his response to Tugendhat, "Noch einmal in Zirkeln," in C. Bellut and U. Müller Schöll (eds.), *Mensch und Moderne* (Würzburg: Königshausen and Neumann, 1989), pp. 89–128.

20 Henrich concedes that Kant's use of the term "reflection" is quite different from the use which became prevalent in post-Kantian philosophy in D. Henrich, "Kant's Notion of a Deduction and the Methodological Background of the First *Critique*," in E. Förster (ed.), *Kant's Transcendental Deductions* (Stanford University Press, 1989), p. 42. It is unclear, however, whether

he identifies the later usage with his talk of the reflection of self-consciousness.

21 I borrow the term "reflexively self-referential" from Robert Nozick, *Philosophical Explanations* (Cambridge, Mass.: Harvard University Press, 1981), pp. 71ff.

22 Allison, "Reflections on the B-Deduction," p. 37. Space and time are unifiable according to the Aesthetic, since they are all parts of one unitary space and time. A categorially determined synthesis is, however, necessary in order for the understanding to represent space and time as unitary. Kant goes on to argue that space and time as intuited derive their unity from a synthesis of the understanding that precedes all use of concepts. In conversation, Allison has pointed out to me that he reads the claim that the synthesis of space and time precedes all concepts as restricted to concepts of space and time. For Allison, even the determination of sensibility by the powers of what Kant calls the productive imagination involves the actual application of categories. On my view, by contrast, this determination of sensibility by spontaneity accords with the unity of self-consciousness and thus makes categories applicable to experience, but it does not involve the use of categories. There is a passage in section 16 (not cited by Allison) that seems to support this view. After insisting that the mineness of intuitions means that those representations are self-ascribable in one consciousness, Kant concludes that: "Synthetic unity of the manifold of intuitions as a priori given is therefore the basis for the identity of apperception itself which must precede all *my* determinate thought" (section 16, B 134). This suggests that the identity of self-consciousness itself presupposes a unity of intuition that is given a priori. But Kant goes on in the next sentence to trace the synthesis upon which this synthetic unity is based to an activity of the understanding.

23 Allison, "Reflections on the B-Deduction," in *Idealism and Freedom*, p. 37, and also *Kant's Transcendental Idealism*, p. 162.

24 Allison, "Reflections on the B-Deduction," p. 36.

25 Henrich, "The Proof Structure of Kant's Transcendental Deduction," p. 70.

26 The connection between the unity of space and time and the synthetic unity of self-consciousness for Kant is undeniable. In a reflection dating from the mid seventies, Kant even more directly expresses the thought that the unity of time and space is based on their relation to self-consciousness: "Time is unitary <*einig*>. (For there is one sub.) <(*Denn es ist ein Sub.*)> Which means as much as: I can know all objects (know them immediately according to the form of inner intuition) only in myself and in representations to be found in my unitary <*einigen*> subject . . . Space is nothing but the intuition of a mere form and without given matter, hence pure intuition. It is a singular intuition due to the unity of the subject (and the capacity) in virtue of which all representations of external objects can be placed (next to) each other" (Reflection 4673, Ak. XVII, p. 638). A reflection dating from the 1780s goes in the same direction: "The unity of intuition a priori is only

possible through the connection of the manifold in one apperception" (Ak. XVIII, p. 282).

27 Béatrice Longuenesse describes the dependence of inner sense on the understanding as a dependence on the understanding's capacity to judge, *Kant et le pouvoir de juger*, pp. 247ff. This seems right to me, but what needs to be pointed out is that this capacity for judgment itself depends for its existence on our capacity for impersonal (transcendental) self-consciousness. It is the unity that experiences have for such self-consciousness that is responsible for the kind of implicit unity in what we experience that makes our judgments applicable to what we experience.

28 Robert Pippin has pointed out that B 161n was a tremendous inspiration to the development of German idealism, since it seems to break down the distinction between the spontaneity through which we interpret experience and the receptivity through which it is given to us in the first place, see R. Pippin, *Hegel's Idealism* (New York: Cambridge University Press, 1989), pp. 29–30. Talk of what is different from the self as a posit of the self was indeed suggested to Fichte by Kant's talk of time as nothing but the mode in which the mind affects itself "through this positing [setzen] of the representation of its own activity" (B 68). While it is true that Kant does make our reception of space and time as intuitions in a certain sense dependent on the spontaneity of the understanding, he does not intend to absorb receptivity completely by spontaneity. For he explicitly distinguishes space and time which have been constructed by our spontaneity from the forms and, *a fortiori*, the content of our receptivity. In the passage in which Kant uses the language of self-positing, he also distinguishes the form or, rather, the mode according to which self-positing occurs from that activity itself. He is also careful to assign the unity of space and time to space and time a priori and not to concepts of the understanding. Since understanding is operating through imagination, concepts are not being explicitly applied to objects. This is why Kant then refers to section 24. If there were no forms of receptivity for Kant that were independent of imagination, he would indeed have fallen into the Fichtean idea of self-positing. Wayne Waxman actually argues, in his *Kant's Model of the Mind* (New York: Oxford University Press, 1991), that transcendental idealism commits one to the denial "not merely of super*sensible* reality to space and time, but super*imaginational* as well (here construing 'sensible' in a sense exclusive of imagination – contrary to Kant's regular practice). All spatial and temporal relations must then be supposed to exist only in and through imagination, and in no way to characterize sensations; there can be no 'flux' of representations in inner sense, and not even color 'patches' can be regarded as genuine *data*," p. 14.

29 Anthony Quinton, "Spaces and Times," *Philosophy* 37 (1962), 130–147, is the first paper to defend the possibility of experiential spaces that might be disconnected. M. Hollis, "Times and Spaces," *Mind* 76 (1967), 524–536, extends the possibility of disconnected experiences to experiences of disconnected times. Richard Swinburne attacks the incoherence of such partially

connected times in his *Space and Time* (London: Macmillan, 1969), pp. 198ff. In "Time," *Analysis* 26 (1965), 189–191, he maintains that the notion of partially connected times is not coherent because it would not preserve personal identity. But, of course, this assumes that personal identity is something that we know must be preserved. I have already argued that Kant rejects such an assumption.

30 The theory upon which the existence of singularities is based is developed in Stephen Hawking and Brian Ellis, *The Large Scale Structure of Spacetime* (Cambridge University Press, 1973).

31 "When we combine quantum mechanics with general relativity, there seems to be a new possibility that did not arise before: that space and time together might form a finite, four-dimensional space without singularities or boundaries, like the surface of the earth but with more dimensions." Stephen Hawking, *A Brief History of Time* (New York: Doubleday, 1988), p. 173.

6 TIME-CONSCIOUSNESS IN THE ANALOGIES

1 There is a helpful discussion of the connection between the subject–predicate structure in judgment and the Kantian notion of substance in Dieter Scheffel, "Der Anfang der transzendentalen Deduktion im Falle der Kategorie der Substanz," in G. Funke (ed.), *Akten des 5ten Internationalen Kant-Kongresses* (Bonn: Bouvier, 1985), pp. 292–301.

2 Guyer, *Kant and the Claims of Knowledge*, pp. 218–219.

3 Strawson, *The Bounds of Sense*, pp. 129–130.

4 Kant's reference to substances in appearance rules out Gordon Nagel's suggestion that the argument against multiple time-series is directed against the possibility of different time-series implicit in Leibniz's monadology and in his notion of pre-established harmony, *The Structure of Experience*, (University of Chicago Press, 1983), p. 182. The time-series of a monad are not series that either Kant or Leibniz would ascribe to appearances, but rather to things as they are in themselves. Leibniz anticipates Kant's insistence that phenomenal objects are subject to changes that must be empirically determinable. So Leibniz's views concerning phenomenal substance are not a good target for Kant either.

5 Strawson, *The Bounds of Sense*, pp. 128–129. The argument is also criticized by Broad, "Kant's First and Second Analogies of Experience," 189–210; Wolff, *Kant's Theory of Mental Activity*, p. 251; and Bennett, *Kant's Analytic*, p. 200.

6 Carl Friedrich von Weizsäcker, "Kant's 'First Analogy of Experience' and Conservation Principles of Physics," *Synthese* 23 (1971), 75–95; Allison in *Kant's Transcendental Idealism*, pp. 210ff; Guyer in *Kant and the Claims of Knowledge*, pp. 215ff; and Van Cleve, "Substance, Matter and Kant's First Analogy," *Kant-Studien* 70 (1979), 158–161.

7 Franz Brentano, *Kategorienlehre* (Hamburg: Meiner, 1968), pp. 90–97. A helpful discussion of Brentano's critique of Kant's proof is to be found in

Roderick Chisholm, "Beginnings and Endings," in P. van Inwagen (ed.), *Time and Cause* (Dordrecht: Reidel, 1980), esp. pp. 21ff.

8 James van Cleve, "Substance, Matter and Kant's First Analogy'" 149–161.

9 Unlike physical states, mental states are, for Kant, inherently anomalous. This is a function of their inherently perspectival character. But, as long as mental states have physical counterparts, an objective correlate may be found for all statements ascribing inner states to oneself, even though there is no way of reducing inner (mental) states to outer (physical) states. There are two excellent discussions of Kant's denial of lawlike properties to psychological states: Theodore Mischel, "Kant and the Possibility of a Science of Psychology," *Monist* 51 (1967), 599–622, and Meerbote, "Kant on the Nondeterminate Character of Human Actions," pp. 155ff.

10 Kant's appeal to the successiveness of representations has led Arthur Melnick, *Kant's Analogies of Experience* (University of Chicago Press, 1973), p. 84, and Guyer, *Kant and the Claims of Knowledge*, p. 254, to argue that Kant takes our (putative) lack of direct experience of temporal succession as a key premise in his argument for the need for causal connection to determine the temporal relations between representations. This is based on an interpretation of the synthesis of apprehension at A 99 that I have already rejected in my discussion of the A-Deduction. In the second edition of the Second Analogy, Kant contrasts my consciousness that my imagination posits one state before the other with knowledge of the objective relation between states (B 233–234). This strongly suggests that we are or can be directly conscious of succession, while we do not have direct knowledge of the objective relations between parts of an event, or between different events. It does not mean, of course, that we therefore have knowledge of the order even of subjective succession by introspection alone.

11 Van Cleve, "Four Recent Interpretations of Kant's Second Analogy," 71ff.

12 The idea that perceptions are bound down to the order of changes in the object perceived may be a critical allusion to section 58 of Hume's *Enquiry Concerning Human Understanding*, E. Steinberg (ed.) (Indianapolis: Hackett, 1981): "All events seem entirely loose and separate. One event follows another; but we never can observe any tie between them. They seem conjoined, but never connected. And as we can have no idea of anything which never appeared to our outward sense or inward sentiment, the necessary conclusion seems to be that we have no idea of connexion or power at all, and that these words are absolutely without any meaning, when employed either in philosophical reasonings or common life."

13 Broad, "Kant's First and Second Analogies of Experience," 195. Wolff, *Kant's Theory of Mental Activity*, p. 268, and Bennett, *Kant's Analytic*, pp. 221–222, among others, have understood Kant to be confusing subjective sequence with objective sequence.

14 Thus Harper and Van Cleve have argued that the reconstruction of the argument in D. P. Dryer, *Kant's Solution for Verification in Metaphysics* (London: Allen and Unwin, 1966), esp. pp. 418ff., fails to show that causal connections

are necessary to distinguish the occurrence of an event. The objection first appears in the review article by Van Cleve, "Four Recent Interpretations of Kant's Second Analogy," 86. He attributes it to William Harper. Harper and Meerbote take up the objection in their very helpful introductory essay to *Kant on Causality, Freedom and Objectivity* (Minneapolis: University of Minnesota Press, 1984), pp. 12–13.

15 Harrison, "Transcendental Arguments and Idealism," pp. 215–218, accuses Kant of shifting in his defence of causation from a *de dicto* to a *de re* necessity. Strawson famously diagnoses "a non-sequitur of numbing grossness" in Kant's analysis, in his *The Bounds of Sense*, p. 138. This point is related, but somewhat different. As Strawson sees it, Kant shifts from a conceptual necessity based on the fact of a change, to a causal necessity that a change occur. Strawson's justification of the *non-sequitur* is based in part on a modal fallacy pointed out by Van Cleve in "Four Recent Interpretations," 82. Strawson treats the consequent of the conditional necessity involved in event perception (whose antecedent is not itself necessary) as a conceptual necessity, thus confusing it with the conceptual necessity of the conditional which must be fulfilled, if a perceptual sequence is to be a perception of a change.

16 According to Arthur Lovejoy, "On Kant's Reply to Hume," *Archiv für Geschichte der Philosophie* (1906), 380–407, Kant falsely infers a synthetic necessity connecting states of objects from the analytic necessity of the irreversibility of the sequence of perceptions in the perception of an event. Lovejoy is correct that the perceptual isomorphism holding between the sequence of perceptions of a ship going downstream and that objective occurrence is based on analysis of what it means to be an event. But Kant's argument is not analytic as Lovejoy maintains. Causal connections are conditions for the recognition of events, not part of the meaning of an event. Without objective changes we could not have any knowledge of subjective changes either. It is a substantive precondition of experience for Kant, and not a matter of an analysis of the meaning of the concept of an event, as Graham Bird, *Kant's Theory of Knowledge*, pp. 157ff., interprets the Second Analogy. For Bird, the causal law is a "conceptual truth" that determines the meaning of the terms "cause" and "event", see esp. pp. 162, 165–166.

17 Arthur Melnick seems to be the first commentator to emphasize the importance of the idea that changes must be recognizable in the argument of the Second Analogy, cf. *Kant's Analogies of Experience*, pp. 89ff.

18 Allison, *Kant's Transcendental Idealism*, p. 229.

19 Arthur Schopenhauer, *Über die vierfache Wurzel vom zureichenden Grund. Kleinere Schriften:Sämtliche Werke III* (Frankfurt: Cotta-Insel, 1962), p. 115.

7 CAUSAL LAWS

1 A quite different reading of this passage may be found in Buchdahl, who insists on the independence of the kind of necessity involved in specific causal laws from the necessity involved in the general causal principle; see Gerd Buchdahl, "Causality, Causal Laws, and Scientific Theory in the

Philosophy of Kant," *British Journal for the Philosophy of Science* 16 (1965), 187–208.

2 Melnick, *Kant's Analogies of Experience*, pp. 82, 90–91; Guyer, *Kant and the Claims of Knowledge*, pp. 254–255, 258–259.

3 Henry Allison defends the view that Kant does not require the existence of specific causal covering laws in *Kant's Transcendental Idealism*, pp. 232–234, and more recently in considerably modified form in "Causality and Causal Law in Kant: A Critique of Michael Friedman," in *Idealism and Freedom*, pp. 80–91. He appears to have been strongly influenced by papers of Gerd Buchdahl.

4 The view that causal connections need not imply the existence of causal laws for Kant is defended by Henry Allison, *Kant's Transcendental Idealism*, p. 230.

5 Buchdahl, "Causality, Causal Laws, and Scientific Theory in the Philosophy of Kant," 187–208.

6 *Ibid.*, 193.

7 *Ibid.*, 187–208.

8 Allison, *Kant's Transcendental Idealism*, p. 230.

9 Allison in "Causality and Causal Law in Kant," p. 86.

10 Paton, *Kant's Metaphysic of Experience*, vol. 2, pp. 275–278.

11 *Ibid.*, p. 276.

12 Michael Friedman, "Causal Laws and the Foundations of Natural Science," in *The Cambridge Companion to Kant*, pp. 164 and 170.

13 *Ibid.*, p. 170.

14 Allison, "Causality and Causal Law in Kant," p. 87.

15 The view that the necessity of specific causal laws is not due to the understanding and the general causal principle is defended by Buchdahl in *Metaphysics and the Philosophy of Science* (Cambridge, Mass.: MIT Press, 1969), pp. 651–665, "Causality, Causal Laws, and Scientific Theory in the Philosophy of Kant," 200–201, and 204, and "The Kantian 'Dynamic of Reason' with Special Reference to the Place of Causality in Kant's System," in L. Beck (ed.), *Kant-Studies Today* (LaSalle Ill.: Open Court, 1969), pp. 340–346. Guyer also argues that necessity is derived from reason or reflective judgment, *Kant and the Claims of Knowledge*, p. 241, and also, Paul Guyer, "Kant's Conception of Empirical Law," *Proceedings of the Aristotelian Society* supp. vol. 64 (1990), 221–242. The effort to prise apart the necessity of specific causal laws from the necessity of the general causal principle is criticized by Friedman, "Causal Laws," pp. 170–174, 190ff. Susan Neiman argues plausibly that the need for the existence of causal regularities in order to be able to apply the concept of causation implies that the regulative principles of reason are required in order for the understanding to function correctly, *The Unity of Reason*, p. 57. This is the conclusion that suggests itself from my analysis of the connection between specific forms of lawlikeness in nature and the general lawlikeness of nature that Kant postulates in the A-Deduction in terms of the transcendental affinity of nature.

16 Guyer, *Kant and the Claims of Knowledge*, p. 258.
17 Friedman, *Kant and the Exact Sciences*, pp. 171ff.
18 Melnick, *Kant's Analogies of Experience*, p. 135; Guyer, *Kant and the Claims of Knowledge*, p. 240.
19 Kant's thesis that incompatibilism and compatibilism are compatible is emphasized by Allen Wood, "Kant's Compatibilism," in A. Wood (ed.), *Self and Nature in Kant's Philosophy* (Ithaca: Cornell University Press, 1984), pp. 73–101.
20 The most extensive account of the Davidsonian interpretation of Kant's account of agency is Hud Hudson, *Kant's Compatibilism* (Ithaca: Cornell University Press, 1994), esp. pp. 43ff. But the view originates with Ralf Meerbote, "Kant on the Nondeterminate Character of Human Actions," pp. 138–163.
21 The view that thought is only relatively spontaneous for Kant is defended by Ingeborg Heidemann, "Der Begriff der Spontaneität in der *Kritik der reinen Vernunft*," esp. p. 29; D. Henrich, "Die Deduktion des Sittengesetzes," in A. Schwan (ed.), *Denken im Schatten des Nihilismus* (Darmstadt: Wissenschaftliche Buchgesellschaft, 1975), pp. 55–112; W. Sellars, "This I or he or it (the thing) which thinks," esp. p. 20; Ameriks, *Kant's Theory of Mind*, p. 217; Kitcher, *Kant's Transcendental Psychology*, p. 253.
22 Allison defends absolute spontaneity for thought in "Kant's Refutation of Materialism," in *Idealism and Freedom* (New York: Cambridge University Press, 1996), pp. 92–108, and in his *Kant's Theory of Freedom* (New York: Cambridge University Press, 1990), pp. 80–81. It is also defended by Robert Pippin, "Kant on the Spontaneity of Mind," *Canadian Journal of Philosophy* 17 (1987), esp. 466–467. The interpretation of Kant's theory of spontaneity that assimilates freedom in judgment to free will goes back to Fichte, but the substantive view that judgment requires an incompatibilist interpretation of freedom is already defended by Descartes in his Fourth Meditation.

8 SELF-CONSCIOUSNESS AND THE PSEUDO-DISCIPLINE OF TRANSCENDENTAL PSYCHOLOGY

1 Kant did not free himself from commitment to the project of rational psychology until quite late in his career. Kant still thought of the subject of thought as theoretically knowable in the substantial terms suggested by the four basic paralogisms that he identifies in rational psychology into the middle of the 1770s. His discovery of the fallacies involved in inferences from self-consciousness to substantive claims about the nature of the self or the soul was the last important innovation in his thinking prior to publication of the *Critique* in 1781. The evidence for this claim is assembled in Wolfgang Carl, *Der Schweigende Kant* (Göttingen: Vandenhoek and Ruprecht, 1989), pp. 101ff.
2 Karl Ameriks shows more interest in the metaphysical side of Kant than most interpreters of the Paralogisms, emphasizing the extent of agreement between the positive conception of mind that underlies Kant's critique of rationalism in the Paralogisms and traditional rationalists' views. "The

Critique of Metaphysics: Kant and Traditional Ontology," in P. Guyer (ed.), *The Cambridge Companion to Kant* (New York: Cambridge University Press, 1992), pp. 249–279, and especially *Kant's Theory of Mind: An Analysis of the Paralogisms of Pure Reason*. Ameriks links his approach to the metaphysical approach to Kant that was in favor in the 1920s in Germany. "Understanding Apperception Today," in P. Perrini (ed.), *Kant and Contemporary Epistemology* (Dordrecht: Kluwer, 1994), pp. 331–347. At the same time, however, he defends a metaphysical deflationary epistemological interpretation of the "I think." For instance, Ameriks rejects the thesis that Kant requires a notion of absolute freedom or spontaneity to make sense of theoretical reasoning and self-consciousness in favor of a relatively spontaneous conception of self-consciousness. Ameriks criticizes Guyer's interpretation of the "I think" as requiring a *de re* necessity, linking an analytic interpretation of the principle that representations must be self-ascribable to the synthetic assumption that we have empirical knowledge in his "Kant and Guyer on Apperception," *Archiv für Geschichte der Philosophie* 65, 106n. Ameriks then circumvents the problem of how knowledge is to be justified by dropping any presumption that the possibility of knowledge is to be established in the Deduction in "Kant's Transcendental Deduction as a Regressive Argument," *Kant-Studien* 69 (1978), 273–87. Kant is taken simply to assume the existence of empirical knowledge.

3 One may call the self that is the logical object of self-consciousness a quasi-object to distinguish it from objects subject to third-person criteria of identification, cf. Dieter Sturma, *Kant über Selbstbewußtsen* (Hildesheim: Olms, 1985), p. 10.

4 R. Descartes, *La Recherche de la vérité*, in *Oeuvres complètes*, Charles Adam and Adam Tannery (eds.) (Paris: Leopold Cerf, 1887–1913), vol. 10, p. 518.

5 Patricia Kitcher takes the First Paralogism as well as the Third to be about the permanence of the "I," *Kant's Transcendental Psychology*, p. 194. But I have tried to show that the First Paralogism is not about permanence or persistence, but about being a basic particular. It is the task of the Third Paralogism to deal with persistence and permanence. I discuss the Third Paralogism in more detail in my paper, "Personal Identity and Kant's Third Person Perspective," *Idealistic Studies* 24 (1994), pp. 123–146.

6 I owe the term "immunity to reference failure owing to misidentification" to Sydney Shoemaker, "Persons and their Pasts," *Identity, Cause, and Mind* (New York: Cambridge University Press, 1984), pp. 19–48, esp. pp. 40ff. Shoemaker restricts immunity to reference failure to non-deviant causal and representational circumstances governing personal identity. The possibility of branching and fusion of persons is thus excluded. This restriction reflects his exclusive interest in the empirical notion of a person, that is, the notion of a person linked to a particular representational history.

7 Paul Guyer takes Kant to be committed in the Third Paralogism to the actual existence of other minds that exist outside of me; Paul Guyer, "Placing Myself in Time: Kant's Third Paralogism," p. 531. But there is no

compelling reason to interpret Kant this way. Kant talks of one taking the standpoint of another, and of how, in order for one to take another's standpoint, one need not assume that the other person actually exists. Indeed, Kant's notion of a problematic use of the "I think" in the ascription of thoughts would suggest that we cannot infer that another exists from the fact that we can take the other's perspective. There is thus also no reason to see a conflict between Kant's project in the Refutation of Idealism of showing that inner experience presupposes outer experience and the argument in the first edition version of the Third Paralogism, as Guyer does. Kant does not claim that one could not have the notion of a temporal order for one's experiences without the actual existence of another mind. Instead, he argues that we could not have such a notion without the possibility of taking the point of view of another possible mind. It seems plausible to argue that the very notion of the kind of outer object presupposed in the Refutation of Idealism as a condition under which inner experience is possible is, in turn, only intelligible to us if we can abstract from our present point of view and thus place ourselves in time and space relative to other actual and possible objects.

8 This possibility is discussed by Sydney Shoemaker, "Persons and their Pasts," 40.

9 Contemporary controversy over "repressed memories," for instance in cases of alleged child molestation, has become focused on the extent to which putative memories of abuse might be the result of suggestion by the therapists questioning the purported victims; see E. F. Loftus, "The Reality of Repressed Memories," *American Psychologist* 48 (1993), 518–537. The important point is that the individuals in question believe themselves to have a certain history, and this is as far as immunity to reference failure extends.

10 A critical discussion of Leibniz's views on immortality and continuity of consciousness may be found in Margaret Wilson, "Leibniz, Self-Consciousness and Immortality: In the Paris Notes and After," *Archiv für Geschichte der Philosophie*, Sonderheft 58 (1976), 335–352.

9 HOW INDEPENDENT IS THE SELF FROM ITS BODY?

1 The importance of the simplicity of I thoughts for Kant's argument in the Deduction is emphasized by D. Henrich, "Identity and Objectivity," pp. 162ff.

2 Jonathan Bennett brings this first-personal perspective out in his essay "The Simplicity of the Soul," *The Journal of Philosophy* (1968), 654. Unfortunately, Bennett's ascription of methodological solipsism to Kant leads him to argue that "Kant is wholly inattentive . . . to all aspects of the notion of an embodied mind," p. 655. But Kant's view is that I have an *empirical* self only as a human being, and hence an embodied mind. This mind is indirectly accessible to the third-person point of view through its connection with the human being's body.

3 Henry Allison takes the argument from simplicity to the self to go against non-reductive as well as reductive materialism in "Kant's Refutation of Materialism," in his *Idealism and Freedom*, p. 97.

4 René, Descartes, *Oeuvres complètes*, vol. VII, p. 81. A helpful discussion of embodiment in Descartes may be found in Paul Hoffman, "The Unity of Descartes's Man," *The Philosophical Review* 54 (1984), 339–370.

5 Allison, "Kant's Refutation of Materialism," p. 97.

6 Leibniz, *On the Manner of Distinguishing Real Phenomena from Imaginary*, in *Philosophische Schriften*, C. J. Gerhard (ed.) (Hildesheim: Georg Olms, 1978), VII, p. 319. See Nicholas Jolley, "Leibniz and Phenomenalism," *Studia Leibniziana* 18 (1986), 49.

7 It has been suggested that the Fourth Paralogism's critique of "dogmatic idealism" (A 377) is directed at Leibniz rather than Berkeley; see George W. Miller, "Kant's First Edition Refutation of Dogmatic Idealism," *Kant-Studien* 62 (1971), 298–318. But this is hardly plausible. Leibniz never maintains that matter is a self-contradictory notion, despite his interest in the "labyrinth of the continuum" and in a reduction of matter to force. The dogmatic idealism of the first edition has also been identified with the position of Bayle and Charles Collier, whose *Clavis Universalis* was bundled with a German translation of Berkeley's *Three Dialogues* in a collection by Johann Christian Eschenbach, *Samlung der vornehmsten Schriftsteller die die Wirklichkeit ihres eignen Körpers und der ganzen Körperwelt leugnen* (Rostock: Anton Ferdinand Röse, 1756). Lewis Robinson, "Contributions à l'histoire de l'évolution philosophique de Kant," *Revue de metaphysique et de morale* 31 (1924), 319–321, argues for regarding Bayle and Collier as the targets of the criticism of dogmatic idealism. Heinz Heimsoeth, "Arthur Collier und der Durchbruch des neuzeitlichen Bewußtseinsidealismus," *Studien zur Philosophiegeschichte* (Köln: Kölner Universitätsverlag, 1961), identifies Kant's notion of skeptical idealism with Bayle's skepticism. Heimsoeth maintains that Kant has Descartes's methodical doubt in mind when Kant refers to problematic idealism, p. 297. But, as Wolfgang Müller-Lauter, "Kants Widerlegung des materialen Idealismus," *Archiv für Geschichte der Philosophie* 46 (1964), points out on p. 64, Kant never explicitly distinguishes between skeptical and problematic idealism, as he should have done. Skeptical idealism would actually deny the existence of the external world, whereas problematic idealism would merely entertain that denial as a hypothesis.

8 However, Leibniz and Wolff provide obvious targets for the First and Second Paralogisms; cf. Margaret Wilson, "Leibniz and Materialism," *Canadian Journal of Philosophy* (1974), 509ff.

9 The controversy between Kant and Garve and Feder is discussed in helpful detail by Frederick C. Beiser, *The Fate of Reason* (Cambridge, Mass.: Harvard University Press, 1987), pp. 172ff.

I O THE ARGUMENT AGAINST IDEALISM

1 Martin Heidegger has suggested in *Being and Time*, trans. Joan Stambaugh (New York: State University of New York Press, 1996), "that the 'scandal of

philosophy' is not that this proof has yet to be given, but that such proofs are expected and attempted again and again," p. 205 (cited according to the original pagination of the 1926 German edition reprinted in the translation). On the other hand, Heidegger offers what amounts to an argument for the existence of objects outside of us. His argument for the assumption that Being-in-the-World is a condition for the possibility of the temporal existence of the self, has at least some similarity with Kant's argument in the Refutation of Idealism. There are two key differences. Heidegger attempts to avoid the use of any assertions in his argument. This is only a superficial advantage, since in order to have conviction his argument needs to be reformulatable in terms of premises involving assertions. Heidegger also rejects Kant's assumption that there is a theoretical approach to the world that is independent of our practical involvements. This raises too many questions to answer here. It will have to suffice to say that it is not clear that the problem of skepticism about the external world is substantially changed by shifting to the perspective of an agent. For the agent must also have some reason to believe that he or she is able to have a genuine effect in the external world.

2 The allusion is to F. H. Jacobi, *David Hume über den Glauben, oder Idealismus und Realismus, ein Gespräch* (Breslau: Löwe, 1785). Unlike Hume, Jacobi does not deny that our belief in the existence of the external world is true, instead he argues only that it is indemonstrable. The problem is that we cannot infer from what we perceive that objects exist even when they are not perceived.

3 Edwin McCann, "Skepticism and Kant's B-Deduction," 77ff. McCann argues that the second step of the B-Deduction shows that one cannot even think of oneself as an individual subject of conscious states without having the determinate self-knowledge that is the basis for Kant's argument in the Refutation.

4 H. J. Paton takes the empirical determination of consciousness to exclude pure apperception in favor of objects of inner sense (*Kant's Metaphysic of Experience*, pp. 377–378).

5 Bennett identifies empirical consciousness with empirical knowledge of one's own history, *Kant's Analytic*, p. 205. Meerbote, identifies empirically determined consciousness with the empirical cognition of our sensation-states (and thought-states), "Kant's Refutation of Problematic Material Idealism," pp. 116–117. Similar views are expressed by Richard Aquila, "Personal Identity and Kant's 'Refutation of Idealism,'" *Kant-Studien* 70 (1979), 261; McCann, "Skepticism and Kant's B-Deduction," 84; and Baum, "The B-Deduction and Kant's Refutation of Idealism," p. 95. Allison's interpretation of the Refutation seems also to favor an appeal to self-knowledge as the lead-off premise in the argument. He identifies the consciousness presupposed in this premise as actual self-knowledge rather than mere self-consciousness (*Kant's Transcendental Idealism*, p. 297). He also maintains that Kant identifies this consciousness of inner states with inner experience (B 275). But, on the other hand, he claims that the argument is

committed to the real possibility of empirical self-knowledge. The notion of real possibility in Kant is somewhat obscure, but Allison interprets real possibility as being possible in or over a period of time in accordance with the Analogies of Experience (*Kant's Transcendental Idealism*, pp. 189–190). It is thus somewhat unclear what strength Allison gives to the first premise. The first premise might presuppose that one has actual self-knowledge or that one is only in a position to acquire such self-knowledge.

6 Bennett maintains *Kant's Analytic* that the Refutation does not presuppose the argument of the First Analogy, or at least that it ought not to. Part of his argument for this claim is that the Refutation would have to be linked "to the latter's [the First Analogy's] least comprehensible part – not to the analysis of existence-change but to the obscure doctrine that time is permanent and unperceivable," p. 202. Bennett does not argue for this mistaken claim, so I shall pass over it in favor of his major criticism. "Most important of all: if the Refutation of Idealism presupposes the First Analogy, then the 'proof' of the latter must be taken as offering, in support of the conclusion that self-consciousness requires experience of something permanent, an argument which is neutral as to whether the 'something permanent' is inner or outer. This is an impossible reading of the First Analogy, which is clearly stated in both editions as a thesis about the division of 'appearances', i.e. of the objective realm, into substances and properties" (*Kant's Analytic*, pp. 202–203). Bennett's point is based on the dubious assumption that Kant straightaway identifies the objective with the outer. But this identification is precisely part of the task of the Refutation. Neither the Deduction nor the Analogies require such an identification in any sense.

7 Allison, *Kant's Transcendental Idealism*, p. 305.

8 This also seems to be the way the argument is understood by Herbert Blunt, "La Réfutation kantienne de l'idéalisme," *Revue de métaphysique et de morale*, pp. 482–483.

9 The thing outside of me is to be taken here not only as a permanent perceptible, but as something that belongs with me to a unitary experience. And this experience is as much something external as it is something internal to my consciousness.

10 Erling Skorpen, "Kant's Refutation of Idealism," *Journal of the History of Philosophy*, maintains that "permanence cannot be a strict *a priori* concept if, as Kant claims in the Refutation, permanent objects can be directly perceived as such without the help of representations of permanence. If they can, then the concept of permanence begins to look like an *a posteriori* concept, and so too the concepts of time and substance which are analytically bound up with it," p. 28. But permanent objects may be directly perceived despite the fact that permanence itself is not directly perceptible or even something of which one can have strictly empirical knowledge. Skorpen goes on to suggest that Kant's transcendental idealism is incompatible with the thesis of direct perception that is crucial to the Refutation of Idealism: "What would have to be modified in keeping with the Refutation

is the claim that the object of perception and knowledge is fashioned in its essentials by the sensibility and understanding of man and is therefore different from the thing-in-itself," p. 30. This also seems to me to be mistaken for similar reasons.

11 Broad, *Kant: An Introduction*, p. 198.

12 Douglas Langston has criticized the thesis that the arguments of the Fourth Paralogism and the Refutation are incompatible in "The Supposed Incompatibility between Kant's Refutations of Idealism," *Southern Journal of Philosophy*, 359–369. Langston focuses on the issue of whether the claim in the Fourth Paralogism that I am immediately conscious of my representations is incompatible with the claim in the Refutation that external objects are anything in me at all. The incompatibility is asserted both by Kemp-Smith, *A Commentary on Kant's "Critique of Pure Reason"* pp. 312–313, and A. C. Ewing, *A Short Commentary on Kant's "Critique of Pure Reason"* (Chicago University Press, 1938), p. 34n. Surprisingly, Langston has nothing to say about the crucial fact that the Fourth Paralogism argument asserts a symmetry of immediacy between external and internal experience that is rejected in the Refutation.

13 Moore rejects the need for an argument for things that no sane person would doubt. But this is not even compelling on Moore's own terms, since he admits the possibility of having inferential or indirect knowledge of things that can also be known directly or immediately. Moore agrees with Kant that our knowledge of external objects is immediate. This is why he thinks that raising his hands provides a proof of the existence of external objects. One has direct perceptual knowledge of these objects. Barring some further knowledge of unusual causal conditions such as hallucination, knowledge that these hands are mine is as certain as anything is. We know that these hands are here immediately, although we may confirm or disconfirm our judgment through appeal to much more indirect sources of evidence. "We can now see that Kant insists on our possession of just the kind of knowledge G. E. Moore thought he was exhibiting in his proof of an external world ... No theory that represents our knowledge of external things as indirect or inferential could account for that knowledge; it could not show that we are in the very position Moore unquestioningly took himself to be in," Barry Stroud, *The Significance of Philosophical Skepticism* (Oxford: Clarendon Press, 1984), p. 132.

14 Guyer, *Kant and the Claims of Knowledge*, p. 326.

15 Erling Skorpen maintains in "Kant's Refutation of Idealism," pp. 23–24, that "Kant's implication in the Refutation is not only that self-knowledge is inseparable for world-knowledge, but that there is nothing we know about ourselves which is not *already* reference to an external world. Any autobiographical or biographical reference, including those growing out of psychoanalysis, is confirmation for this. For even reports like 'I was hostile,' 'I am hallucinating,' etc., are elliptical for longer reports starting where, when, and under what circumstances," p. 33. In "Kant's Refutation of Idealism," *Journal of the History of Philosophy* 12 (1974), 195–206, Myron

Gochnauer criticizes Skorpen's attempt to make all knowledge of inner states not only dependent upon, but actually inclusive of, knowledge of outer states (see p. 204). Gochnauer maintains that it should be possible to know that one is performing a logical inference or a mathematical calculation without also referring to the outside world. "I might feel sick and I might solve equations even if there were no external world. But what I could not do without an external world is to know the temporal ordering of these two items of consciousness," p. 204. The dependence of Kant's theory of arithmetic (and of mathematics in general) on spatial sequence undercuts this alleged independence from spatial models for arithmetic. Mathematics is based on schemata – generative rules – for producing inherently spatial objects of perception in imagination (A 140/B 179: "Bilder"). The issue must be pushed back to the general status of objects of imagination. Raw feelings are difficult for another reason. It is not obvious that the connection between raw feelings such as pains and the body is a contingent one. This is at least a controversial issue and one that Kant does not express an explicit opinion on. Even the independence of logic from spatial objects is less clear cut than it might seem to be, since Kant thinks that without any implicit reference to objects of experience, logic cannot make any bona fide commitments to the existence of objects.

16 An exhaustive survey of the relevant evidence is to be found in a chapter on "The Application of the Categories to the Self," in A. C. Ewing, *Kant's Treatment of Causality* (London: Kegan Paul, 1924), pp. 124–168.

17 This interpretation has been pursued recently by Ralf Meerbote in his article "Kant's Refutation of Problematic Material Idealism," in B. den Ouden and M. Moen (eds.), *New Essays on Kant* (New York: Peter Lang, 1986), pp. 111–135. Meerbote derives inspiration for his view from Donald Davidson's anomalous monism. The ascription of lawlike relations to mental events only under a physical description need not entail a commitment to physicalism. The identity relation is, after all, a symmetrical one. Some further premise is needed beyond the anomalous monist thesis to lead one to physicalism. The physicalism that Davidson and Meerbote defend requires not only that the physical states instantiating animal representations (and indeed human representations) be subject to the causal principle, but also the further premise that mental events are only subject to causal laws under a physical description. It does not, to be sure, require that mental events are only caused or causal under a physical description, since, for Davidson, causation is an extensional notion. However, I cannot find a premise in Kant that would justify the ascription to him of physicalism.

18 Guyer, *Kant and the Claims of Knowledge*, p. 326.

19 *Ibid.*, p. 314.

20 *Ibid.*, p. 324.

21 *Ibid.*, p. 326.

22 *Ibid.*, p. 315.

23 *Ibid.*, p. 297.

24 P. Guyer, "Placing Myself in Time," p. 533.

25 Eckart Förster, "Kant's Refutation of Idealism," p. 295. Förster's objection of a contradiction between the theory of space in the Transcendental Aesthetic and the externality claim of the Refutation goes back to Hans Vaihinger's article "Zu Kants Widerlegung des Idealismus," *Strassburger Abhandlungen zur Philosophie* (Tübingen: J. C. B. Mohr, 1884), pp. 131–132. An extensive criticism of Vaihinger's claim that the argument of the Refutation is inconsistent with transcendental idealism is to be found in a postscript to Anton Thomson, "Bemerkungen zur Kritik des Kantischen Begriffs des Dinges an sich," *Kant-Studien* 8 (1903), 248–257.

26 Eckart Förster seems to be attracted to the view that the refutation entails a form of extreme idealism, since he argues that the "full-fledged idealism" he finds in Kant's incomplete work, the so-called *Opus Postumum*, is unavoidable, if the Refutation is to be integrated into Kant's philosophy as a whole, Förster, "Kant's Refutation of Idealism," esp. p. 302.

27 H. A. Pritchard, *Kant's Theory of Knowledge* (Oxford: Clarendon Press, 1901), maintains that Kant means: "a thing external in the sense of independent of mind, i.e. a thing in itself. For the nerve of the argument consists in the contention that the permanent the perception of which is required for consciousness of my successive states must be a thing external to me, and a thing external to me in opposition to a representation of a thing external to me can only be a thing in itself," pp. 322–323. Pritchard goes on to find a contradiction between this notion of externality and that of the phenomenal externality of things in space. Perhaps he does not give "dependence on my mind" the normal connotation of privacy. But even then he has failed to make out his claim of contradiction. Robert Dostal, "Kant's Refutation of Idealism: Transcendental Idealism and Phenomenalism," in G. Funke (ed.), *Akten des 5ten Internationalen Kant-Kongresses* (Bonn: Bouvier, 1981), discusses and rejects the phenomenalism that Pritchard attributes to Kant, as well as Pritchard's view that the reference to things in themselves is unintentional in the Refutation (p. 417). Although it may be unclear whether Pritchard argues from the privacy of all appearances to the need for external things that are things in themselves, the argument is explicit in Broad (*Kant: An Introduction*, pp. 198–199).

28 There is a tendency in the literature to gloss transcendental realism as synonymous with any awareness of things in themselves. "But Kant does not accept realism, understood 'transcendentally.' For him it is not true 'transcendentally' that we are aware of things that are independent of us. The correct 'transcendental' position is idealism: what we perceive and know are all 'appearances,' things that are dependent on us," Barry Stroud, "Kant and Skepticism," in M. Burnyeat (ed.), *The Skeptical Tradition* (Berkeley: University of California Press, 1983), p. 421. Stroud's discussion of the role of transcendental idealism in Kant's argument against skepticism is quite helpful. But some direct awareness of things as they exist in themselves is necessary if Kant's inference from the existence of appearances to the

existence of things as they exist in themselves is to be valid. This is consistent with the restriction of all descriptive knowledge to appearances.

29 According to J. Findlay, there is the same demand for something outside of the subject to act on the subject in the case of transcendental self-consciousness, as in the case of empirical self-consciousness. Kant studiously used the terms "outside" and "external" in an ambiguous manner so as to cover *both* the phenomenal outsidedness of bodies in space and the meta-empirical, transcendental outsidedness of things-in-themselves to that thing-in-itself which is our own transcendental self: John N. Findlay, *Kant and the Transcendental Object* (Oxford: Clarendon Press, 1981), pp. 184–185.

30 Guyer, *Kant and the Claims of Knowledge*, p. 328.

31 I have criticized this view in my discussion of the synthesis of apprehension in chapter three. It is also rejected by Anthony Bruckner in his critical discussion of Guyer's reconstruction of the Refutation in "The Anti-Skeptical Epistemology of the Refutation of Idealism," *Philosophical Topics* 19 (1991), 34–5.

I I EMPIRICAL REALISM AND TRANSCENDENTAL IDEALISM

1 A parallel claim is made for time (A 35–36/B 52).

2 Against such interpreters as Allison and Strawson, Guyer maintains that the non-spatiality of things in themselves is the premise from which Kant argues here for the subjectivity of space, rather than a conclusion drawn from the premise that space is inherently subjective "the passage concisely displays the order of Kant's inference *from* the nonspatiality of things in themselves *to* the merely subjective nature of space, as well as the claim about knowledge of necessity on which the premise of this inference itself is based," *Kant and the Claims of Knowledge*, p. 355. However, the phrase "that is" in the second sentence does not seem to introduce an inference from the claim made in the first sentence, but rather a mere explication of the meaning of that first sentence. The a priori, and hence necessary, character of intuition seems to be the claim about knowledge of necessity to which Guyer also refers as the basis of Kant's argument. However, it should be noted that Kant appeals to a distinctive intuitive necessity rather than some general notion of necessity as the basis for his argument. Since intuition is a form of representation, some notion of the subjectivity of space is involved in the initial premise of the argument.

3 Kant addresses the problematic character of a priori intuition in the *Prolegomena* (section 8–10, Ak. IV, pp. 218–283). He notes that, since intuition depends for its existence on the immediate presence of its object, this seems to rule out the very existence of a priori intuition. For *a priori* intuition cannot depend on the previous or present object that intuition requires. Intuition would have to depend on the presence of givenness of the object, if the object were a thing in itself. Thus, any intuition of things in themselves would have to be empirical. A priori intuition is possible as an intuition of the form according to which objects immediately present to the mind must

be ordered. It is possible to intuit the form according to which a thing in itself is immediately present to the mind. But what one is intuiting according to that form is not the thing as it exists in itself. It is only the thing as it appears to us a priori. This is the thing as that thing must appear to us in absolutely all situations.

4 Guyer, *Kant and the Claims of Knowledge*, pp. 362ff.

5 Allison, *Kant's Transcendental Idealism*, p. 110.

6 *Ibid.*, p. 109.

7 Morris Lipson attempts to articulate a variant of Allison's mode of presentation account of transcendental idealism that does not fall victim to the problem in question. He argues that space is "a mode of presentation of ontological independence." Morris Lipson, "On Kant on Space," *Pacific Philosophical Quarterly* 73 (1992), 74. Kant does think of space as a mode in which objects are presented or given to us (A 42/B59, A35/B52). Lipson maintains that it makes no sense to argue that a thing in itself is in space, if one understands space to be a mode of presentation. For, once we see that space is the way in which ontological independence is presented to us, "we find that we have no basis for suspecting that space is anything else than this," 97. Even if we have no basis for suspecting space is anything but the form according to which ontological independence is presented to us, space might well also itself be genuinely independent of us. Our very ability successfully to structure the objects of our experience spatio-temporally suggests that there is some independent basis for the existence of space and time.

8 Allison, "Transcendental Idealism: A Retrospective," *Idealism and Freedom*, p. 10.

9 Allison, "Incongruence and Ideality," *Topoi* 3 (1984), 169–175; cf. also J. Buroker, *ibid.*, 177–180.

10 Lorne Falkenstein, "Kant's Argument for the Non-Spatiotemporality of Things in Themselves," *Kant-Studien* 80 (1989), 265–283.

11 A helpful discussion of this evidence may be found in J. Buroker, *Space and Incongruence: The Origins of Kant's Idealism* (Dordrecht: Reidel, 1981).

12 Guyer, *Kant and the Claims of Knowledge*, p. 366.

Bibliography

Adickes, Erich, *Kants Lehre von der doppelten Affektion unseres Ichs* (Tübingen: Mohr, 1929).
Allison, Henry, *Idealism and Freedom* (New York: Cambridge University Press, 1996).
  Kant's Theory of Freedom (New York: Cambridge University Press, 1990).
  Kant's Transcendental Idealism (New Haven: Yale University Press, 1983).
  "Apperception and Analyticity in the B-Deduction," in *Idealism and Freedom* (New York: Cambridge University Press: 1996), pp. 41–52.
  "Causality and Causal Law in Kant: A Critique of Michael Friedman," in *Idealism and Freedom*, pp. 80–91.
  "Locke's Theory of Personal Identity: A Re-Examination," in I. C. Tipton (ed.), *Locke on Human Understanding: Selected Essays* (Oxford University Press, 1977), pp. 105–122.
  "Kant's Refutation of Materialism," in *Idealism and Freedom*, pp. 92–108.
  "Transcendental Affinity – Kant's Answer to Hume," in L. W. Beck (ed.), *Kant's Theory of Knowledge* (Dordrecht: Reidel, 1974), pp. 120–127.
  "Incongruence and Ideality," *Topoi* 3 (1984), 169–175.
  "Review of *Kant and the Claims of Knowledge*," *The Journal of Philosophy* 86 (1989), 214–221.
  "Reflections on the B-Deduction," Spindel Conference 1986: The B-Deduction, *Southern Journal of Philosophy* 25 (1986), Supplement, 1–15.
  "Transcendental Idealism and Descriptive Metaphysics," *Kant-Studien* 60 (1969), 216–223.
Ameriks, Karl, *Kant's Theory of Mind: An Analysis of the Paralogisms of Pure Reason* (Oxford: Clarendon Press, 1982).
  "The Critique of Metaphysics: Kant and Traditional Ontology," in P. Guyer (ed.) *The Cambridge Companion to Kant* (New York: Cambridge University Press, 1992), pp. 249–279.
  "Understanding Apperception Today," in Paolo Perrini (ed.), *Kant and Contemporary Epistemology* (Dordrecht: Kluwer, 1994), pp. 331–347.
  "Kant and Guyer on Apperception," *Archiv für Geschichte der Philosophie* 65 (1983), 174–184.
  "Kant's Transcendental Deduction as a Regressive Argument," *Kant-Studien* 69 (1978), 273–287.

"Recent Work on Kant's Theoretical Philosophy," *American Philosophical Quarterly* 19 (1982), 1–24.

Aquila, Richard, *Matter in Mind: A Study of Kants Transcendental Deduction* (Bloomington, Indiana: University of Indiana Press, 1989).

Representational Mind: A Study of Kant's Theory of Knowledge (Bloomington, Indiana: University of Indiana Press, 1983).

"Personal Identity and Kant's 'Refutation of Idealism,'" *Kant-Studien* 70 (1979), 259–278.

Baum, Manfred, *Deduktion und Beweis in Kants Transzendentalphilosophie: Untersuchungen zur 'Kritik der reinen Vernunft'* (Meisenheim: Königstein, 1986).

"The B-Deduction and the Refutation of Idealism," *Southern Journal of Philosophy* 25 (1986), Supplement, 89–107.

Baum, Manfred and Rolf P. Horstmann, "Metaphysikkritik und Erfahrungstheorie in Kants theoretischer Philosophie," *Philosophische Rundschau* 26 (1979), 62–91.

Beck, Lewis White, "Kant's Theory of Definition," *The Philosophical Review* 67 (1956), 179–191.

Beck, Lewis White (ed.), *Kant's Theory of Knowledge* (Dordrecht: Reidel, 1974).

Beiser, Frederick C., *The Fate of Reason* (Cambridge, Mass.: Harvard University Press, 1987).

Bennett, Jonathan, *Kant's Analytic* (Cambridge University Press, 1966).

Kant's Dialectic (Cambridge University Press, 1974).

"The Simplicity of the Soul," *The Journal of Philosophy* (1968).

"Analytical Transcendental Arguments," in P. Bieri and R.-P. Horstmann (eds.), *Transcendental Arguments and Science* (Dordrecht: Reidel, 1981).

Bird, Graham, *Kant's Theory of Knowledge* (London: Routledge and Kegan Paul, 1962).

"Kant's Transcendental Idealism," in G. Vesey (ed.), *Idealism Past and Present*, Royal Institute of Philosophy Lecture Series 13 (Cambridge University Press, 1982), pp. 71–92.

"Recent Interpretations of Kant's Transcendental Deduction," in G. Funke (ed.), *Akten des 4ten Internationalen Kant-Kongresses* (Berlin: De Gruyter, 1974), pp. 1–15.

Bittner, Rüdiger, "Transzendental," in H. Krings, H. M. Baumgartner, and C. Wild (eds.), *Handbuch der Philosophischen Grundbegriffe* (Munich: Kössel, 1974), vol. 5, pp. 1524–1539.

Blunt, Herbert, "La réfutation kantienne de l'idéalisme," *Revue de Métaphysique et de Morale* 12 (1904), 477–491.

Brandt, Reinhardt, *Die Urteilstafel* (Hamburg: Meiner, 1989).

Brentano, Franz, *Kategorienlehre* (Hamburg: Meiner, 1968).

Brittan, Gordon G., Jr., *Kant's Theory of Science* (Princeton University Press, 1978).

Broad, C. D., *Kant: An Introduction* (Cambridge University Press, 1976).

"Kant's First and Second Analogies of Experience," *Proceedings of the Aristotelian Society* 25 (1926), 189–210.

Brook, Andrew, *Kant and the Mind* (New York: Cambridge University Press, 1994).

Brouillet, Raymond, "Dieter Henrich et 'The Proof-Structure of Kant's Transcendental Deduction.' Réflexions critiques," *Dialogue* 14 (1975), 639–648.

Bruckner, Anthony, "The Anti-Skeptical Epistemology of the Refutation of Idealism," *Philosophical Topics* 19 (1991), 31–46.

Buchdahl, Gerd, *Kant and the Dynamics of Reason* (Oxford: Blackwell, 1992).

Metaphysics and the Philosophy of Science (Cambridge, Mass.: MIT Press, 1969).

"Causality, Causal Laws, and Scientific Theory in the Philosophy of Kant," *British Journal for the Philosophy of Science* 16 (1965), pp. 187–208.

"The Kantian 'Dynamic of Reason' with Special Reference to the Place of Causality in Kant's System," in L. W. Beck (ed.), *Kant Studies Today* (LaSalle, Ill.: Open Court, 1969).

Buroker, Jill Vance, "The Role of Incongruent Counterparts in Kant's Transcendental Idealism," in J. Van Cleve and R. E. Frederick (eds.), *The Philosophy of Right and Left* (Dordrecht: Kluwer, 1991), pp. 34–36.

Carl, Wolfgang, *Der Schweigende Kant. Die Entwürfe zu einer Deduktion der Kategorien vor 1781*. Abhandlungen der Akademie der Wissenschaften in Göttingen: Philologisch-Historische Klasse, Series 3, Number 189 (Göttingen: Vandenhoek and Ruprecht, 1989).

Die Transzendentale Deduktion der Kategorien in der ersten Auflage der "Kritik der reinen Vernunft": Ein Kommentar (Frankfurt: Klostermann, 1992).

"Kant's First Drafts of the Deduction of the Categories," in E. Förster (ed.), *Kant's Transcendental Deductions in the Three Critiques and the Opus Postumum* (Stanford University Press, 1989), pp. 3–20.

Castañeda, Hector-Neri, "The Role of Apperception in Kant's Transcendental Deduction of the Categories," *Nous* 24 (1990).

Chisholm, Roderick, "Beginnings and Endings," in Peter van Inwagen (ed.), *Time and Cause* (Dordrecht: Reidel, 1980), pp. 17–25.

Davidson, Donald, *Inquiries on Truth and Interpretation* (New York: Oxford University Press, 1984).

Descartes, René, *Oeuvres complètes*, Charles Adam and Adam Tannery (eds.) (Paris: Leopold Cerf, 1887–1913, and Vrin, 1964–1975).

Dostal, Robert, "Kant's Refutation of Idealism: Transcendental Idealism and Phenomenalism," in G. Funke (ed.), *Akten des 5ten Internationalen Kant-Kongresses* (Bonn: Bouvier, 1981), pp. 407–417.

Dryer, D. P., *Kant's Solution for Verification in Metaphysics* (London: George Allen and Unwin, 1966).

"The Second Analogy," in W. Harper and R. Meerbote (eds.), *Kant on Causality, Freedom and Objectivity* (Minneapolis: University of Minnesota Press, 1984), pp. 58–65.

Eschenbach, Johann Christian, *Samlung der vornehmsten Schriftsteller die die Wirklichkeit ihres eignen Körpers und der ganzen Körperwelt leugnen* (Rostock: Anton Ferdinand Röse, 1756).

Evans, J. Claude, "Two-Steps-in-One-Proof: The Structure of the Transcendental Deduction of the Categories," *Journal of the History of Philosophy* 28 (1990), 553–570.

Ewing, A. C., *A Short Commentary on Kant's 'Critique of Pure Reason'* (Chicago University Press, 1938).

Kant's Treatment of Causality (London: Kegan Paul, 1924).

Falkenstein, Lorne, "Kant's Argument for the Non-Spatiotemporality of Things in Themselves," *Kant-Studien* 80 (1989), 265–283.

Kant's Intuitionism: A Commentary on the Transcendental Aesthetic (University of Toronto Press, 1995).

Findlay, John N., *Kant and the Transcendental Object* (Oxford: Clarendon Press, 1981).

Förster, Eckart, "Kant's Refutation of Idealism," in A. J. Holland (ed.), *Philosophy and Its History and Historiography* (Dordrecht: Reidel, 1985), pp. 287–303.

Förster, Eckart (ed.), *Kant's Transcendental Deductions in the Three Critiques and the Opus Postumum* (Stanford University Press, 1989).

Frank, Manfred, " 'Intellektuelle Anschauung'. Drei Stellungnahmen zu einem Deutungsversuch von Selbstbewußtsein: Kant, Fichte, Hölderlin, Novalis," in E. Behler and J. Hörisch (eds.), *Die Aktualität der Frühromantik* (Paderborn: Schöningh, 1987), pp. 96–126.

Friedman, Michael, *Kant and the Exact Sciences* (Cambridge, Mass.: Harvard University Press, 1992).

"Causal Laws and the Foundations of Natural Science," in Paul Guyer (ed.), *The Cambridge Companion to Kant* (New York: Cambridge University Press, 1992), pp. 161–199.

Garve, Friedrich, *Göttingscher Gelehrten Anzeiger* 3 (January 19, 1782), 40–48.

Gibbons, Sarah, *Kant's Theory of Imagination* (New York: Oxford University Press, 1994).

Gloy, Karen, *Studien zur theoretischen Philosophie Kants* (Würzburg: Königshausen and Neumann, 1990).

Gochnauer, Myron, "Kant's Refutation of Idealism," *Journal of the History of Philosophy* 12 (1974), 195–206.

Gram, Moltke S. (ed.), *Kant: Disputed Questions* (Chicago: Quadrangle Press, 1967).

Guyer, Paul, *Kant and the Claims of Knowledge* (Cambridge University Press, 1987).

"Placing Myself in Time: Kant's Third Paralogism," in G. Funke (ed.), *Akten des 5ten Internationalen Kant-Kongresses* (Bonn: Bouvier, 1985), pp. 524–533.

"The Transcendental Deduction of the Categories," in P. Guyer (ed.), *The Cambridge Companion to Kant* (New York: Cambridge University Press, 1992), pp. 123–160.

"Kant's Conception of Empirical Law," *Proceedings of the Aristotelian Society*, Supplementary Volume 64 (1990), 221–242.

"Kant on Apperception and *A Priori* Synthesis," *American Philosophical Quarterly* 17 (1980), 205–212.

Review of *Identität und Objektivität*, *The Journal of Philosophy* 76 (1979), 151–167.

Guyer, Paul (ed.), *The Cambridge Companion to Kant* (Cambridge University Press, 1992).

Hamann, J. G., *Briefwechsel*, A. Henkel (ed.) (Frankfurt: Suhrkamp, 1986).

Harper, William and Ralf Meerbote (eds.), *Kant on Causality, Freedom, and Objectivity* (Minneapolis: University of Minnesota Press, 1984).

Harrison, Ross, "Transcendental Arguments and Idealism," in G. Vesey (ed.), *Idealism Past and Present*. Royal Institute of Philosophy Lecture Series: 13 (Cambridge University Press, 1982).

Hawking, Stephen, *A Brief History of Time* (New York: Doubleday, 1988).

Hawking, Stephen and Brian Ellis, *The Large Scale Structure of Spacetime* (Cambridge University Press, 1973).

Heidegger, Martin, *Being and Time* (Tübingen: Max Niemeyer, 1972[12]).

   Kant and the Problem of Metaphysics (Bloomington: University of Indiana Press, 1962).

   Phänomenologische Interpretation von Kants "Kritik der reinen Vernunft" (Frankfurt: Klostermann, 1977).

Heidemann, Ingeborg, "Der Begriff der Spontaneität in der *Kritik der reinen Vernunft*," *Kant-Studien* 47 (1955–1956), 3–30.

Heimsoeth, Heinz, "Arthur Collier und der Durchbruch des neuzeitlichen Bewußtseinsidealismus," *Studien zur Philosophiegeschichte* (Köln: Kölner Universitätsverlag, 1961).

   "Consciousness of Personality and the Thing in Itself in Kant's Philosophy," in M. Gram (ed.), *Kant: Disputed Questions* (Chicago: Quadrangle Press, 1967), pp. 237–278.

Henrich, Dieter, *The Unity of Reason* (Cambridge, Mass.: Harvard University Press, 1994).

   "Die Anfänge des Subjekts (1789)," in A. Honneth et al. (eds.), *Zwischenbetrachtungen im Prozeß der Aufklärung* (Frankfurt: Suhrkamp, 1989), pp. 106–170.

   "Die Beweisstruktur der transzendentalen Deduktion der reinen Verstandesbegriffe – eine Diskussion mit Dieter Henrich," in B. Tuschling (ed.), *Probleme der 'Kritik der reinen Vernunft'* (Berlin: De Gruyter, 1984), pp. 35–96.

   "Die Deduktion des Sittengesetzes," in Alexander Schwann (ed.), *Denken im Schatten des Nihilismus* (Darmstadt: Wissenschaftliche Buchgesellschaft, 1975), pp. 55–112.

   "Fichtes 'Ich,'" in *Selbstverhältnisse* (Stuttgart: Reclam, 1982).

   "Identity and Objectivity: An Inquiry into Kant's Transcendental Deduction," in *The Unity of Reason* (Cambridge, Mass.: Harvard University Press, 1994), pp. 123–210.

   "The Identity of the Subject in the Transcendental Deduction" in E. Schaper and W. Vossenkuhl (eds.), *Reading Kant* (Oxford: Blackwell, 1989), pp. 250–280.

   "Kant's Notion of a Deduction and the Methodological Background of the First *Critique*," in E. Förster (ed.), *Kant's Transcendental Deductions in the Three Critiques and the Opus Postumum* (Stanford University Press, 1989), pp. 29–46.

   "Noch einmal in Zirkeln," in C. Bellut and U. Müller-Schöll (eds.), *Mensch und Moderne* (Würzburg: Königshausen and Neumann, 1989), pp. 89–128.

"The Proof Structure of Kant's Transcendental Deduction," in R. C. Walker (ed.), *Kant on Pure Reason* (Oxford University Press, 1982), pp. 66–81.

"Self-Consciousness, A Critical Introduction to a Theory," *Man and World* 4 (1971), 3–28.

Hoffman, Paul, "The Unity of Descartes's Man," *The Philosophical Review* 54 (1984).

Hollis, M., "Times and Spaces," *Mind* 76 (1967), 524–536.

Howell, Robert, *Kant's Transcendental Deduction* (Dordrecht: Kluwer, 1992).

"Apperception and the 1786 Transcendental Deduction," *Synthese* 47 (1981), 385–448.

Hudson, Hud, *Kant's Compatibilism* (Ithaca: Cornell University Press, 1994).

Hume, David, *A Treatise of Human Nature*, L. E. Selby-Bigge (ed.) (Oxford: Clarendon Press, 1888).

Enquiry Concerning Human Understanding, E. Steinberg (ed.) (Indianapolis: Hackett, 1981).

Jacobi, Friedrich H., *David Hume über den Glauben, oder Idealismus und Realismus, ein Gespräch* (Breslau: Löwe, 1785).

Jolley, Nicholas, "Leibniz and Phenomenalism," *Studia Leibniziana* 18 (1986).

Kalter, Alfons, *Kants vierter Paralogismus. Eine entwicklungsgeschichtliche Untersuchung zum Paralogismenkapitel der ersten Auflage der 'Kritik der reinen Vernunft'* (Meisenheim am Glan: Königstein, 1975).

Keller, Pierre, "Personal Identity and Kant's Third Person Perspective," *Idealistic Studies* 24 (1994), 123–146.

Kemp-Smith, Norman, *A Commentary on Kant's "Critique of Pure Reason"* (London: Macmillan, 1923²).

Immanuel Kant's 'Critique of Pure Reason' (London: Macmillan, 1929).

Kitcher, Patricia *Kant's Transcendental Psychology* (New York: Oxford University Press, 1990).

"Kant's Real Self," in Allen W. Wood (ed.), *Self and Nature in Kant's Philosophy* (Ithaca: Cornell University Press, 1984), pp. 113–147.

"Connecting Intuitions and Concepts at B 160n," *Southern Journal of Philosophy* 25 (1986), Supplement, 137–149.

"Kant on Self-Identity," *The Philosophical Review* 91 (1982), 41–72.

"Kant's Patchy Epistemology," *The Pacific Philosophical Quarterly* 68 (1987), 306–316.

Kitcher, Philip, "Projecting the Order of Nature," in Robert Butts (ed.), *Kant's Philosophy of Physical Science* (Dordrecht: Reidel, 1986), pp. 210–235.

Krüger, Gerhard, "Über Kants Lehre von der Zeit," in *Philosophie und Moral in der Kantischen Kritik* (Tübingen: J. C. B. Mohr, 1967²), pp. 269–294.

Krüger, Lorenz, "Wollte Kant die Vollständigkeit seiner Urteilstafel beweisen?," *Kantstudien* 59 (1968), 333–355.

Lachièze-Rey, Pierre, *Idéalisme kantien* (Paris: Vrin, 1972³).

Langston, Douglas, "The Supposed Incompatibility between Kant's Refutations of Idealism," *Southern Journal of Philosophy* 17 (1979), 359–369.

Larmore, Charles, Review of E. Tugendhat, "Selbstbewußtsein und Selbstbestimmung," *The Philosophical Review* 98 (1989), 104–109.

Leibniz, Gottfried Wilhelm, *Logical Papers*, G. H. R. Parkinson (ed.) (Oxford: Clarendon Press, 1966).

Mathematische Schriften, C. J. Gerhard (ed.) (Hildesheim: Georg Olms, 1978).

Philosophische Schriften, C. J. Gerhard (ed.) (Hildesheim: Georg Olms, 1978).

Lipps, Theodor, *Leitfaden der Psychologie* (Leipzig: Engelmann 1903).

"Inhalt und Gegenstand; Psychologie und Logik," in *Sitzungsberichte der philosophischen-philologischen und der historischen Klasse der Königlichen Bayerischen Akademie der Wissenschaften* 4 (1905).

Lipson, Morris, "On Kant on Space," *Pacific Philosophical Quarterly* 73 (1992), 73–99.

Loftus, E. F., "The Reality of Repressed Memories," *American Psychologist* 48 (1993), 518–537.

Longuenesse, Béatrice, *Kant et le pouvoir de juger* (Paris: Presses Universitaires de France, 1993).

Lovejoy, Arthur, "On Kant's Reply to Hume," *Archiv für Geschichte der Philosophie* (1906), 380–407.

Mackie, John L., *The Cement of the Universe* (Oxford University Press, 1974).

Malcolm, Norman, "Whether 'I' is a Referring Expression," in C. Diamond and J. Teichman (eds.), *Intention and Intentionality* (Brighton: Harvester Press, 1979), pp. 15–24.

Matthews, H. E., "Strawson on Transcendental Idealism," *Philosophical Quarterly* 19 (1969), 204–220.

McCann, Edwin, "Skepticism and Kant's B-Deduction," *History of Philosophy Quarterly* 2 (1985), 71–89.

Meerbote, Ralf, "Kant on the Nondeterminate Character of Human Actions," in W. P. Harper and R. Meerbote (eds.), *Kant on Causality, Freedom, and Objectivity* (Minneapolis: University of Minnesota Press, 1984), pp. 138–163.

"Kant's Functionalism," in J.-C. Smith (ed.), *Historical Foundations of Cognitive Science* (Dordrecht: Kluwer, 1990).

"Kant's Refutation of Problematic Material Idealism," in B. den Ouden and M. Moen (eds.), *New Essays on Kant* (New York: Peter Lang, 1986), pp. 111–135.

"The Unknowability of Things in Themselves," in L. W. Beck (ed.), *Kant's Theory of Knowledge* (Dordrecht: Reidel, 1974), pp. 166–174.

Melnick, Arthur, *Kant's Analogies of Experience* (University of Chicago Press, 1973).

Space, Time, and Thought in Kant (Dordrecht: Kluwer, 1989).

Miller, George W., "Kant's First Edition Refutation of Dogmatic Idealism," *Kant-Studien* 62 (1971), 298–318.

Mischel, Theodore, "Kant and the Possibility of a Science of Psychology," *Monist* 51 (1967), 599–622.

Mittelstaedt, Peter, *Philosophical Problems of Modern Physics* (Dordrecht: D. Reidel,

1976).

Moore, G.E., "The Refutation of Idealism," *Proceedings of the British Academy* 25 (1939), 273–300.

Müller-Lauter, Wolfgang, "Kants Widerlegung des materialen Idealismus," *Archiv für Geschichte der Philosophie* 46 (1964), 60–82.

Nabert, J., 'L'expérience interne chez Kant," *Revue de Métaphysique et de Morale* 31 (1924), 205–266.

Nagel, Gordon, *The Structure of Experience* (University of Chicago Press, 1983).

Nagel, Thomas, *Mortal Questions* (Cambridge University Press, 1979).

The View From Nowhere (Oxford University Press, 1986).

"Brain Bisection and the Unity of Consciousness," in *Mortal Questions* (Cambridge University Press, 1979), pp. 147–164.

"What is it like to be a bat?," in *Mortal Questions* (Cambridge University Press, 1979), pp. 165–180.

Naragon, S., "Kant on Descartes and the Brutes," *Kant-Studien* 81 (1990), 1–23.

Natorp, Paul, "Kant und die Marburger Schule," *Kant-Studien* 17 (1926).

Neiman, Susan, *The Unity of Reason* (New York: Oxford University Press, 1994).

Newton-Smith, W. H., *The Structure of Time* (London: Routledge and Kegan Paul, 1980).

Nietzsche Friedrich, *On the Genealogy of Morals*, trans. Walter Kaufmann (New York: Random House, 1967).

Nolan, J. P., "Kant on Meaning: Two Studies," *Kant-Studien* 70 (1979), 113–130.

Nozick, Robert, *Philosophical Explanations* (Cambridge, Mass.: Harvard University Press, 1981).

O'Neill, Onora, "Space and Objects," *The Journal of Philosophy* 83 (1976), 29–44.

Parsons, Charles, *Mathematics in Philosophy* (Ithaca: Cornell University Press, 1983).

"Kant's Philosophy of Arithmetic," in R. C. S. Walker (ed.), *Kant on Pure Reason* (Oxford University Press, 1982), pp. 13–40.

"Commentary: Remarks on Pure Natural Science," in Allen Wood (ed.), *Self and Nature in Kant's Philosophy* (Ithaca: Cornell University Press, 1984), pp. 216–227.

"The Transcendental Aesthetic," in P. Guyer (ed.), *The Cambridge Companion to Kant* (New York: Cambridge University Press, 1992), pp. 62–100.

"Arithmetic and the Categories," *Topoi* 3 (1984), 109–121.

"Infinity and Kant's Conception of the 'Possibility of Experience,'" *The Philosophical Review* 73 (1964), 183–197.

"Objects and Logic," *Monist* 65 (1982), 491–516.

Paton, Herbert J., *Kant's Metaphysic of Experience* (London: George Allen and Unwin, 1936).

Patten, S. C., "An Anti-Skeptical Argument at the Deduction," *Kant-Studien* 67 (1976), 550–569.

Perrini, Paolo (ed.), *Kant and Contemporary Epistemology* (Dordrecht: Kluwer, 1994).

Pippin, Robert, *Hegel's Idealism: The Satisfactions of Self-Consciousness* (New York:

Cambridge University Press, 1989).

Kant's Theory of Form (New Haven: Yale University Press, 1982).

"Kant on the Spontaneity of Mind," *Canadian Journal of Philosophy* 17 (1987), 449–476.

Pistorius, A., "Review of Kant's *Prolegomena zu einer jeden künftigen Metaphysik*," *Allgemeine Deutsche Bibliothek* 59 (1784), 322–357.

Plaass, Peter, *Kant's Theory of Natural Science*, trans. A. and M. Miller (Dordrecht: Kluwer, 1994).

Porter, Lindsay, "Does the Transcendental Deduction Contain a Refutation of Idealism?," *Kant-Studien* 74 (1983), 487–499.

Pothast, Ulrich, *Über einige Probleme der Selbstbeziehung* (Frankfurt: Suhrkamp, 1971).

Powell, C. Thomas, *Kant's Theory of Self-Consciousness* (New York: Oxford University Press, 1990).

Prauss, Gerold, *Erscheinung bei Kant* (Berlin: De Gruyter, 1971).
    Kant und das Problem der Dinge an sich (Bonn: Bouvier, 1974).

Pritchard, H. A., *Kant's Theory of Knowledge* (Oxford: Clarendon Press, 1901).

Quinton, Anthony, "Spaces and Times," *Philosophy* 37 (1962), 130–147.

Rademacher, Franz, "Kants Lehre vom innern Sinn in der 'Kritik der reinen Vernunft,'" *Kant-Studien, Ergänzungshefte* 9 (1908), 1–45.

Reich, Klaus, *The Completeness of Kant's Table of Judgments*, trans J. Kneller and M. Losonsky (Palo Alto: Stanford University Press, 1992).

Rickert, Heinrich, *Der Gegenstand der Erkenntnis* (Tübingen: Mohr, 1928³).

Robinson, Hoke, "Intuition and Manifold in the Transcendental Deduction," *Southern Journal of Philosophy* 22 (1984), 403–412.

Robinson, Lewis, "Contributions à l'histoire de l'évolution philosophique de Kant," *Revue de métaphysique et de Morale* 31 (1924), 269–353.

Rohs, Peter, "Über Sinn und Sinnlosigkeit von Kants Theorie der Subjektivität," *Neue Hefte für Philosophie* 27/28 (1988), 56–80.

Rorty, Richard, "Strawson's Objectivity Argument," *Review of Metaphysics* 24 (1970), 208–244.

Rosenberg, Jay, *The Thinking Self* (Philadelphia: Temple University Press, 1986).
    "I Think: Some Reflections on Kant's Paralogisms," *Midwest Studies in Philosophy* 10 (1986), 503–532.

Scheffel, Dieter, "Der Anfang der transzendentalen Deduktion im Falle der Kategorie der Substanz," in G. Funke (ed.), *Akten des fünften Internationalen Kant-Kongresses* (Bonn: Bouvier, 1985), pp. 292–301.

Schopenhauer, Arthur, *Über die vierfache Wurzel vom zureichenden Grund*, in *Kleinere Schriften: Sämtliche Werke III* (Frankfurt: Cotta-Insel, 1962).

Sellars, Wilfrid, *Science and Metaphysics: Variations on Kantian Themes* (London: Routledge and Kegan Paul, 1968).
    "Kant's Transcendental Idealism," in P. Laberge (ed.), *Proceedings of the Ottawa Congress on Kant* (University of Ottawa Press, 1976), pp. 165–181.

"Metaphysics and the Concept of a Person," in Karel Lambert (ed.), *The Logical*

Way of Doing Things (New Haven: Yale University Press, 1969), pp. 219–232.

"This I or he, or it (the thing) which thinks," *Proceedings and Addresses of the American Philosophical Association* 44 (1971), 5–31.

Shoemaker, Sydney, *Self-Knowledge and Self-Identity* (Ithaca: Cornell University Press, 1963).

"Commentary: Self-Consciousness and Synthesis," in Allen W. Wood (ed.), *Self and Nature in Kant's Philosophy* (Ithaca: Cornell University Press, 1984), pp. 148–156.

"Persons and their Pasts," in *Identity, Cause, and Mind* (New York: Cambridge University Press, 1984), pp. 19–48.

"Self-Reference and Self-Awareness," *The Journal of Philosophy* 65 (1968), 555–567.

Skorpen, Erling, "Kant's Refutation of Idealism," *Journal of the History of Philosophy* 6 (1968), 23–34.

Sommers, Fred, *The Logic of Natural Language* (Oxford: Clarendon Press, 1982).

Strawson, Peter F., *Persons: An Essay in Descriptive Metaphysics* (London: Methuen, 1958).

The Bounds of Sense: An Essay on Kant's 'Critique of Pure Reason' (London: Methuen, 1966).

Stroud, Barry, *The Significance of Philosophical Skepticism* (Oxford: Clarendon Press, 1984).

"Kant and Skepticism," in M. Burnyeat (ed.), *The Skeptical Tradition* (Berkeley: University of California Press, 1983), pp. 413–434.

"Transcendental Arguments," *Journal of Philosophy* 65 (1968), 241–256.

Stuhlmann-Laeisz, Rainer, "Kants Thesen über sein Kategoriensystem und ihre Beweise," *Kant-Studien* 77 (1986), 5–24.

Sturma, Dieter, *Kant über Selbstbewußtsein* (Hildesheim: Georg Olms Verlag, 1985).

Swinburne, Richard, *Space and Time* (London: Macmillan, 1968).

"Time," *Analysis* 26 (1965), 189–191.

Tenbruck, Friedrich, "Die transzendentale Deduktion der Kategorien nach der zweiten Auflage der 'Kritik der reinen Vernunft'" (Marburg: Dissertation, 1948).

Thöle, Bernhard, *Kant und die Gesetzmäßigkeit der Natur* (Berlin: De Gruyter, 1991).

"Die Beweisstruktur der transzendentalen Deduktion in der zweiten Auflage der 'Kritik der reinen Vernunft,'" in G. Funke (ed.), *Akten des 5ten Internationalen Kant-Kongresses 4.-8. April 1981* (Bonn: Bouvier, 1981), pp. 302–312.

Thompson, Manley, "Epistemic Priority, Analytic Truth, and Naturalized Epistemology," *American Philosophical Quarterly* 18 (1981), 1–12.

Thomson, Anton, "Bemerkungen zur Kritik des Kantischen Begriffs des Dinges an sich," *Kant-Studien* 8 (1903), 248–257.

Tugendhat, Ernst, *Self-Consciousness and Self-Determination* (Cambridge, Mass.: MIT Press, 1986).

Vaihinger, Hans, *Commentar zu 'Kants Kritik der reinen Vernunft'* (Stuttgart: Union

Deutsche Verlagsgesellschaft, 1892).

"Die transzendentale Deduktion in der ersten Auflage der *Kritik der reinen Vernunft*," in *Abhandlungen* (Halle: 1902).

"Zu Kants Widerlegung des Idealismus," *Strassburger Abhandlungen zur Philosophie* (Tübingen: J. C. B. Mohr, 1884), pp. 87–164.

Van Cleve, James, "Substance, Matter, and Kant's First Analogy," *Kant-Studien* 70 (1979), 149–161.

"Four Recent Interpretations of Kant's Second Analogy," *Kant-Studien* 64 (1973), 69–87.

Vleeschauwer, Hermann J. de, *La Déduction transcendentale dans l'œuvre de Kant* (Antwerp: De Sikkel, 1937).

Wagner, Hans, "Der Argumentationsgang in Kants Deduktion der Kategorien," *Kant-Studien* 71 (1980), 348–366.

Walker, Ralph C. S., *Kant* (London: Routledge and Kegan Paul, 1978).

"The Status of Kant's Theory of Matter," in L. W. Beck (ed.), *Kant's Theory of Knowledge* (Dordrecht: Reidel, 1974), pp. 151–158.

"Review of *Identität und Objektivität*," *Grazer Philosophische Studien* 4 (1977), 189–197.

Walker, Ralph C. S.,(ed.), *The Real in the Ideal* (New York: Garland, 1989).

Walsh, W. H., *Kant's Criticism of Metaphysics* (Edinburgh University Press, 1978).

Waxman, Wayne, *Kant's Model of the Mind* (New York: Oxford University Press, 1991).

Weizsäcker, Carl Friedrich von, "Kant's 'First Analogy of Experience' and Conservation Principles of Physics," *Synthese* 23 (1971), 75–95.

Weldon, D., *Kant's 'Critique of Pure Reason'* (Oxford: Clarendon Press, 1956).

Weyl, Hermann, *Philosophie der Mathematik und Naturwissenschaft* (Darmstadt: Wissenschaftliche Buchgesellschaft, 1969[6]).

Whitehead, Alfred North, *An Enquiry Concerning the Principles of Natural Knowledge* (Cambridge University Press, 1921).

Science in the Modern World (Cambridge University Press, 1924).

Wilkerson, Terence, "Kant on Self-Consciousness," *Philosophical Quarterly* 30 (1980), 47–60.

Williams, Bernard, *Descartes: The Project of Pure Enquiry* (Atlantic Highlands, N.J.: Humanities Press, 1978).

"Imagination and the Self," in *Problems of the Self* (Cambridge University Press, 1973), pp. 40–56.

"Wittgenstein and Idealism," in G. Vesey (ed.), *Understanding Wittgenstein*. Royal Institute of Philosophy Lectures 6 (New York: St. Martin's Press, 1974).

"Knowledge and Meaning in the Philosophy of Mind," *Philosophical Review* 77 (1968), 216–228.

Wilson, Margaret. "On Kant and the Refutation of Subjectivism," in L. W. Beck (ed.), *Kant's Theory of Knowledge* (Dordrecht: Reidel, 1974), pp. 208–217.

"Leibniz and Materialism," *Canadian Journal of Philosophy* (1974), 495–513.

"Leibniz, Self-Consciousness and Immortality: In the Paris Notes and

After," *Archiv für Geschichte der Philosophie*, Sonderheft 58 (1976), 335–352.

Wolff, Michael, *Die Vollständigkeit von Kants Urteilstafel* (Frankfurt: Klostermann, 1995).

Wolff, Robert Paul, *Kant's Theory of Mental Activity* (Cambridge, Mass.: Harvard University Press, 1963).

"Kant's Debt to Hume via Beattie," *Journal of the History of Ideas* 21 (1960), 117–123.

Wood, Allen, *Kant's Moral Religion* (Ithaca: Cornell University Press, 1970).

"Kant's Compatibilism," in A. Wood (ed.), *Self and Nature in Kant's Philosophy* (Ithaca: Cornell University Press, 1984), pp. 73–101.

Wood, Allen (ed.), *Self and Nature in Kant's Philosophy* (Ithaca: Cornell University Press, 1984).

Young, J. Michael, "Kant's View of the Imagination," *Kant-Studien* 79 (1988), 140–164.

Index